ABOUT ISLAND PRESS

Island Press, a nonprofit organization, publishes, markets, and distributes the most advanced thinking on the conservation of our natural resources— books about soil, land, water, forests, wildlife, and hazardous and toxic wastes. These books are practical tools used by public officials, business and industry leaders, natural resource managers, and concerned citizens working to solve both local and global resource problems.

Founded in 1978, Island Press reorganized in 1984 to meet the increasing demand for substantive books on all resource-related issues. Island Press publishes and distributes under its own imprint and offers these services to other nonprofit organizations.

Support for Island Press is provided by Apple Computers, Inc., Mary Reynolds Babcock Foundation, Geraldine R. Dodge Foundation, The Educational Foundation of America, The Charles Engelhard Foundation, The Ford Foundation, Glen Eagles Foundation, The George Gund Foundation, The William and Flora Hewlett Foundation, The Joyce Foundation, The J. M. Kaplan Fund, The John D. and Catherine T. MacArthur Foundation, The Andrew W. Mellon Foundation, The Joyce Mertz-Gilmore Foundation, The New-Land Foundation, The Jessie Smith Noyes Foundation, The J. N. Pew, Jr., Charitable Trust, Alida Rockefeller, The Rockefeller Brothers Fund, The Florence and John Schumann Foundation, The Tides Foundation, and individual donors.

Recycling and Incineration

Recycling and Incineration

EVALUATING THE CHOICES

EDITED BY

Richard A. Denison
John Ruston
ENVIRONMENTAL DEFENSE FUND

Foreword by Senator John H. Chafee

ISLAND PRESS

WASHINGTON, D.C. □ COVELO, CALIFORNIA

AKR 9208-4/1
S-100

"This publication is designed to provide accurate and authoritative information in regard to the subject matter covered. It is sold with the understanding that the publisher and the author are not engaged in rendering legal, accounting, or other professional service. If legal advice or other expert assistance is required, the services of a competent professional person should be sought."

From a Declaration of Principles jointly adopted by a Committee of the American Bar Association and a Committee of Publishers and Associations.

Library of Congress Cataloging-in-Publication Data

Recycling and incineration : evaluating the choices / edited by
   Richard A. Denison and John Ruston.
      p.   cm.
   Includes index.
   ISBN 1-55963-055-8 (alk. paper). — ISBN 1-55963-054-X (pbk. :
alk. paper)
   1. Incineration—Evaluation.   2. Recycling (Waste, etc.)—
Evaluation.   I. Denison, Richard A.   II. Ruston, John.
   TD796.I5   1990
   363.72'85—dc20   90-37971
                                                         CIP

Printed on recycled, acid-free paper

Manufactured in the United States of America

10 9 8 7 6 5 4 3 2 1

A Project of the EDF's Environmental Information Exchange

CONTRIBUTORS

The assembly of this book involved the time and effort of many people at the Environmental Defense Fund. A brief description of each's contribution and what he/she does at EDF follows.

Dr. Richard A. Denison, a senior scientist in EDF's Washington, DC office, was coeditor of the book, and oversaw it through the various phases of publication. He coordinated the sections on environmental impacts, wrote Chapter 5, and contributed to the Introduction and Chapters 1, 2, 6, 7, and 10.

John Ruston, an economic analyst in EDF's New York office, was also coeditor of the book and largely conceived its economic comparison approach. He wrote Chapter 4 and the bulk of Chapter 2, and heavily contributed to the Introduction and Chapters 1 and 3.

Karen Florini, a senior attorney in EDF's Washington, DC office, undertook the unenviable task of editing and redrafting most of the first draft, especially Chapter 7.

Sarah Clark, a scientist in EDF's New York office, oversaw the early stages of project coordination, from outline to first draft, and aided in compiling and producing figures and appendices.

Daniel Kirshner, a senior economic analyst in EDF's California office, was responsible for much of the economic comparison of recycling and incineration presented in Chapter 3.

David Roe, a senior attorney in EDF's California office, wrote Chapter 8, which discusses some innovative approaches to holding incinerator proponents to their promises about facility performance.

Michael Herz, formerly an attorney in EDF's New York office, wrote the guide through the myriad federal and state laws on incineration, presented in Chapter 10.

Dr. Ellen K. Silbergeld, a senior scientist and chair of EDF's Toxic Chemicals Program, drafted Chapter 7, a layperson's guide to risk assessment, and helped in the writing of the introduction to Part II.

Madeline Grulich, formerly a scientist in EDF's Virginia office, wrote most of Chapter 9, which deals with the issues of incinerator siting and solid waste management planning.

ACKNOWLEDGMENTS

The Environmental Defense Fund wishes to acknowledge the following foundations, grants from which made the writing of this handbook possible:

The Catto Foundation
Robert Sterling Clark
    Foundation, Inc.
Geraldine R. Dodge Foundation
The Educational Foundation of
    America
The George Gund Foundation
The Joyce Foundation
The Moriah Fund

Jessie Smith Noyes Foundation,
    Inc.
The New York Community
    Trust
Public Welfare Foundation
True North Foundation
Union Foundation
Victoria Foundation, Inc.

We also wish to acknowledge the generosity of the following individuals who undertook the unenviable task of reviewing various drafts of this handbook:

Jenny Bagby, Seattle Solid Waste Utility
Marjorie Clarke, INFORM
Robert Ginsburg, formerly with Citizens for a Better Environment
Kevin Greene, Citizens for a Better Environment
Pete Grogan, R. W. Beck and Associates
Ed Hopkins, Ohio Public Interest Campaign
Kevin Mills, East Michigan Environmental Action Council
Emily Moore, Environmental Defense Fund
Lorie Parker, Seattle Solid Waste Utility
Tim Searchinger, Environmental Defense Fund

CONTENTS

FIGURES

FOREWORD

WITH LITTLE WARNING, managing our garbage has become a problem of immense proportions. This has traditionally been a task that few of us thought twice about, content to leave it to our municipal public works or sanitation managers to choose how and where to haul it away. Events in just the last few years, however, have made it apparent that there is no "away." Both the costs and environmental consequences of dealing with garbage in our own communities have skyrocketed. The growing number of attempts to export it to other states or even other countries are, understandably, bitterly opposed by their residents. Increasingly, we are recognizing the need for wholly new approaches to addressing this old problem.

Americans now generate 160 million tons of garbage every year, approaching one ton per person. This amount is growing every year and greatly exceeds that produced by citizens in most of the other developed countries of the world. Congress has heard loud and clear from municipalities across the country about a solid waste disposal crisis. If not every community, a substantial number of our towns, cities, and counties are struggling with the problems of waste disposal and facing formidable hurdles. Typically, the crisis initially manifests itself in the form of landfill shortages. Underlying such shortages, however, is not only the fact that many landfills have simply filled up, but also that many have been forced to close because they cannot meet today's environmental standards or are contaminating groundwater or surface water. The resulting local opposition to the siting of new—even if more safely designed—landfills further magnifies these factors.

Whatever its cause, the crisis is causing a revolution in the way we handle our solid waste. One part of that revolution is a new effort to make recycling, composting, and waste reduction, and, in many cases, waste-to-energy incineration work for communities.

While solid waste has always been viewed as a local problem, it is increasingly clear that there are major issues that state and federal governments must help local governments to resolve if they are to move toward sound waste management practices. First and most important, what steps can we begin to institute now to reduce the amount of waste we each generate? How much of our waste can we recycle, and how can we create sufficient markets for these materials? What role should incineration play in waste management, and how can we ensure that when incineration is chosen by a community as a waste management option, it is done in an environmentally sound manner? Are recycling and incineration inherently in conflict? And finally, how can we reduce the need for landfilling and make landfills safer?

The sheer number of dollars involved makes it clear how much is at stake. Municipal waste management has become one of the largest items in local budgets, in some cases approaching the cost of such staples as police and fire protection and even education. Those communities that have built incinerators are often finding that the facilities represent one of the largest capital investments they have ever made—even before considering that the costs of air pollution controls and ash management are expected to rise dramatically with increasing regulation.

The challenge facing concerned citizens and decision-makers at all levels of government is a formidable one: to identify and implement long-term solutions that are safe, socially acceptable, *and* cost-effective, often in the face of tremendous pressure to do something immediately. Making wise choices under such conditions requires access to information that allows a thorough evaluation and comparison of options on both environmental and economic grounds. *Recycling and Incineration: Evaluating the Choices* not only provides the needed information, but puts it into a comprehensive context that is so urgently needed in this area.

Recycling and Incineration, written by the Environmental Defense Fund's team of nationally recognized solid waste experts, critically examines the abilities and suitability of two of the major approaches that are being used to tackle our solid waste problem. EDF's scientists, economists, and attorneys present the technology, the basis for economic comparison, the environmental concerns, and the legal intricacies surrounding these approaches in a manner that both educates and provides the reader with a strong basis for making sound choices.

But even more valuable is the framework the authors provide for assessing the vast amounts of information now available on solid waste management. The book presents and convincingly defends the need to adopt a holistic, yet hierarchical, approach to managing our wastes. While acknowledging the utility of a broad array of management methods, the authors argue that they cannot be viewed as all equal. Special emphasis must be placed first on developing and implementing those methods—source reduction, recycling, and composting—that not only effectively manage solid waste, but do so in a manner that is the most safe, most conserving of resources and energy, and most cost-effective.

This book is certain to prove an indispensable tool for all of us faced with making the tough choices about how to manage our waste.

John H. Chafee
United States Senator from Rhode Island

Recycling and Incineration

INTRODUCTION

SEEMINGLY OVERNIGHT, America's communities have found themselves taking a new and worried look at an old chore—taking out the trash.

With the help of the media, some of the dimensions of the problem have become well known. On the nightly news, the image of tractors crawling across huge mounds of trash as sea gulls swirl overhead has come to symbolize the imminent closing of landfills. Newspapers report community protests and political stalemate over proposals to build huge garbage-burning incinerators. As recycling grows in popularity, concern is expressed that too many households diligently sorting their discards are swamping markets for recovered materials. Long-held assumptions about disposability and convenience are being questioned, as city councils consider putting limits on packaging in fast-food restaurants and grocery stores, and debates about whether plastics can be recycled or should be made degradable are widely broadcast.

The United States produces more garbage—per person and in total—than any other nation on earth. We currently accrue municipal solid waste (MSW) at the rate of 160 million tons per year: more than 100,000 pounds in the ten seconds it might take you to read this paragraph. And these amounts are growing: Unless something is done, by the turn of the century, we are projected to be generating at least 190 million tons annually.[1]

This handbook is intended for citizens, government officials, and business people who want to help resolve the solid waste crisis. It provides the facts and reasons—scientific, economic, and legal—for making fundamental changes in the way we generate, handle, and dispose of MSW. More specifically, the handbook covers:

- the basics of waste reduction, recycling, and incineration technologies and methods, and a comparative evaluation of their ability to manage MSW;

3

- detailed cost comparisons of large-scale recycling and incineration, and a discussion of economic reforms needed to push recycling to its maximum potential;
- an evaluation of the health and environmental impacts of incineration, including a critical review of the role of risk assessment in incinerator proposals and an extensive discussion of the measures needed to reduce incinerator risks; and
- a road map through the myriad regulations and permitting processes governing MSW management planning and incinerator construction and operation, intended to facilitate full public participation in local decisions affecting all aspects of solid waste management.

SOLID WASTE: DIMENSIONS OF THE PROBLEM

The most prominent evidence of changing tides in solid waste management comes from our growing understanding of the public health, environmental, and economic shortcomings of our traditional reliance on landfilling. Throughout the 1960s and 1970s, virtually all (an estimated 93 percent) of our MSW was landfilled.[2] By 1986, growth in recycling and waste combustion had reduced this figure somewhat, to about 83 percent. The U.S. Environmental Protection Agency's (EPA) goal is to reduce landfilling to about 55 percent by the year 1992, through increases in reduction, recycling, and waste combustion.[3]

THE DECLINE OF LANDFILLING

The decline in landfilling reflects several factors. First, in many areas of the country, a majority of landfills have been closed as they pose unacceptable environmental risks because of their location, design, or operation, or simply because they have filled up. Since 1978, EPA estimates that more than 14,000 MSW landfills (70 percent of the total operating at that time) have closed, leaving today about 6,000 operating landfills. Further reductions in existing landfill capacity are expected: About half of the landfills operating today will be closed within 5 years and almost three-quarters within the next 15 years.[4]

New landfills are being sited and built at a much slower rate than in the 1970s, resulting in a net decrease in landfill capacity; a 30 percent drop in capacity is projected to occur nationally between 1988 and 1993.[5]

Because these trends are concentrated in areas of the country that generate the most waste, the capacity crunch has taken on crisis proportions for some municipalities.

Growing Environmental Concerns

Environmental concerns over landfilling have also increased dramatically in recent years. Landfills can pollute the environment through several routes: release of contaminated leachate directly into groundwater or indirectly into surface water; runoff of contaminated rainwater or melted snow directly into surface water; and air emissions of toxic or explosive gases. As the waste in landfills decays, leachates are generated that can contain a broad range of hazardous chemicals, including metals such as lead, cadmium, and mercury, and organic chemicals such as benzene, vinyl chloride, and tetrachloroethylene. Air emissions can include methane, which is both toxic and explosive, as well as other volatile, carcinogenic compounds, such as benzene, chloroform, and carbon tetrachloride.

EPA has documented widespread contamination of both groundwater and surface water that has resulted from the inadequate design, location, or operation of municipal landfills. EPA's most recent survey[6] documented these negative trends:

- Nationally, only about 25 percent of existing MSW landfills have the capability to monitor groundwater; of these, 36 percent have documented deficiencies in their groundwater monitoring programs.
- Despite these data-gathering deficiencies, at least one-quarter of those MSW landfills monitoring their groundwater are known to be contaminating groundwater.
- A separate EPA-sponsored study of 163 landfill case studies chosen to be nationally representative found groundwater contamination or adverse trends in groundwater quality at 146 sites.[7]
- Fewer than 12 percent of existing MSW landfills monitor for surface-water contamination; of these, however, 60 percent are known to be contaminating surface waters.
- Only 1 out of every 6 existing MSW landfills is lined, and only 1 out of 20 has a leachate collection system.
- Only about one-third of the states have regulations specifying liners, which can be natural or synthetic, for new MSW landfills, and less than two-thirds specify any leachate controls.

- More than 20 percent of the toxic waste sites on the Superfund National Priority List (NPL) are MSW landfills (249 of 1,177 NPL sites as of June 1988); of the 20 worst NPL sites, 8 are MSW landfills.[8]

Even the best-designed landfills suffer inherent deficiencies. All of the structures built into the landfill to contain the waste—liners, leachate collection systems, and final cover materials—have finite lifetimes, whereas the wastes and their toxic emissions will continue to exist for decades or longer. EPA has recently proposed to require MSW landfills to monitor groundwater and surface water and to maintain leachate collection systems and final covers for a minimum of 30 years, but has acknowledged that this time period is, in all likelihood, too short. Indeed, EPA recognized that the need for extended postclosure maintenance and monitoring is actually made more acute in landfills employing more-advanced containment systems because "even the best liner and leachate collection systems will ultimately fail due to natural deterioration," and such technologies may delay releases by many decades.[9]

Skyrocketing Costs

The worst general shortage of landfill space is in the Northeast, with the West Coast and large cities of the northern Midwest close behind. As public and private landfill operators in these regions have recognized the true value of their remaining landfill capacity, tipping fees have risen dramatically. In New Jersey, for example, typical tipping fees have escalated from $30 to $125 per ton between 1983 and 1987; a tipping fee is the charge levied for unloading solid waste at a landfill, incinerator, or transfer station.[10]

Greater capacity remains in the underpriced and underregulated landfills of the industrial Midwest, the South, and the Rocky Mountain states. As tipping fees rise, however, garbage becomes fluid, flowing from high-cost disposal options toward cheaper ones. New Jersey, once a destination for Philadelphia's trash, now ships over half of its solid waste to other states. Solid waste from the Northeast is turning up in Arkansas, Alabama, and Virginia. Under one scheme, baled garbage from the Northeast would be shipped by rail to a huge proposed landfill in New Mexico, and under another, Paraguay would be the recipient.[11]

Along with large profits for private waste haulers, long-distance shipment of MSW has engendered political controversy. In August 1989, for instance, the governor of Pennsylvania stood at a highway roadblock as state troopers turned back trucks delivering trash from out of state. He later signed an executive order freezing the amount of out-of-state waste that can be accepted at Pennsylvania landfills.[12] Jokes about the situation are common, such as the suggestion that garbage exports are New Jersey's revenge on Ohio for acid rain, but so are bitter local protests against proposed new megalandfills that would make rural towns accept waste from hundreds of miles away.

THE WAVERING PROMISE OF INCINERATION

Although we never will be rid of landfills entirely, it is clear that our reliance on them for almost all of our disposal needs cannot last. For example, the Fresh Kills landfill on Staten Island, which opened in 1948, accepts about 25,000 tons of waste a day from New York City, but it will close in about ten years. No nearby towns have entered the sweepstakes to host the next Fresh Kills; in fact, the landfill is simply irreplaceable.

One major response of solid waste managers to the decline of landfilling has been the actual or proposed construction of large incinerators. Almost 160 incinerators are operating today, with another 100 or more in the planning stages. These facilities generally accept either an unprocessed waste stream, accepted at mass-burn facilities, or a refuse-derived fuel (RDF) from which a large fraction of heavy noncombustible materials have been removed through mechanical preprocessing.

Incinerators are large, very complex facilities, with main buildings standing over 15 stories high, smokestacks hundreds of feet tall, and sophisticated computerized control systems that rival the space shuttle. Building and operating these plants has become the province of a handful of large, specialized engineering/construction firms, such as Ogden-Martin, Wheelabrator Technologies, Combustion Engineering, and Westinghouse; the latter two firms moved into the field from the nuclear-power-plant industry.

Because of their complexity, the prevailing means of selling incinerators is a "turnkey operation." This means that following a competitive bidding process an incinerator vendor, allied consultants, and investment bankers arrange to build and finance—either privately or through public bonding authority—the plant and operate it under contract with a municipality or regional solid waste authority. The key to making this arrangement work is a service contract that guarantees the private operator delivery of an established minimum quantity of waste and a substantial fee for processing it. A contract with a local utility for sale of steam or electricity produced by the plant is also an important part of the revenue picture. To attract vendors, minimize financial risks, and reduce the apparent tipping fee, the public sector usually offers a range of additional subsidies to private vendors. These may include contract clauses that pass on various financial risks to the municipality, donations of land, assistance with ash disposal, and large state grants.

For a price, incineration promises to handle waste without changing the way it is collected. The standardized packaging of such deals accounts for a large part of the popularity of incineration among solid waste professionals and local officials. In many cases, incinerator proponents sweeten the deal by offering direct or indirect financial inducements to the host community, such as reduced-cost or even free garbage processing, a per-ton royalty on imported garbage, or aid to local development projects, such as parks.

Incinerators offer the advantages of significant volume reduction, thereby extending landfill capacity, as well as destruction of much of the organic material in MSW, which otherwise would contribute significantly to the production of toxic leachates and air emissions as this material decomposes in a landfill. On the other hand, incineration greatly increases the mobility of toxic metals present in MSW, releasing them through air emissions or ash in forms that are generally much more bioavailable, that is, more readily absorbed by living organisms, than the same metals in the unburned waste. Large amounts of gaseous pollutants—nitrogen oxides, sulfur oxides, carbon monoxide, and hydrogen chloride—are released to the air. Incinerators can also create toxic organic by-products of combustion, including chlorinated dioxins, furans, and PCBs.

Though widely advertised as waste-to-energy facilities, incinerators equipped with energy-recovery technology should not be portrayed as power plants that burn garbage.[13] To begin with, MSW is not a good fuel—about 45 percent of the materials in our waste, such as glass, metal, and yard wastes, do not burn or burn poorly in incinerators.[14] Unprocessed MSW contains about 38 percent of the heating value of bituminous coal and 26 percent of the heating value of distillate fuel oil.[15] Power plants operated by electrical utilities make their profits by generating electricity from purchased coal or oil, but incinerator operators depend primarily on payments for accepting garbage. Revenues from the sale of electricity or steam typically cover only a fraction of the costs of both operating an incinerator and paying off the bonds required to build it.

As one would expect from a technology designed to control the high-temperature combustion and emission of pollutants from large volumes of mixed solid waste, incineration is also very expensive. For example, the required bond issue for a plant proposed to burn about 13 percent of New York City's solid waste—3,000 tons per day—is estimated at over $562 million, not including a $47 million direct grant from New York State.[16]

Finally, incineration is not a complete replacement for landfilling. Incinerators require both scheduled and unscheduled maintenance, amounting to at least a 15 percent downtime; at many facilities, waste received during such periods must be bypassed directly to a landfill. Many wastes, such as construction debris and large appliances, cannot be processed at incinerators and may also require landfilling. Finally, the large amounts of ash produced by incinerators—one-quarter to one-third by weight and one-tenth to one-fifth by volume of the input waste—must also be landfilled.

THE ENVIRONMENTAL CONSEQUENCES OF INCINERATION

The recent focus on incineration has been on environmental consequences, not on performance. In particular, the limitations, as well as the advantages, of incineration are being increasingly recognized. Incineration is not a waste disposal method but rather a waste processing technology. Although it reduces the amount of waste requiring disposal, it creates air pollution and leaves behind its own substantial burden of toxic ash, which requires very careful management and disposal.

Despite the clear perception that incineration poses health risks, the major focus of the risk debate is only beginning to encompass the full range of such risks. Public and regulatory concern has focused on chlorinated dibenzodioxins and dibenzofurans (commonly referred to as simply "dioxins") to the exclusion of other toxic constituents of incinerator by-products. There has been a similar fixation on cancer to the exclusion of other adverse health effects, despite the fact that several of the major pollutants released by incinerators (e.g., lead and mercury) are of primary concern because of noncarcinogenic health effects (e.g., their effects on neurological development and their ability to cause birth defects).

In addition, incinerators primarily have been characterized as stationary sources of toxic air pollutants that may cause harm through direct inhalation. Only recently have risk analyses for proposed incinerators begun to quantitatively assess pathways of exposure to air emissions in addition to direct inhalation, such as ingestion of food crops contaminated through deposition of airborne contaminants (see further discussion of routes of exposure in chapter 6). And even preliminary characterizations of the risks from the even larger number of pathways of exposure to incinerator ash are virtually nonexistent (see chapter 5).

The appropriate consideration of risk issues includes a comprehensive assessment not only of the individual impacts of a specific new source, such as an MSW incinerator, but, more important, consideration of this source in the context of ongoing exposures to other environmental releases of pollutants. The evaluation of incremental inputs—even if they are apparently small when considered in isolation—is critical. Consideration of the cumulative nature of both exposure to and the health effects induced by many incinerator-associated pollutants may be critical to the siting of such facilities.

Incineration differs from other methods of waste management, such as compaction and direct landfilling, in that major portions of the waste stream are physically and chemically transformed during the combustion process. Moreover, the products of this process—both solids and gases—differ markedly from the original waste in their environmental and biological behavior. Opportunities for release of the incinerator by-products arise from the moment of their generation, through the release of air pollutants, and continue during on-site management, handling, storage, and transport, as well as disposal, of ash.

Rational management of our trash requires that we understand what is in it and how best to manage each component. Incineration poses health risks in no small part because it is being used to manage materials that are uniquely unsuited to incineration—most notably, toxic metals, which are made more mobile and bioavailable through incineration.

Many communities are attempting to replace mass landfills with mass-burn incinerators. Both approaches suffer the same defect. Each perpetuates two myths that compromise our ability to find workable solutions to the solid waste dilemma: first, that we can manage trash without considering its individual components, and second, that a single method can successfully manage our entire waste stream. If trash is anything, it is diverse. It contains some materials that are readily recyclable, others that aren't; some that burn, others that don't; and some materials that are probably best buried; others that should never be.

Yet most of our incinerators, like our landfills, give equal treatment to lead-acid batteries and last week's leftovers. Indeed, mass-burn incinerators consume trash as if it were a homogeneous fuel like coal, when, in actuality, it is comprised of materials such as cans and bottles, which don't burn but can be readily recycled; yard wastes and paper, which burn but can be readily composted or recycled; and still other materials that contain toxic metals, such as batteries and many plastics. In short, incinerators pollute the air and create toxic ash in large part because they don't discriminate in the waste they handle.

THE RISE OF WASTE REDUCTION AND RECYCLING

The growing expense of solid waste management has primed the growth of recycling: the circuit of collection, processing, manufacture, and consumption that diverts raw materials from the waste stream and returns them to productive use in the economy. Although recycling was extolled on Earth Day, 1970, because it saves trees, by the twentieth anniversary of Earth Day in 1990, city managers supported it because it saves money. Most recyclable commodities are not enormously valuable, and few municipal programs pay for themselves through sales alone. The real economic advantages of recycling stem from the disposal costs that recycling avoids.

Of course, recycling is still good for the environment, and is so popular partly because it helps individuals solve environmental problems in their daily lives.

The recent growth of recycling has been substantial. For example, over 27 million tons of paper were collected in the United States and recycled into new products in 1989, compared to 21.6 million tons in 1986.[17] This amount represents 50 percent more waste than was burned in all MSW incinerators operating in 1988 (see chapter 2). With over 1,000 convenient residential curbside collection programs and about 650 yard-waste composting programs operating in the United States (see chapter 2), many older myths about recycling have been overcome. High-performance recycling programs can be systematically planned, and the field is full of innovation and entrepreneurial activity, in addition to being a longtime tradition in certain industries.

Though recycling recalls the curbside collection of newspapers, bottles, and cans in a middle-class suburb or college town, it is far more than this. Successful recycling programs can be found in the inner city, in rural areas, in office towers, at construction sites, in restaurants, in high-rise apartments, at private waste transfer stations, at scrap yards, and even at amusement parks. For example, the Six Flags Theme Park in New Jersey recycles or composts 76 percent of its waste.[18]

A vast variety of additional materials are now being recycled in substantial quantities, including office paper, magazines, plastic soda bottles and milk jugs, corrugated boxes, construction and demolition debris, wood, aluminum and other nonferrous metals, and iron and steel (in auto bodies, tin-coated steel cans, large appliances, and other scrap). Leaves, grass clippings, branches, and animal wastes are composted on a large scale, producing a useful soil amendment. Efforts to recycle or compost even more materials, such as additional plastics, commercial and residential food waste, and food-contaminated paper, are well underway. In fact, over 80 percent of our waste *technically* can be recycled or composted.

Waste reduction—making products more recyclable and producing less volume and toxic constituents in products to begin with—is also growing in practice. Citizens and local officials have realized that producing at least twice as much garbage per person as most other industrialized nations does not make life in the United States twice as comfortable or as convenient as anywhere else. Manufacturers are beginning to recognize that many of the toxic metals used in their products can be replaced by more benign substances.

As businesses seek to gain advantage from consumers' interest in buying less trash when they shop, "environmental marketing" has become a retailers' catchphrase for the 1990s. Some cities and states are not leaving the choices solely up to the private sector, however, and are passing ordinances that seek to regulate the composition and recyclability of parts of the local waste stream. As of late 1989, 15 to 20 cities and towns had passed ordinances that restrict the use of certain packaging materials or require that the materials be integrated into local recycling programs. Similar proposals are under consideration in at least another 50 to 60 communities and several states.[19]

RECYCLING REALITIES

Two problems continue to limit the growth of recycling to its full potential. First, recycling has not received the financial support merited by its status as a viable, large-scale waste management alternative. Although a contractual disposal charge—the tipping fee—is the norm for incineration and landfilling, it is rare in recycling, which must depend on the uncertain annual municipal-budget cycle for funds.

One recent survey of currently planned expenditures among 18 states in the Northeast and Midwest found that recycling and composting will handle 25 percent of these states' waste by 1995, assuming currently legislated recycling goals are met. At the same time, if all currently planned facilities are constructed, incineration is projected to handle 43 percent of these states' solid waste by the same year. Anticipated state spending on recycling is estimated from $525 to $790 million; spending on incineration is estimated at roughly $7 billion, or eight to ten times as much.[20] Though obviously subject to change, if these intentions are realized, local spending on recycling and incineration will be even more disparate.

More important than even outright spending, the development of large-scale recycling will require the use of public-sector financial resources and tools to support and leverage private investment. In fact, governments' current fiscal policy toward solid waste management works against realizing the substantial environmental and economic benefits of recycling, and instead favors continued reliance on the options of lesser resort—landfilling and incineration. In short, this policy has the effect of turning the widely accepted solid waste management hierarchy—reduce and recycle first, landfill and incinerate last—on its head.

This imbalance in funding directly influences the stability of markets for recovered materials, which, at least perceptually, is the largest current constraint on recycling. Though markets for almost all other secondary materials are expected to remain strong, the late-1988 collapse in the price for recovered newsprint agitated many would-be recyclers. This price decline resulted from three factors that hit the secondary-newsprint market simultaneously: increased municipal and private carter collections, a cyclical, short-term drop in Asian export buying (exports comprise about 20 percent of the market), and labor difficulties at a major U.S. paper mill that consumes old news. Combined with an inherently volatile international commodity market, these forces caused prices paid by private processors for municipally collected used newsprint to drop significantly. To cite a generalized example from the Northeast, processors' prices fluctuated from paying $50 per ton to charging $25 per ton in less than nine months. The negative price now supports processors' costs to clean and bale newsprint; they sell accumulated large quantities to domestic or foreign mills at a higher, positive price.

Under these circumstances, a few towns stopped marketing their newsprint, and landfilled it instead and often at landfills with depletion costs far in excess of what towns would have had to pay to move the newsprint. In some midwestern and rural communities, or towns new to recycling, markets dried up entirely for a number of weeks.[21]

These episodes were widely reported in the media; less recognized were subsequent moves by a number of paper companies to retrofit their plants to make greater use of the abundant new supplies of cheap raw material. In fact, as paper manufacturers began to retrofit their plants to handle more recovered fiber, they made it clear that new supplies of high-quality materials will be key to the success of their investments.[22] Again, this is why a strong financial policy toward recycling is essential—to show industry that the public sector is serious about recycling, and to provide the resources to process materials to specifications.

COMMUNITIES AT THE CROSSROADS

As space in landfills dwindles, communities are considering investments in recycling and incineration. Unfortunately, in many respects, these options are in competition for financial and political support and, most basically, for trash.

The profit structure of designing and operating incinerators presses heavily for building plants as large as can be justified. However, unlimited pursuit of solid waste combustion may dramatically undermine recycling efforts. To obtain financial backing, incinerator vendors require contractually guaranteed supplies of waste. In the typical put-or-pay contract, if municipalities are unable to deliver waste, they must make up the operator's financial shortfall resulting from lost tipping fees.

Commitments to large-scale incineration may work as long-term commitments *not* to recycle, even as recycling markets grow. For large cities, incinerators require investments on the scale of other public works projects in transportation, water delivery, and sewerage. For smaller cities or regional entities, an incinerator may be the biggest public investment in local history. If overall spending on incineration makes funds unavailable to pay for recycling, the consequences will be the same as removing materials by burning them.

Finally, successful recycling and incineration require the political commitment of local leaders. Local officials may often, though not always, find it difficult to advocate both at the same time. Marshaling popular and state agency approval to site and build an incinerator now requires years of intensive public relations and advocacy work on the part of local officials and their consultants. Unfortunately, this process sometimes seems to require that incinerator boosters must denigrate recycling to show that they have no choice but to build their plants. Not surprisingly, some of recycling's greatest skeptics are incinerator vendors.[23]

SEVEN STEPS TOWARD PRACTICAL SOLUTIONS

The United States is poised on the verge of a major shift in its trash management policies. Clearly, much is at stake in the hundreds of pending local decisions that will decide what means of solid waste management are utilized. The Environmental Defense Fund (EDF) believes that safe, economically sound solid waste management practices will not be created simply by taking pro- or anti-incineration stances. We need to move beyond this dichotomy to fundamentally reform the political institutions, economic ground rules, and environmental regulations that govern solid waste management.

If enacted in concert, the following recommendations will allow market forces to help settle the balance between recycling and incineration, and in the process create thriving recycling businesses, more efficient and resource-conserving industries, and a substantial number of new jobs. The incinerators and landfills that are built will be much safer and much more thoughtfully integrated into an overall waste management strategy.

Though powerful in combination, these changes do not have to be wrenching or socially disruptive. In many cases, we are simply recommending that households and businesses receive stronger economic signals as to the consequences of their waste-generating activities, and that tax dollars allocated to solid waste management be spent more prudently.

1. *Waste reduction must be a top priority.*

The flip side of our profligacy in generating solid waste is that we have substantial opportunities for waste reduction. Some see implementation of waste reduction as an intractable cultural problem, but a number of concrete steps are available to begin reducing the amount of trash we produce.

Basic education programs aimed at manufacturers and individuals can put good intentions toward the environment to work, making products more durable, reusable or recyclable, and less toxic in their composition. Experience in Europe, Canada, and California shows that creating labels for packages that inform consumers about their recyclability, recycled content, or other environmental consequences can channel consumer spending and can prompt manufacturers to redesign their products. Letting households and businesses see the bill for waste collection disposal services they already pay for—and charging for these services based on volume discarded, rather than a flat rate—can put economic incentives to work in favor of waste reduction and recycling.[24]

More complicated policies, such as differentially taxing the use of recyclable, recycled, and difficult-to-recycle materials by manufacturers could also play a role in waste reduction policies, as could repealing the federal tax and budget subsidies for the exploitation of virgin minerals, timber, and energy resources. Even prior to state or federal action, local restrictions on products that pose particular disposal problems may prompt industry to respond on a national scale. The possible design and effects of such policies are elaborated upon in chapter 1.

2. *Planners should conduct a fair and thorough environmental and economic comparison of all waste reduction, recycling, treatment, and disposal methods.*

Our institutional tendency to shortchange waste reduction and recycling can be preempted by insisting that any proposals to build new incinerators or landfills include a full and fair comparative evaluation of the potential of waste reduction and recycling. Such evaluations have been done for a number of large American cities, and, in some cases, have dramatically changed the direction of solid waste management. For example, in the mid-1980s, Seattle was considering construction of a large mass-burn incinerator to replace its two badly leaking landfills. In 1988, the city and its consultants undertook a review of the possible achievements that might result from a comparable level of investment in recycling. Seattle found that recycling levels of 50 to 78 percent were within reason, and estimated that they could be achieved with an overall system cost that was less than that for plans that included even a relatively small incinerator. Seattle has since adopted the goal of recycling 60 percent of its waste by 1998, and is more than halfway to that point already.

The criteria for measuring the performance of recycling and incineration should evaluate how much each option reduces dependence on landfilling. This approach considers not just what can be fed into a processing plant or incinerator, but the residues that are left over and materials that cannot be accepted.

Solid waste managers must compare all available options on economic grounds as well. Managing garbage costs tax dollars; New Jersey now spends close to $1 billion each year to handle its solid waste, and Elizabeth, New Jersey, pays more for waste management than for police or education. Poor investments in waste management can be a major drain on the local economy.

Even with uncertainty about the future, it is possible to compare recycling and incineration on practical and economic grounds, and draw firm conclusions for the course of local waste management. Chapters 1 through 3 explain how to compare in detailed terms, and give examples of comparisons that have already been conducted and acted upon.

3. *Regulation of incineration, landfilling, and recycling should comprehensively address the environmental consequences of improper waste management.*

For the substantial amounts of waste that can be expected to remain even after maximum recycling, reliance on landfilling and incineration will continue, so that their significant health and environmental risks must be directly addressed. Proper design of facilities using the best-available technology is critical. For landfills, impermeable liners and covers and collection systems for leachate can greatly reduce risks to water supplies; methane recovery systems can reduce the risks posed by landfill gas emissions, and provide the added benefit of turning landfills into sources of energy.

For incinerators, advanced combustion systems and state-of-the-art air pollution controls, coupled with restrictions on the kinds of waste that may be burned, can reduce air pollution significantly. Comprehensive monitoring (continuous whenever technology allows) of stack emissions and periodic testing of ambient air and soils are necessary to assess whether the permitted, but continual releases are resulting in accumulation in the environment. Proper training of facility operators is critical to ensuring that the presence of state-of-the-art equipment translates into actual state-of-the-art reduction in emissions. Chapter 6 discusses these recommendations in detail.

With respect to incinerator ash, provision should be made for separate testing of fly and bottom ash, and the capability to manage these two wastes separately should be engineered into all facilities. Especially for fly ash, chemical and/or physical treatment may be needed prior to disposal because of its dispersive nature and high heavy metal leachability. An assurance of capacity to disposal of all ash separate from other wastes, and only in lined landfills equipped with leachate collection and leak-detection systems, must be an integral part of the approval of any incinerator project. Chapter 5 further discusses these recommendations.

Recycling is by no means without its environmental impacts, as evidenced by the serious contamination of air, soil, and water surrounding secondary-lead smelters. Recycling operations, whether at a paper mill, plastics formulator, steel furnace, or aluminum smelter, all produce wastes in the form of releases to air and water, as well as solid wastes. Promotion of recycling cannot take place at the expense of full regulation and environmental control over recycling facilities. Current regulations applying to air and water pollution and solid waste generated by recycling facilities should be fully enforced. Existing loopholes that exempt certain recycling facilities from regulation need to be carefully scrutinized to determine if they are justified with respect to environmental hazards, yet, at the same time, consider the need to maintain strong incentives for recycling.

To some extent, better regulation of all types of solid waste management will also lead to more valid comparisons of the costs of different approaches. Lax regulation of incinerator air emissions, for example, could lead to substantial and costly damage to the public health. However, these costs would not show up in the price tag for operating the plant. Making incinerator, landfill, and recycling operators incorporate the cost of appropriate pollution control equipment or residue disposal charges in their balance sheets will not completely internalize these external costs but can improve comparisons significantly.

4. *Solid waste management efforts must be expanded to include source reduction of toxic constituents and maximum waste segregation.*

Traditionally, pollution control has been thought of as beginning at the "end of the pipe," that is, at the point of discharge of a waste to the air, water, or land. Requirements to install air and water pollution control equipment and requirements to design landfills to certain specifications represent typical approaches to pollution control. However, the issue of solid waste management provides an excellent opportunity to expand the scope of what is considered pollution control to include a much broader range of strategies, beginning with efforts toward pollution prevention.

One conceptual constraint to viewing the waste problem in sufficiently broad terms is that we have traditionally considered the waste cycle to begin at the point when a product or material has fulfilled its intended function and is discarded. The subsequent steps of collecting, transporting, processing, and disposing of these materials constitute our present view of MSW management. Yet the safety, efficiency, and economics of waste management are dramatically affected by decisions made by manufacturers concerning the chemical and physical composition, packaging, marketing, and distribution of their products. Components or characteristics of a product that are useful or incidental to its function may increase the costs or hazards or constrain the available means of managing the product once it becomes waste.

As one example, the use of cadmium-based pigments as colorants in many consumer plastics is a major contributor of cadmium to MSW.[25] A manufacturer's decision to use cadmium-based pigments, which is based largely on increasing a product's attractiveness to a potential consumer, is made entirely without regard to its postconsumer impacts. Yet the cadmium present in such plastics is liberated during incineration of the MSW, increasing both the toxicity of and costs of managing incinerator air emissions and/or ash residues.

Rational waste management is, in essence, materials management. It begins with a thorough understanding of waste composition, with regard to which waste constituents or properties pose environmental and health risks or constrain the management of various waste components. Source-based measures to reduce either the amount or the toxicity of materials entering the waste stream represent the most efficient means of waste management. Restricting the use of heavy metal colorants in manufacturing consumer plastics is one such measure.

In several European countries, government initiatives have been directed toward reducing the use of certain metals (e.g., cadmium) in consumer products, particularly those that are used and discarded in large amounts after limited use, such as disposable plastic items.[26] Given the use of toxic metals in the manufacture of a very broad range of consumer materials (e.g., printing inks, plastic stabilizing agents), as well as in more easily identified materials such as lead-acid batteries, only comprehensive source-based strategies are likely to prove successful in achieving significant reductions in the metal content and toxicity of our waste and incineration by-products.

Our present approach to MSW management has avoided solving difficult problems only by transferring them to later stages in the waste cycle. It is unreasonable to expect the economics and technologies of waste disposal to efficiently manage risks whose origins lie far upstream. For example, the most difficult and expensive method of reducing the risk of exposure to toxic metals in products is to delay action until after incineration has refined metals into a highly bioavailable and concentrated form. Both efficiency and the generally accepted goal of promoting prevention over remediation dictate that we examine alternatives to the use of such metals at the production stage. Chapter 1 discusses source reduction approaches that are currently applied or could be applied to solid waste.

After pursuing source reduction approaches, every opportunity to maximize segregation of the waste stream into its various components should be utilized. Developing methods include household-based materials separation programs supported by curbside collection and mixed-waste processing technologies. These emerging waste management approaches are discussed in chapter 2. Waste segregation provides the means to direct individual materials to the management methods most appropriate for them. For example, yard wastes (e.g., leaves and grass clippings) represent one-fifth or more of the American waste stream. Such waste only takes up valuable space in landfills, and contributes to nitrogen oxide emissions if burned. If kept separate from other wastes, however, yard wastes can be readily composted, reducing their volume and yielding a useful, clean soil amendment that need not be disposed of at all.

Nor does it make any sense to send noncombustible materials, such as cans and bottles to incinerators, since they only serve to reduce incinerator efficiency and add to the volume of ash that is produced. Moreover, such materials are eminently recyclable. Waste components containing toxic metals, such as batteries, are best separated from waste headed for landfills or incinerators. Where possible, recycling of such materials is the ideal option; in the alternative, stockpiling, treatment, or controlled disposal in hazardous waste facilities are preferable to handling such toxic materials as ordinary garbage.

Recycling and recovery of waste materials can yield substantial reductions in energy and raw materials requirements and wastes associated with acquisition of raw materials and product manufacturing, and should be the options of first resort. With respect to waste management, large-scale separation and recycling can provide the dual benefit of reducing the amount of waste that must be managed, and increasing the safety of any landfilling or incineration that is carried out, by removing materials that should not be buried or burned. Seen in this light, recycling is itself pollution control, since it translates directly into a reduced need for landfills or incinerators.

5. *Incinerator vendors should be held accountable for their promises about plant performance through contracts.*

Incinerator proposals are virtually always accompanied by claims or promises as to how the facility will perform. In theory, operating permits provide public assurance that such promises will be met. In practice, however, permits are not a sufficient guarantee of adequate, let alone optimal, performance.

Even a perfect permit will be useless without adequate enforcement, which, in turn, is dependent on the frequently meager resources of regulatory agencies. And once an incinerator is up and running, with a fleet of loaded garbage trucks arriving every day, government officials are understandably reluctant to interfere too often or too much, even if the incinerator only intermittently honors its permit.

Nonetheless, citizens and officials have a right to know whether the promises they are hearing are realistic, and whether those promises will actually be kept. The surest way to find out whether a project's proponents are serious about their assurances is to arrange for the project—not the municipality or the public—to bear the risk if the assurances turn out to be wrong. Such an approach has the benefit of producing more realistic promises than might otherwise be offered, and also assures that if promises are later broken, it will not be only the public who pays.

Chapter 8 discusses some simple legal tools that can be used to ensure that promises made by incinerator vendors are actually kept. These tools are applied to three critical areas of incinerator operation—ash toxicity, interference with recycling, and air emissions.

6. *Recycling should be supported by fiscal policies that reflect its full potential as a solid waste management alternative.*

Assuming comprehensive environmental regulation of incineration, landfilling, and recycling, a "level playing field" for financing recycling can be provided. For example, major investment banks have shown a serious interest in issuing revenue bonds to support very large materials processing operations, just as they now do for incinerators. The repayment of these bonds would be guaranteed by municipal tipping fees to the processing plant operator. Revenues from sales of secondary commodities would be split between the participants on a formula basis, decoupling successful plant operations from swings in commodity market prices but preserving an incentive for market development. This is essentially an incinerator finance model applied to recycling, which could be in use by the early 1990s.

The state and local fiscal policies that would establish the basis for such an arrangement could take several forms. One possibility would be to revise the bidding rules on municipal incinerator or landfill contracts to allow recycling proposals to compete for funding. Cities would issue a request for proposals (RFP) for a given quantity of waste management services, allow recyclers to bid on specified material streams, and select the lowest responsible bid. If recyclers needed materials delivered in segregated form, the costs would be factored into the bid-selection equation.

State legislation can support private recycling and condition the policies of local government. For example, Assembly Bill 2020, California's experiment in container deposits, requires beverage distributors to subsidize the scrap value of secondary glass and plastic. In essence, this policy makes recycling operations profitable by making these materials too valuable to throw away. Under the New York State Solid Waste Management Act of 1988, by 1992, municipalities must undertake programs to collect for recycling all materials for which there are so-called economic markets. This condition is defined to exist when the costs of collection and processing, minus revenue from material sales, are less than the costs of disposal by other means.

Finally, cities can simply conduct detailed comparative studies of the cost and feasibility of different solid waste management options, select appropriate recycling goals, and then develop funding mechanisms to get the job done. For example, waste management costs in Seattle, including landfill tipping fees, cleanup costs for closed landfills, and projected recycling costs, are all built into the rates the city charges for trash collection. States can also do much more to create dedicated funding sources for recycling, using instruments such as general obligation bonds, landfill tipping-fee surcharges, reclaimed bottle deposits, or taxes on difficult-to-recycle materials. Chapter 4 explains these approaches.

7. *Expanded recycling collection programs must be accompanied by market development initiatives.*

Ensuring stable markets for recovered materials will require joint action by government and industry, and can benefit both substantially. To begin with, the public sector must make clear its motivations and intentions in undertaking recycling programs, commit to meeting market specifications for materials, and inform industry of the timing and expected quantity of delivering new materials. The best way for the public sector to show its commitment to this process is by funding recycling on par with other waste management options. At the same time, businesses need to understand that secondary commodity markets are being inexorably altered by rising costs in solid waste disposal, and that this may provide major opportunities for lowering manufacturing costs. For some but not all materials, these steps will be sufficient to ensure viable markets.

Public policies to support industries that use more problematic recovered materials can take a variety of forms. Government purchasing offices can "prime the pump" and demonstrate the acceptable performance of recycled products by instituting price preferences for items with recycled content. The tools of economic development agencies—for example, low-interest loans, loan guarantees, research and development (R&D) support, industrial revenue bonds, and siting assistance—can be used to support industrial expansion. Investment in infrastructure, such as port facilities, can improve transportation and exports. Chapter 2 elaborates on the workings of secondary commodity markets and the potential of these and other market development instruments.

Thematically, these seven principles can be reduced even further to just two: We must approach solid waste management more evenly and more comprehensively. More evenly, because we have helped to create the present solid waste crisis through fiscal policies and a mentality among solid waste managers that favor continued landfilling and incineration over waste reduction and recycling, and that allow manufacturers and consumers to escape the full costs of their waste-generating behavior. More comprehensively, because we cannot reduce the environmental risks of solid waste management without examining all stages of the product life cycle. Decisions concerning the introduction of toxic chemicals or the types and amounts of packaging used in product manufacture, marketing, and distribution have profound impacts on our ability to manage those materials once they become waste—impacts we can no longer afford to ignore.

BEYOND NIMBY: PUTTING THIS HANDBOOK TO USE

Efforts to build new solid waste management facilities have unquestionably led to political conflict and stalemate in many communities. To some, this is the result of the not-in-my-backyard (NIMBY) syndrome, used to invoke images of misinformed citizens egged on by "environmental evangelists."[27] To others, NIMBY is "the incinerator vendors' term for democracy."[28]

We are not surprised that citizens who are offered poor information and limited choices feel compelled to act in opposition, especially given the history of glaring environmental disasters in waste management. In any case, we must all accept the costs and consequences of disposing of our waste, whatever the chosen method. To the extent that a local stalemate is the result of the lack of systematic, thorough information on the full range of available solid waste management options, we hope that this handbook helps to clarify and resolve the debate. To those of you in all occupations who use this handbook, please let us know whether it helped or not, and how. Comments, preferably in writing, should be addressed to EDF's offices in New York City (recycling) and Washington, DC (incineration).[29]

NOTES

1. U.S. Environmental Protection Agency, *The Solid Waste Dilemma: An Agenda for Action* (Washington, DC: Office of Solid Waste, February 1989), p. 1. Hereafter cited as EPA.
2. Franklin Associates, *Characterization of Municipal Solid Waste in the United States, 1960 to 2000 (Update 1988)*, *Final Report* prepared for EPA (Washington, DC: Office of Solid Waste and Emergency Response, 1988), p. S-4.
3. EPA, *The Solid Waste Dilemma*, p. 23, see also: U.S. Congress, Office of Technology Assessment (OTA), *Facing America's Trash: What Next for Municipal Solid Waste* (Washington, DC: U.S. Government Printing Office, 1989 OTA-0-424).
4. National Solid Wastes Management Association, "Landfill Capacity in the Year 2000" (Washington, DC, 1989), reporting data from EPA, "Municipal Solid Waste Landfill Survey," draft (Washington, DC: Office of Solid Waste, 1986); and EPA, *Report to Congress: Solid Waste Disposal in the United States* (Washington, DC: Office of Solid Waste and Emergency Response, October 1988).
5. EPA, "Municipal Solid Waste Landfill Survey," draft (Washington, DC: Office of Solid Waste, 1986).

6. EPA, *Census of State and Territorial Subtitle D Non-Hazardous Waste Programs* (Washington, DC: Office of Solid Waste and Emergency Response, October 1986).

7. *Federal Register* 53 (August 30, 1988): 33366.

8. See U.S. Government Accounting Office, "State Management of Municipal Landfills and Landfill Expansions," (Washington, DC: Resources, Community, and Economic Development Division, June 1989), p. 15. Although many of those sites accepted hazardous wastes before RCRA hazardous waste system took effect, for several reasons the implementation of this system cannot justify dismissal of the lessons to be learned from the Superfund sites. First, hazardous wastes from households and small quantity generators routinely wind up in MSW landfills. Indeed, the proportion of such wastes as a percentage of total waste in MSW landfills may increase in the future, as recycling programs broaden their scope to include larger geographic regions and quantities of wastes. Also, leachates from pre- and post-RCRA MSW landfills appear to differ little in their toxicity. See EPA, "Summary of Data on Municipal Solid Waste Landfill Leachate Characteristics," draft background document (Washington, DC: Office of Solid Waste, July 1988). For these reasons, lessons from old landfills still have much to teach us about design standards for new ones.

9. *Federal Register* 53 (August 30, 1988): 33345.

10. In Newark, the city budget for waste disposal increased from $6 million in 1987 to $30 million in 1988. Plainfield, New Jersey, was paying tipping fees of $18 per ton at the Edgeboro landfill near New Brunswick in 1987, but in 1988, the city was required by the state to send its trash to the Linden transfer station, where the tipping fee is $137 per ton; the trash is subsequently shipped to Ohio and Pennsylvania for disposal; "Hauling Costs Soaring, Jerseyans Turn to Dumping Trash Illegally," *New York Times*, March 18, 1988, pp. A1, B2.

11. "Waste Spurs Uncivil War Between the States; As Landfills Close, Debate Grows Over Shipping Garbage," *Wall Street Journal*, November 17, 1989, p. A9C; "Alabama Rule Requires Bond on Out-of-State Waste," *Solid Waste Report*, September 26, 1988, p. 306; "Philly Garbage May Be Headed for Arkansas," *Solid Waste Report*, June 27, 1988, p. 205; "Paraguayans Balk at Lucrative Trash Deal from New York City," *Christian Science Monitor*, January 9, 1990, p. 5; Joan V. Schroeder, "Northern Trash," *New York Times*, August 16, 1989, op-ed page.

12. *Wall Street Journal*, November 17, 1989, p. A9C.

13. For the reasons laid out in this paragraph, we will generally use the term "incinerator" throughout this handbook.

14. Glass, metals, and miscellaneous inorganic wastes were estimated to comprise 19.1 percent of the U.S. waste stream in 1986. Food waste and yard waste comprised an estimated 29 percent of the waste stream. Franklin Associates, *Characterization of Municipal Solid Waste in the United States, 1960 to 2000 (Update 1988), Final Report*, p. 7.

15. T. Randall Curlee, *The Economic Feasibility of Recycling*. (New York: Praeger, 1986), p. 28.

16. New York City Office of Management and Budget, *Message of the Mayor: The City of New York Executive Budget, Fiscal Year 1988*, May 5, 1987, p. 141. The 1987 figure of $535 million bond issue for the Brooklyn Navy Yard plant was updated in 1989 to $562 million.

17. Personal communication with Rod Edwards, American Paper Institute, New York City, 1988, who supplied preliminary data for 1989.

18. Personal communication with Mary Sheil, Deputy Director, New Jersey Department of Environmental Protection, 1989.

19. Pete Rathbun, "And the Ban Plays On," state report on environment (Washington, DC: National Center for Policy Alternatives, January 1990).

20. Northeast-Midwest Institute, "A Bad Burn; States Are Depending on Incineration Instead of Recycling," *Northeast Midwest Economic Review* September 5, 1989, pp. 9–11. Available from NMI, 218 D Street, SE, Washington, DC 20003.

21. In some cases, local officials decided to dump collected newspaper in their nearly full landfills rather than pay to have it shipped to paper mills; "Extra Paper Is Bad News; Recycling of Paper Dropped in Smithtown," *New York Newsday*, June 11, 1989, p. 7.

22. G. Pierce Goad, "Recycling Siren Lures Newsprint Makers; Profit Outlook is Weak, But Demand Is Soaring," *Wall Street Journal*, November 11, 1989.

23. The incinerator industry has recently diversified into recycling operations. For example, Wheelabrator Technologies holds the license for U.S. distribution of Buhler-Miag solid waste composting and recycling systems. Wheelabrator also plans to convert an old cement plant in Northhampton, Virginia, into a linerboard mill that will consume old corrugated containers. At the same time, incinerator vendors are unenthusiastic about high levels of recycling. For example, a spokesperson for Westinghouse stated that recycling over 25 percent of the waste stream would be "extremely aggressive and unrealistic"; Tom Watson, "Here Comes the Burner Brigade," *Resource Recycling*, March/April 1989, pp. 44–45, 71–73.

24. David Riggle, "Only Pay for What You Throw Away," *BioCycle*, February 1989, pp. 39–41.

25. Franklin Associates, *Characterization of Products Containing Lead and Cadmium in Municipal Solid Waste in the United States, 1970 to 2000* (Washington, DC: EPA Office of Solid Waste, January 1989).

26. Mats Bothen and Ulla-Britta Fallenius, *Cadmium: Occurrence, Uses, and Stipulations* (Solna, Sweden: National Swedish Environmental Protection Board 1982 report no. SNV PM 1615); Ministry of Housing, Physical Planning, and Environment, Chemical Substances Act: Cadmium Decree, *Government Gazette* 60 (The Netherlands: Leidschendam 1987); Commission of the European Communities, *Environmental Pollution by Cadmium: Proposed Action Programme* (Brussels, Belgium, April 1987 report no. COM [87] 165).

27. George Melloan, "Waste Disposal and the 'Environmental Evangelists,' " *Wall Street Journal*, July 26, 1988, op-ed. p. 35.
28. For a trenchant evaluation of the NIMBY syndrome from the standpoint of a citizen activist group, see: Environmental Research Foundation, "What Have the NIMBYS Done for Me Lately?" *Rachel's Hazardous Waste News*, no. 140 (August 1, 1989). Available from Environmental Research Foundation, P.O. Box 3541, Princeton, NJ 08543-3541.
29. The addresses for EDF are:
    EDF
    257 Park Avenue South
    New York, NY 10010

    EDF
    1616 P Street, NW
    Washington, DC 20036

PART I

Recycling and Incineration: The Basis for Comparison

THE CURRENT GARBAGE CRISIS has focused nationwide attention on MSW management; one result is the formal adoption of the now-familiar waste management hierarchy into legislation and regulations governing solid waste. Under this hierarchy, our waste should be managed according to a set of preferences: waste reduction and reuse first, followed by recycling, incineration, and landfilling.

Despite its common-sense countenance, this hierarchy is not self-implementing. In many communities, proposals to build mass-burn incinerators that would process the majority of the waste stream are under active consideration; reduction and recycling initiatives lag far behind. Before a community can know whether a commitment to incineration is prudent or even necessary, several key questions must be considered, including:

- What is the ability of incineration to reduce dependence on landfilling?
- To what extent can alternatives such as recycling and waste reduction achieve the same end?
- What are the real costs of each approach, budgetary and otherwise?

The next four chapters present an analytical approach that communities can use to address each of these questions.

"Ability to reduce dependence on landfilling" is emphasized for an important reason. Both recycling and incineration are waste *processing*—not disposal—technologies, and neither completely eliminates the need to landfill some portion of the waste stream. Though mass-burn incinerators, in particular, are designed to accept mixed solid waste, some materials are not suitable for incineration. These materials include construction and demolition debris and bulk waste, such as discarded stoves, refrigerators, and couches. This material accounts for roughly one-quarter of the waste stream (by weight). In addition, a sizable portion of what is fed into mass-burn incinerators is noncombustible and remains behind as ash, which must also be landfilled under carefully managed conditions, as discussed in Part II. Ash comprises 25 percent or more by weight, about 10 percent or more by volume of the input waste. Finally, bypass waste—material that cannot be burned when the incinerator is shut down for maintenance or repairs, which is typically 15 to 30 percent of the time—must also be sent to the landfill.

Some waste materials are impractical or expensive to recycle, and all recycling processing operations generate some amount of residue that also must be landfilled; for example, shredding old cars for use as scrap metal produces a plastic residue known as "shredder fluff." Thus, the best measure of these approaches to solid waste management is not how much trash can be fed into an incinerator or a materials processing plant but how effectively each technology reduces *overall* dependence on landfilling.

To establish the basis for comparing incineration and recycling, a number of factors must be known or estimated for each alternative.

For an incineration proposal, these factors include:

1. The amount of waste generated in a locality, and the fraction of this waste that can be accepted for processing at an incinerator; the assumption is that the proposed incinerator will not greatly alter waste collection methods.
2. The composition of the waste stream, defined in terms of suitability for combustion: material size, abrasiveness, moisture, energy content, and so on.
3. The specific type of incinerator technology that is proposed (e.g., mass burn, refuse-derived fuel, modular).
4. The fraction of input refuse that will remain as ash after combustion.
5. The overall cost of building and operating the incinerator, including the costs of ash disposal, air pollution control equipment, and compliance with environmental regulations.
6. Financial and technical risks and uncertainties associated with the proposal.
7. The status of local energy markets and prices (and price subsidies) for electricity or steam produced by incineration.

For recycling, a similar, but not entirely equivalent, set of factors must be understood:

1. The amount of waste generated in a locality, and how it is currently collected (e.g., the mix of public collection, private collection, and public-private contracts).
2. The composition of the waste stream in terms of specific materials (e.g., aluminum, glass, yard waste) and where it is generated (e.g., businesses, residential neighborhoods).
3. The specific materials targeted for recycling and the design of programs intended to recover them.
4. The expected effectiveness of proposed household and commercial recycling programs in diverting targeted materials from the waste stream; this is primarily a function of public participation.
5. The type of additional processing required to prepare recovered materials for marketing (e.g., intermediate processing centers, composting facilities, mixed solid waste processing facilities).
6. The overall costs of recycling collection and processing systems, including savings in conventional refuse collection and disposal expenses that result from the diversion of materials from the waste stream.
7. Financial and logistical risks and uncertainties associated with the proposal.
8. The availability of markets for recovered materials, prevailing prices, price volatility, and the potential effect of market development programs.

Chapters 1 through 4 explain how to compare recycling and incineration along each of the parameters described above. Chapter 1 begins with a discussion of the composition of MSW, noting the differences between waste composition studies oriented toward recycling and incineration, and contrasting the results of several such studies that have been conducted in the United States.

Chapter 1 also addresses the enormous potential to reduce the amount of waste we generate through a variety of technological, economic, and social approaches. Such waste reduction measures occupy the highest tier in the so-called waste management hierarchy and, therefore, deserve consideration as the options of first resort. Despite this preference, chapter 1 indicates that much of the potential to reduce our wastes is largely untapped.

Chapter 2 compares the ability of incineration and recycling to manage portions of the waste stream. This comparison begins with an overview of incinerator technology, the reduction in solid waste weight and volume that can be achieved through incineration, the amount of ash produced in the incineration process, and the scope of present and anticipated incinerator use in the United States.

Chapter 2 evaluates the waste management potential of large-scale recycling. In practice, large-scale recycling includes a number of different types of recycling programs that work in concert, each recovering materials generated by the various economic activities that coexist in a large city or region. Estimating the potential of large-scale recycling for a given city usually means extrapolating from the performance of local pilot programs and fully developed programs in other cities. This kind of estimation requires an understanding of the mechanics of different collection methods, which the chapter surveys, including curbside and apartment-house collection, composting, commercial recycling, rural recycling, and buy-back centers. In describing each of these approaches, chapter 2 also gives representative data from cities where they have been successfully implemented.

Chapter 3 concentrates on costs. Large incinerators require financing through large bond issues, sometimes as much as several hundred million dollars, which must be paid off over the life of the incinerator. Proper ash disposal, air pollution controls, and other regulatory costs, such as testing and monitoring, add to the operating expense. These costs are partially offset by revenues from the sale of steam or electricity produced by the plant. Recycling also requires significant public expenditures, which can vary dramatically depending on how programs are designed and operated.

In an era of tight budgets, it is critical to compare the costs of recycling and incineration side by side when selecting waste management options. Chapter 3 explains the economic concepts and calculations necessary to make this financial comparison, and works step-by-step through sample cost calculations for recycling and incineration programs. Chapter 3 also describes some of the financial and practical risks associated with recycling and incineration, and explains how these can be accounted for, both in program design and in comparative analysis.

The ability to directly compare recycling and incineration as waste management alternatives has important consequences for communities, which are summarized in chapter 4. The recent growth of large-scale recycling in the United States has made new data available, allowing increasingly sophisticated comparisons between the two alternatives. Chapter 4 begins by summarizing comparative analyses of waste management options conducted by city agencies, consulting firms, and nonprofit groups for three regions—New York City, Seattle, Washington, and a collection of towns on Long Island, New York. Each of these studies shows that recycling can play a major role in waste disposal, at a cost that is substantially less than comparably sized incineration programs.

Chapter 4 concludes with three important recommendations for solid waste policy that stem from our growing recognition of the economic advantages of recycling. First, as a condition for considering any proposed incinerator, municipal officials should thoroughly study and compare the environmental and economic risks and the waste management and economic potentials of recycling and incineration. Second, and more to the point, recycling should be supported by public investment under the same economic ground rules now almost exclusively reserved for incineration. This fiscal stance toward recycling extends naturally from the recognition that one major purpose of recycling is to avoid the higher costs of incineration and long-distance landfilling.

Currently, most state and local governments offer a number of subsidies and contractual guarantees that reduce financial risks and improve profits for the large companies that build incinerators and for the investment banks that support them. Mechanisms that do the same for private and nonprofit concerns that process and market recyclable materials are in their infancy. To remove this inequity, and to give market forces greater influence in the selection of waste disposal options, recycling and incineration proposals should be allowed to compete on at least equal terms for public support. Indeed, if recycling is a preferred option, as indicated in the waste management hierarchy, it should be afforded greater economic preference.

Waste Generation and Waste Reduction

RELIABLE DATA on both the quantities and qualities of our trash are of central importance in planning for solid waste management; the discussion in this chapter is intended to provide the basics on what makes up our waste and how much of it we generate.

The chapter discusses what is increasingly recognized, though yet to be seriously acted upon, as the option of first resort in dealing with our trash: reducing the amount we generate in the first place, so that we needn't worry about how to manage it. Waste reduction encompasses a broad array of strategies and approaches—some technological, some social, some economic—for reducing both the amount and toxicity of MSW.

SOLID WASTE QUANTITIES

Americans generate more MSW—both in terms of the total amount and on a per capita basis—than any other nation on earth. Although definitions of what materials constitute waste can vary greatly among nations, available waste generation data clearly document our lead over all others. In rough terms, Japan and Western European nations generate less than half as much solid waste, per capita, as the United States. Moreover, generation of solid waste is not well correlated with economic output. Many nations have managed to maintain a per capita gross national product close to that of the United States yet produce far less waste per capita. Though precise comparisons between nations are difficult because waste generation data may have been collected differently and in different years, table 1.1 and figure 1.1 display the available international data on waste generation and economic output.

33

TABLE 1.1

Comparative Data on National Solid Waste Generation and Economic Output

Country	Total Annual Waste Generation (1,000 tons)	Annual Per Capita Waste Generation (lbs)	Annual Per Capita GNP, 1984 (US $)	Per Capita Waste Generation/ US Per Capita Waste Generation (%)	Per Capita GNP/Waste Generation ($/lb)	Year Given for Waste Generation Data
Norway	1,543	617	$13,750	37.6%	22.271	1984/85
Switzerland	1,947	741	$15,990	45.2%	21.582	1980
Finland	1,089	545	$10,830	33.2%	19.885	1983
Austria	1,479	476	$ 9,140	29.0%	19.190	1983
Sweden	2,269	664	$11,880	40.5%	17.900	1980
France	12,704	573	$ 9,860	34.9%	17.199	1980
Japan	14,289	754	$10,390	46.0%	13.778	1983
United Kingdom	14,880	642	$ 8,350	39.1%	13.013	1983
Denmark	1,857	880	$11,290	53.6%	12.833	1980
Italy	12,741	549	$ 6,440	33.5%	11.729	1980
Germany, Fed Rep	24,995	986	$11,090	60.1%	11.252	1984/85
Korea, Rep	14,289	1,497	$15,410	91.3%	10.293	1983
United States	161,525	1,641	$15,490	100.0%	9.442	1983
Canada	14,519	1,416	$13,140	86.3%	9.282	1983
Netherlands	6,572	1,103	$ 9,430	67.2%	8.553	1984/85

Country					
Australia	9,074	1,502	$11,890	91.5%	7.918	1980
Spain	9,619	606	$ 4,470	37.0%	7.372	1984/85
Israel	1,270	728	$ 5,100	44.4%	7.009	1984/85
Greece	2,269	571	$ 3,740	34.8%	6.549	1983
Ireland	1,152	792	$ 4,950	48.3%	6.253	1984/85
New Zealand	1,387	1,440	$ 7,240	87.8%	5.028	1984/85
Portugal	2,038	514	$ 1,970	31.3%	3.834	1984/85
Costa Rica	485	465	$ 1,210	28.4%	2.601	1983
Hungary	6,352	1,451	$ 2,050	88.4%	1.413	1984/85

SOURCES: Waste generation: World Resources Institute et al., *World Resources 1988–89* (New York: Basic Books, 1988), table 20.7; derived from Organization for Economic Cooperation and Development, UN, and national data. Year is not specified for 1984/1985 data.

Per capita GNP: International Institute for Environment and Development and World Resources Institute, *World Resources 1987*. Table 15.1 from World Bank data.

NOTE: Because of differences in the year waste generation data is given and in the way waste generation is measured in different countries, data can only be compared among countries on a rough basis.

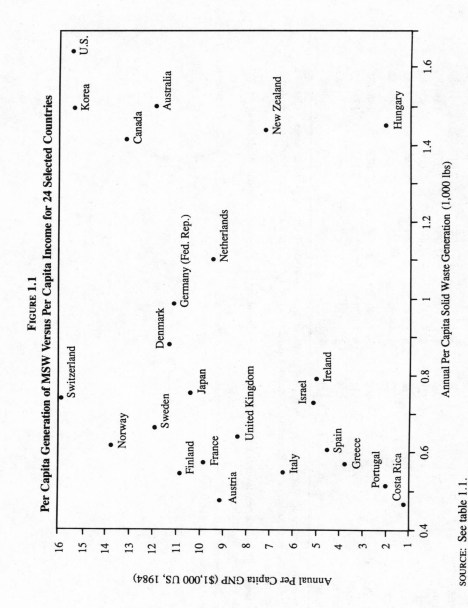

FIGURE 1.1
Per Capita Generation of MSW Versus Per Capita Income for 24 Selected Countries

SOURCE: See table 1.1.

36

The differences in waste generation rates for different countries also make comparisons between different nations' approach to solid waste management more complicated. For example, incineration proponents commonly assert that Japan burns more than half of its waste;[1] recycling proponents claim that Japan recycles at least half of its waste.[2] What Japan really does is produce far less waste to begin with, recycle a high proportion of it, and then burn what's left. Given the fact that Japan is a small, densely populated island with few natural resources and a different political system and culture, it is likely that Japan generates waste with considerably different proportions of recyclables or compostibles (e.g., yard waste) than the United States. This hinders our ability to make meaningful comparisons among waste management practices in the two countries. For this reason, the remainder of this chapter concentrates on representative waste composition, incineration, and recycling data in the United States.

WASTE COMPOSITION

Municipal solid waste consists of many different materials: some burn, some do not; some are readily recyclable, some are not. Many materials, such as newsprint, are candidates for either approach. A detailed understanding of the composition of our garbage—the relative proportions of paper, glass bottles, leaves, etc.—is not terribly important if the mixture is simply tossed into a landfill. To compare the waste management capabilities of incineration and recycling, however, one needs to know more. To address the environmental impacts of different waste management regimes, we also need information on the sources and quantities of toxic materials in our waste, such as lead-acid automotive batteries and household hazardous waste.

The composition of a local waste stream can be estimated in a number of ways. The best waste composition studies rely on sorting actual samples of garbage from specific locales, and are conducted over time to account for seasonal variations in the waste stream, such as surges in yard waste in the fall or increased print advertising and retail packaging around the winter holidays. Ideally, such studies will provide estimates of the composition of waste produced by different sectors of the economy (e.g., commercial versus residential) or different parts of a region (e.g., downtown office districts and residential neighborhoods dominated by multifamily houses or apartments).

Although obtaining detailed waste composition data is ideally the first step in rational planning, it should not serve as an excuse for delaying recycling pilot programs or avoiding pro forma comparisons of recycling

and incineration. Good waste composition data are necessary if a municipality intends to eventually attain a very ambitious level of recycling, and to
minimize overall environmental impacts from waste management, but planning can proceed as waste composition studies are in progress. First-phase
recycling programs can be designed to provide data on waste generation as
they are implemented, and the uncertainty that results from a lack of good
waste composition data can, to some extent, be accounted for in initial
comparisons between recycling and incineration.

Waste composition studies conducted in support of incinerator proposals
are concerned with the amounts of combustible and noncombustible materials, the energy value of the waste or its components, and variables such as
moisture content, size of materials, and their abrasiveness. Table 1.2 shows
the results of such a study conducted in New York City in 1982. A study of

TABLE 1.2
Waste Composition Data from an Incineration-oriented
Waste-sorting Study, New York City

Material Size Category	Waste Classification	Average Composition (%)
+4 inches	Combustibles	57.1
	Magnetics	0.3
	Glass	0.4
	Nonferrous	0.1
	Other	0.3
Middlings (−4 inches)	Light combustibles	13.4
	Heavy combustibles	7.8
	Magnetics	1.6
	Nonferrous	1.5
	Glass	9.7
	Other	0.0
Fines		7.7
Total		100.0

SOURCE: SCS Engineers, *Final Report: Solid Waste Sampling Program, New York City
Resource Recovery Project* (Long Beach, CA: SCS Engineers, November 1982), table 4,
p. 14.

NOTE: The full waste composition study aggregated data from 259 individual waste samples
taken over the course of one year at nine sites. Additional data on the chemical composition of
NYC solid waste was also presented.

Data presented above based on nine samples taken from residential waste at the 52nd Street
Marine Transfer Station, June 22, 1981.

this type is of little use to recycling planners because it does not identify discrete products and materials discarded into the waste stream.

Table 1.3 shows the results of several recycling-oriented waste composition studies conducted for different cities, and illustrates the range of approaches that can be used to estimate the composition of solid waste. The data from Springfield, Missouri, and Portland, Oregon, were extrapolated from statistically representative samples of garbage that were unloaded, sorted, and weighed over the course of a full year. For a given locality, this type of study is generally the most reliable and, unfortunately, the most expensive.

The estimates of the overall composition of the United States waste stream shown in table 1.3 were derived in an entirely different manner; they are based on government and trade association data on product manufacture and consumption. Under this materials-flow methodology, after accounting for imports and exports, assumptions are made about the rate at which of products sold in the United States are eventually discarded, and estimates of these discards are aggregated to give the results as displayed.[3]

The data in table 1.3 for New York City are based on an averaging of data compiled by the city's Department of Sanitation (DOS) from six waste-sorting studies conducted in different neighborhoods between 1971 and 1982. Complicating the effort, each of these six studies used different definitions of waste constituents; for example, some studies treated yard waste and food waste as one category, and three studies did not distinguish between different types of paper. As a result, when the department began curbside collection of newsprint, it discovered that there was roughly twice as much newsprint in residential solid waste as expected.[4] The New York City data displayed in table 1.3 also incorporate the EDF's calculation of the effect of the deposit system implemented through the 1985 New York State Returnable Container Law in reducing the quantities of bottles and cans discarded into the waste stream.

The estimates of residential and commercial waste composition in Seattle in table 1.3 were derived by combining data from Portland's study with preliminary data from an ongoing Seattle waste sort, older Seattle waste composition studies, and records of the Seattle Solid Waste Utility and private waste haulers. An additional estimate of waste produced by various sectors of the economy, such as restaurants and the aerospace industry (not shown in the table), was obtained by incorporating employment and employment growth projections in each industry into statistical functions that predict waste generation. Seattle used this type analysis partly because its *Recycling Potential Assessment* had to be completed before its waste-sorting study. With the benefit of hindsight, table 1.4 compares Seattle's statistical analysis to the results of its waste-sorting study, finished more recently.

TABLE 1.3
Waste Composition Estimates (% by weight)

	National (Combined) 1986	Portland, Oregon (Combined) 1986	Springfield, Missouri (Combined) 1987	Seattle (Residential) 1987	Seattle (Commercial) 1987	New York (Residential) 1983	New York (Commercial) 1983
Combustibles							
Paper							
Newspaper	7.3	4.3	5.8	5.5	3.7	10.0	4.1
Office paper	3.4	4.7	1.4	1.4	7.7	0.0	11.3
Corrugated	9.8	9.9	20.0	5.3	12.7	1.5	36.2
Magazines and books	4.7		2.7			2.7	2.0
Other paper	9.4	15.9	15.8	19.8	18.3	22.8	2.1
Total paper	34.6	34.8	45.7	32.0	42.4	37.0	55.7
Plastics							
Milk jugs		0.4	0.3				
Containers		0.9	0.3				
Durable plastic		0.8	8.8				
Other plastics		5.8					
Total plastics	2.6	7.9	9.4	5.0	7.4	7.3	7.5

Category							
Yard debris							
Prunings		3.0	1.2				
Leaves/grass clippings		7.0	9.6				
Total yard debris	17.6	10.0	10.8	25.3	10.6	22.4	11.3
Food waste	15.4	8.8	5.5	8.0	9.9	3.7	8.3
Wood		8.0		2.7	7.1	5.6	3.6
Textiles		3.8	3.7				
Disposable diapers		1.5	0.8				
Other organics		8.7	13.4	4.5	6.2		
Total combustibles	70.4	83.5	89.3	77.5	83.6	77.4	87.9
Noncombustibles							
Glass							
Beverage containers	5.9	2.1		4.8	1.2		
Food and other	2.9	1.6		5.2	3.5		
Total glass	8.9	3.6	3.1	10.0	4.7	6.6	2.6
Aluminum							
Beverage containers	0.6	0.3	0.7	1.0	0.2		
Other aluminum	0.2	0.6	0.2	0.5	0.4		
Total aluminum	0.8	0.9	0.9	1.5	0.6	1.8	1.0

	National (Combined) 1986	Portland, Oregon (Combined) 1986	Springfield, Missouri (Combined) 1987	Seattle (Residential) 1987	Seattle (Commercial) 1987	New York (Residential) 1983	New York (Commercial) 1983
Ferrous metal							
Food containers	1.6	2.1	3.1	2.3	1.3		
Other ferrous metal	0.5	3.9	0.9	2.5	3.5		
Total ferrous metal	2.2	6.0	4.0	4.8	4.8	10.3	5.0
Other nonferrous metal		0.2	1.0	0.3	1.0		
Durable goods	11.5						
Other inorganics		5.5	1.0			4.2	3.5
Total noncombustibles	23.4	16.1	9.0	16.6	11.1	22.9	12.1
Other	5.7	0.5	1.7	5.9	5.2		
Total	100.0	100.0	100.0	100.0	100.0	100.0	100.0

SOURCES:

National: Franklin Associates, *Characterization of Municipal Solid Waste in the United States, 1960 to 2000 (Update 1988, Final Report)* (Washington, DC: EPA, Office of Solid Waste, March 30, 1988), p. 12.

Portland: Portland Metropolitan Service District, Waste Characterization Study, "Municipal Waste Disposed" (Portland, 1987), table 1.1.

Springfield: State of Missouri Department of Natural Resources, Environmental Improvement and Energy Resources Authority, Solid Waste Characterization Report, Exhibit IV-1, "Springfield Landfill, Spring 1987."

Seattle: Seattle Engineering Department, Solid Waste Utility, *Waste Reduction, Recycling and Disposal Alternatives, Appendix E; Recycling Potential Assessment and Waste Stream Forecast* (1988), tables E-23, E-27.

New York City: Original data from NYC Department of Sanitation, The Waste Disposal Problem in New York City: A Proposal for Action (April 1984), tables 2.1-5, 2.1-7, 3.5-2, 3.5-3. Tabulated by the EDF in EDF, *To Burn or Not to Burn,* (New York: EDF, 1985), tables II-1 and II-2.

TABLE 1.4
Comparison Between a Year-round Waste-Sorting Waste Composition Study and a Statistical Waste Composition Estimate

RESIDENTIAL WASTE STREAM, SEATTLE, WA

Material	Matrix Mgmt Waste Sorting Study March 1988– Feb. 1989 (%) [a]	Seattle Solid Waste Utility Estimate for 1987 (%) [b]	Difference [a]–[b]
Paper	31.24	32.00	0.76
Newspaper	7.10	5.50	−1.60
Corrugated	5.50	5.30	−0.20
Computer/office	0.25	1.40	1.15
Mixed scrap	13.64	13.30	−0.34
Other	4.75	6.50	1.75
Plastics	8.07	5.50	−2.57
Yard waste	17.10	25.30	8.20
Wood	1.22	2.70	1.48
Food	16.32	8.00	−8.32
Organics	5.32	4.50	−0.82
Beverage	2.29	4.80	2.51
Containers	3.94	2.40	−1.54
Other glass	0.19	2.80	2.61
Food cans	1.96	2.30	0.34
Other ferrous	0.47	2.50	2.03
Aluminum beverage	0.86	1.00	0.14
Other aluminum	n/a	0.50	
Other Nonferrous	2.09	0.30	−1.79
Construction debris	0.79	2.70	1.91
Miscellaneous	8.50	3.20	−5.30

SOURCES:

a Matrix Management Group (Seattle, WA, August 1989).

b Seattle Solid Waste Utility, *Waste Reduction, Recycling and Disposal Alternatives, Appendix E-Recycling Potential Assessment and Waste Stream Forecast* (July 1988), p. 238. (Waste composition estimates based on a combined data from six different sources.)

Although the data shown in table 1.3 vary, some patterns are clear. For example, paper constitutes a very large fraction of the commercial waste stream, and, in most cases, yard waste is a major part of the residential waste stream. According to Franklin Associates' waste composition estimates for the United States, conventionally recyclable materials—paper and paperboard, glass, ferrous metals, aluminum, wood and yard waste— comprise over three-quarters of the waste stream. Of course, simply identifying these materials is not the same as separating them from the solid waste stream and finding markets for them.

A key point about all of these studies is that they exclude several large constituents of the waste stream, such as construction and demolition debris and bulk waste. Often these materials are collected separately from the regular garbage and brought to the landfill by private haulers or individuals with their own trucks or trailers. The importance of these materials in any comparison of recycling and incineration is that they are not accepted for processing by incinerators but can, to a large extent, be recycled. The national waste composition estimates in table 1.3 also exclude incinerator ash, imported product packaging, and several other types of waste.

Generation of construction and demolition debris varies substantially depending on the character of a community. Although data on these materials are not especially good, Franklin Associates estimates that roughly 32 million tons of construction and demolition debris were generated in 1984, adding roughly 24 percent to what was otherwise defined as the municipal waste stream for that year.[5]

WASTE REDUCTION[6]

The potential for and benefits of waste reduction in the United States are substantial. In addition to reducing our solid waste disposal costs, thoughtful waste reduction policies may also cut other consumer costs. For example, $1.00 out of every $10.00 Americans spend on food pays for packaging, which amounts to more than U.S. farmers' net income.[7]

With respect to solid waste, the term "waste reduction" is used in a variety of ways. In this handbook, we will consider waste reduction to include any action that reduces the *volume or toxicity* of MSW prior to its processing and disposal in incinerators or landfills. For example, waste reduction can include making packaging more recyclable, by replacing multimaterial packaging with a single material. "Source reduction" we construe more narrowly, meaning policies that reduce the amount of material entering the economy, and hence the waste stream, in the first place. Examples of source reduction would be eliminating excessive layers of packaging around a product or replacing inks containing cadmium with inks that do not.

Some discussions of waste reduction have suggested that the topic is so complicated that, in effect, we cannot do anything about it.[8] How, for example, can we agree upon and account for all of the factors that make a package more or less environmentally sound? In fact, we will probably never be able or even want to microregulate the production of packaging and other goods. We can, however, undertake some waste reduction practices immediately, using a variety of common-sense policies that draw their effectiveness from market forces and consumers' growing interest in protecting the environment.

INFORMATION STRATEGIES: PUBLIC EDUCATION, PRODUCT LABELING, AND VOLUNTARY WASTE REDUCTION

When introducing a new package or product into the marketplace, designers and product managers consider a number of factors, including the cost of materials, the need to protect and transport the product, consumer convenience, how the product will be advertised, and how it will appear on the shelf. When consumers make a purchase, they work through a similar, perhaps more subliminal, calculus relating to the product's cost, advertising, and their perceived needs. To foster voluntary efforts toward waste reduction, environmental and consumer advocates need to inject the consideration of environmental and solid waste impacts of a package or product into both of these processes of evaluation.

The escalating interest in environmental protection among the public offers an excellent opportunity to alter the way manufacturers and consumers think about their products and purchases. Issues like global warming, tropical deforestation, and depletion of the ozone layer may seem scientifically complex, distant, or relevant only in the long term, but everyone relates to garbage because we all produce it. Because reducing waste gives people a way to help protect the environment in their daily lives, solid waste issues are becoming one focus for a wide range of concerns about the degradation of our environment.

Some of the most egregious examples of overpackaging and environmentally unsound product design may be eliminated simply by pointing them out, by giving awards for good and bad packages. Under pressure from environmental groups, a number of major producers of plastic resins have announced that they intend to eliminate the use of cadmium as a pigment or stabilizer in parts of their product lines.[9] After receiving a letter from the New York City Commissioner of Sanitation, the Book of the Month Club stopped using polystyrene foam "peanuts" and shipping books in relatively large boxes, and returned to using smaller corrugated paper containers. Figure 1.2, an insert to Seattle residents' monthly utility bill, provides a good example of simple, direct public education materials on waste reduction. Government agencies and private companies can get involved in waste reduction by buying goods that are more durable or more conserving of resources. The purchase of vehicle tires capable of lasting 60,000 rather than 40,000 miles is a waste reduction measure; so is the use of double-sided rather than single-sided copy machines and the provision of long-term service contracts on home appliances or office machinery.

Retail businesses are recognizing the marketing potential of selling environmentally sound products, from small purveyors of shopping guides like the Seventh Generation Catalog to corporate chains like Walmart discount stores.[10] In the words of one recent business publication:

Thirty-nine percent of Americans strongly identify themselves as environmentalists, according to a Gallup survey for *Times Mirror*. Environmentalists are a bigger market than some of the hottest markets of the 1980s—such as Hispanics (8 percent of the population), married couples with children (20 percent) or even the baby boomers (31 percent).

Not only is the market huge, it's rich. The affluent are more likely than the average American to act on environmental concerns. Fifteen percent of all households—but fully 22 percent of those with incomes of $50,000 or more—donate money to an environmental group, according to the Cambridge Reports survey.

Forty-seven percent of all consumers—but 57 percent of those with household incomes of $50,000 or more—have changed their day-to-day behavior because of environmental concerns.

Sixty-one percent of all consumers—and 68 percent of those with incomes of $50,000 or more—are "much" or "somewhat" more inclined to go to a store or restaurant that is committed to reducing its use of plastic containers and utensils.

Most Americans want to do something to make things better. Your business can profit by showing them the way. It doesn't take much of an investment to turn environmental negatives into marketing pluses: The first step is easy— just promote what the company does right. The next step is to improve your product or change its packaging. Then tell the mass market of Americans that they can do right by doing business with you.[11]

FIGURE 1.2
One Local Government's Effort to Promote Waste Reduction and Recycling: Insert to Seattle Residents' Monthly Utility Bill

Help Seattle STOP BUYING TRASH!

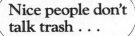

Nice people don't talk trash . . .

 FOR MORE INFORMATION:

Curbside and Alley Recycling
For information on signing up for convenient Curbside and Alley Recycling, call **SEATTLE SOLID WASTE UTILITY, 684-7600**. Or fill out and mail in the sign-up card you may have received in the mail. This recycling service is available for single family through fourplex residents of Seattle.

Other Kinds of Recycling
For information on other kinds of recycling opportunities and locations, call **1-800-RECYCLE**.

Hazardous Household Products
For information on safe substitutes and safe disposal for hazardous household products, call the **HAZARDS LINE, 587-3292**.

Seattle Engineering Department
Solid Waste Utility
710 Second Avenue
Suite 750
Seattle, WA 98104

. . . UNTIL NOW!

Now **everyone** is talking trash:
"Where does all that trash come from?"
"Who is responsible for the trash we can't recycle or dump in a landfill?"

The answer: **all of us.**
"What can we do about it?"

Two steps we can take . . .
- Avoid buying products which use unnecessary plastic and paper packaging. You can remove 10-20% of the waste from your household garbage can.
- Recycle your paper, metal and glass to remove 20-40% of the waste from your garbage can.

On the opposite page is a handy checklist to take along shopping. It can help stop trash before it starts.

THE "STOP BUYING TRASH" SHOPPING CHECKLIST

1. ☐ Is this plastic or paper packaging necessary or just for looks?

2. ☐ Is this packaging recyclable? (Not plastic or mixed materials. Buy paper, metal or glass instead of plastic.)

3. ☐ Can I reuse this container for something else?

4. ☐ Can this beverage container be returned or recycled?

5. ☐ Can I buy this product (detergent, cereal or ?) in a larger container or in bulk quantity?

6. ☐ Can I buy this product (razor, cups, utensils, diapers or ?) in a non-disposable, longer lasting form?

7. ☐ Is there a non-hazardous substitute for this cleaner? (Or pesticide or solvent or ?)

8. ☐ Can I use paper bags instead of plastic bags? (Or a reusable, fabric shopping bag?)

9. ☐ Can I buy this fast food in paper containers instead of plastic or styrofoam?

10. ☐ Is this product worth a higher garbage bill or a more polluted environment?

SOURCE: Seattle Solid Waste Utility.

47

If our experience with "low fat," "natural," and "low cholesterol" foods is any guide, however, retailers will probably abuse what is now being called "environmental marketing." In fact, the introduction of "degradable" plastics, which confound plastics recycling and probably do not degrade effectively in the real-world environment, especially in landfills, suggests that such abuse is well under way.

One way to harness consumer interest in the environment and to limit misleading advertising would be to adopt a coding or labeling system for packaging and products. Consumer labeling is widespread in the United States. Labels tell us about the content of everything from foods to movies, the safety of appliances and tools, the thermal value of insulation, the harms of smoking cigarettes, and, in California, whether foods contain carcinogenic or mutagenic chemicals above certain levels. Based on existing labeling systems in Europe and Canada, it would be possible to develop labeling schemes that give consumers information about recycled content, recyclability, and the presence of hazardous substances in packages and products.[12]

Any such labeling system would have to be carefully thought-out, and would work best on a national or, at least, regional scale. Some labeling schemes could be relatively simple; newspaper publishers, for example, could be required to prominently print in each issue the percentage of recycled fiber they consume in an average printing run. Labels for recycled content and recyclability for a broader range of products could be pegged to the national recycling rate for a given material. For example, the EPA or Department of Commerce could design a symbol that could be used only on containers made of a material that is being recycled at a national rate of 25 percent or higher by 1992 and 50 percent by 1997, with incremental increases in years between. The decision to pursue use of this sort of label might be left up to individual companies, who would have to demonstrate to a special board that their product meets the federal criteria. This board could operate independently and be funded by licensing fees, as is common in Europe. Labels could also be created that identify, in a negative sense, packages introduced on a wide scale that, after a certain number of years, have not attained even a minimal rate of recycling. Other variations are, of course, possible.

ECONOMIC INCENTIVES

Part of the reason that solid waste is such a problem in the United States is that those responsible for its production—designers, manufacturers, consumers, in short, all of us—are not directly responsible for disposal and are unaware of disposal costs. Restructuring the way we pay for activities that create solid waste can change manufacturer and consumer behavior and aid waste reduction.

For example, in the United States, the costs of residential refuse collection have long been covered by property taxes or set for individual households on a flat-rate basis. If instead, households were required to pay for municipal or privately contracted garbage collection services on the basis of the volume of material they discard, municipalities could create incentives for source reduction, such as backyard composting, and recycling. In other words, as long as we are being charged for refuse collection, a pay-as-you-throw accounting system could improve our understanding and provide a strong incentive to reduce the bill.

This approach works in Seattle, where the Seattle Solid Waste Utility charges for waste collection based on a variable-can rate implemented by its private contractor. Under this system, households apply for a particular number of cans, which the city provides to them. The monthly curbside rate for picking up a 19-gallon can, or "minican," is $10.70, the rate for a 30-gallon can is $13.75, and each additional can costs $9.00. Since Seattle also offers curbside collection of separated yard waste, mixed paper, and some plastics, as well as the traditional curbside recyclables, it is possible for conscientious households to significantly cut their garbage collection fee under this system. Twenty-one percent of the households in Seattle have altered their purchasing habits and recycled so effectively as to reduce their weekly garbage to fit into one minican.[13] Other cities and towns in the Northeast have implemented similar schemes, some of which involve selling special stickers that must be affixed to trash bags before they can be collected.[14]

With the intent of influencing manufacturing, bills have been introduced in a number of state legislatures that would tax packages made from virgin or nonrecyclable material at higher levels than recycled or recyclable packages, which might not be taxed at all.[15]

REGULATION OF PRODUCTS AND PACKAGING

Frustrated by the problems posed by growing per capita waste generation, in the last two years, a growing number of communities have moved to regulate retail packaging. As of late 1989, 10 to 15 communities nationwide had passed ordinances banning the use of certain packages or requiring that in order to be marketed locally, certain packages be incorporated into municipal recycling programs. These communities include Berkeley, Hamden, Connecticut, Minneapolis, Newark, New Jersey, Palo Alto, California,

Portland, Oregon, St. Paul and Suffolk County, New York.[16] The most-frequent target of these ordinances is expanded polystyrene foam fast-food packaging, followed by plastic grocery bags, though some ordinances, like those in Minneapolis and St. Paul, are much broader. In August 1989, the North Carolina state legislature passed a bill that will ban the use of polystyrene fast-food packaging and plastic grocery bags if these items are not recycled at a rate of at least 25 percent by January 1, 1993.[17]

Since few of these bills have been implemented, it is hard to judge their effectiveness as waste reduction tools. However, they do seem to enjoy popular support. In the spring of 1989, when the Minneapolis City Council was preparing to vote on that city's ordinance, groups representing the plastics industry and retail grocers ran a full-page ad comparing the proposal to a food tax, listing council members' phone numbers and urging citizens to call. In response to the ad, calls came in as high as 12 to 1 in support of the bill, prompting the council to pass it unanimously.[18]

This ground swell of activity has also led to a major effort by the plastics industry to convince the public that plastics are recyclable, even though the present infrastructure for recycling plastics is highly limited.[19]

SOURCE REDUCTION OF TOXIC MATERIALS IN SOLID WASTE

Waste reduction also entails an equally important emphasis on reducing the toxicity of materials that become waste. Many different materials that we use and discard on a routine basis contain toxic substances, which when disposed of through landfilling or incineration, or when recycled, can pose serious health and environmental risks (see Part II).

These concerns are best illustrated by briefly discussing the various sources of toxic heavy metals in the municipal waste stream. Such metals include lead, cadmium, chromium, mercury, arsenic, copper, tin, and zinc. All of these metals have been demonstrated to be toxic to humans or other organisms. Arsenic is used in wood preservatives and household pesticides; cadmium is used in plastics, colored printing inks, and small rechargeable batteries; lead is used in plastics, colored printing inks, paints, insecticides, and lead-acid automotive batteries; mercury appears in batteries and fungicides; and zinc is present in flashlight batteries and certain rubber products, including tires. Table 1.5 presents more information on the sources of toxic metals in consumer products.

Despite recent increases in lead recycling, we are still disposing of over 200,000 tons of lead each year in the solid waste stream, in the form of lead-acid vehicle batteries, which account for about 75 percent of the lead used in the United States, and approximately 65 percent of the lead in municipal

TABLE 1.5
Sources of Heavy Metals in the Municipal Waste Stream

Metal	General Category	Examples
Lead	Plastic pigments	Garbage bags, margarine tubs, dry cleaner bags
Cadmium	Plastic pigments	Kitchenware (dishes, mugs, utensil handles), towel hangers, clothing hangers, toys (cars, blocks), sporting goods (skis, helmets, sleds), clocks, cameras, plastic lamps, plastic rainware, etc.
	Inks for glossy paper	Magazines, Sunday newspaper supplements, catalogues
	Enamel pigments	Pots, pans, mugs, colored glassware, decorations on porcelain and ceramics
Cadmium	Clothing trim	Zippers, buttons, buckles, belts
Mercury	Paints	Exterior-use latex paint
Zinc, chromium	Pigments	Colored papers and paper coats
Lead, cadmium, tin	PVC plastics stabilizers	Plastic tubes, sheeting, fences, cushioned floor coverings, gutters, packaging, plastic films, plastic "peanuts," linings, housing for switches, car upholstery and trim, hoses, plastic office items (pens, staplers, wastepaper baskets), etc.
Lead, tin	Household construction	Wiring, gutters, downsprouts, roofing, ornamental metalwork; solder
Cadmium	Machinery	Electronics, washing machines, televisions
Lead	Solder	Plumbing (banned for use on drinking-water systems as of June 1988), cans (including 15% of food cans); machinery, cars, electronics
Lead	Batteries	Automotive starting/lighting/ignition
Cadmium	Batteries	Most consumer items, including portable electric appliances and phones, cameras, calculators, toys, flashlights, computer start-up and backup systems

SOURCE: EDF research, unpublished data.

solid waste. Consumer electronics are the next largest source of lead in the waste stream, followed by glass, ceramics, and plastics, where metals are used as pigments or stabilizers. Rechargeable nickel-cadmium batteries account for about one-half of the cadmium in solid waste, followed by plastics (30 percent), and consumer appliances (10 percent).[20]

Taking steps to reduce the amounts of these toxic substances used in consumer products can greatly aid in reducing the risks of managing these materials once they are discarded. For example, there are a number of substitutes for both household and industrial uses of hazardous materials that enter the waste stream, and educational programs on these substitutes should be part of any recycling or household hazardous waste collection program.[21]

Recent federal legislative initiatives have proposed to ban the use of cadmium as a pigment in inks and plastics, a step that has already been taken in Sweden and the Netherlands. Virtually all such uses of cadmium are nonessential to the functioning of the product, but can significantly increase the toxicity of air emissions and ash residues generated by incinerating such cadmium-containing materials. A law passed in 1989 in Connecticut requires that appliances containing rechargeable nickel-cadmium batteries be clearly labeled, and that the batteries be removable.[22]

Where substitutes are not available, such as for lead in lead-acid vehicle batteries, recycling systems can be improved. Several states and communities, including Florida and Suffolk County, New York, have passed laws requiring deposits or other controls on automotive batteries.[23]

An alternative approach to bans and deposits, which tend to take a long time implementing, would be a market-based initiative. One possibility would be to repeal the percentage depletion allowance in the tax code for lead mining, and implement an approach such as marketable depletion rights or a tax on lead imports and virgin lead mined in the United States. The effect would be higher prices for virgin lead ore, which would better reflect the extensive public health damage caused by the wide prevalence of lead use in the United States. Higher prices for lead would improve the competitive position of lead-battery recycling operations and would prompt more extensive and better-controlled recycling. This approach would decrease lead contamination of the environment from careless disposal and compel substitution for lead in the many products where substitutes are available and, at the same time, reduce the total volume of new lead being mined.[24]

"DEGRADABLE" PLASTICS

Despite the current fascination with trying to make plastics disappear, degradable plastics are the wrong answer to the right question.[25] Fueled by an aggressive corn industry lobby eager to find new markets, the developers of degradable plastics tout environmental benefits that are either nonexistent or have yet to be demonstrated. Indeed, serious questions remain about the ability of degradable plastics to solve *any* of the real problems that plastics pose, whether as litter, as solid waste, as a threat to wildlife through entanglement and ingestion, or as a source of hazardous pollutants generated during plastics production.

Degradable plastics come in two basic varieties: photodegradable, capable of being broken down by light, and biodegradable, capable of being broken down by bacteria. But the vast majority of plastic waste winds up in landfills, where the light needed for photodegradation is obviously not present. And even biodegradable plastics that readily degrade in the laboratory are unlikely to break down in a reasonable length of time in landfills. The reason is simple: Well-operated landfills lack the two ingredients critical for biodegradation—air and water. Recent excavations of decades-old landfills have uncovered still recognizable newspaper and even banana peels and hot dogs—materials readily degradable under other conditions.

Serious and heretofore unanswered technical questions have also been raised as to whether degradable plastics will degrade in water, that is, in streams, lakes, or the ocean. Here, degradation—if it occurs—could lessen the risk of wildlife entanglement; but it could also exacerbate the likelihood of animals ingesting plastic by creating small pieces from large ones.

Even assuming degradables work, what do they degrade into? The term "biodegradable plastic" is really a misnomer, since it is not the plastic but the starch or cellulose added to it that degrades, leaving behind a less visible but more dangerous plastic dust. Plastics are manufactured using all sorts of toxic additives: lead and cadmium pigments and stabilizers, for example. Such toxins remain relatively inert in roadside plastic litter or in a landfill, but once the plastic degrades and releases them, they pose a far greater risk to our health and environment.[26]

Worse still, degradable plastics threaten to derail the most promising approaches to managing plastics—reduction and recycling. Many curbside collection programs are beginning to collect various types of plastic for recycling. But contamination of this plastic with photodegradable or biodegradable agents could render durable goods (e.g., plastic lumber) made from them degradable—clearly an undesirable attribute. In addition, starch additives used in biodegradable plastics directly interfere with recycling by gumming up machinery and even catching fire. As a result many plastics recyclers are already refusing to accept any degradable plastics. For example, a plastic bag recycler in North Carolina recently stopped accepting any grocery bags when a local grocery store introduced degradable grocery bags.[27]

Finally, widespread introduction of degradable plastics may actually increase plastics use and even littering. Biodegradable bags and containers on the market today must be made using more plastic resin in order to provide the same strength as ordinary plastic. And fewer people might think twice before buying nonrecyclable plastic packaging or tossing away a candy wrapper if they are led to believe the plastic will magically disappear.

The false promise of degradable plastics threatens to divert our attention from the real solutions to plastics pollution and the solid waste problems we face. The proliferation of plastic packaging, though offering certain advantages such as convenience and light weight, is being increasingly questioned because the plastics are rapidly replacing more readily recyclable materials, such as glass. Recycling of plastics holds promise and is growing, but degradable plastics will only increase the technical and attitudinal barriers that must be overcome.

NOTES

1. See, for example, an editorial entitled "A Glimpse of the Future" in *Solid Waste & Power*, October 1989, p. 10.
2. See, for example, Allen Hershkowitz and Eugene Salerni, *Garbage Management in Japan: Leading the Way* (New York: INFORM, 1987), p. 5.
3. Franklin Associates, *Characterization of Municipal Solid Waste in the United States, 1960 to 2000 (Update 1988), Final Report* (Washington, DC: EPA, Office of Solid Waste and Emergency Response, March 30, 1988), pp. 2–5.
4. For summaries of New York City waste composition data, see: Environmental Defense Fund, *To Burn or Not to Burn: The Economic Advantages of Recycling Over Garbage Incineration for New York City* (New York: EDF, 1985), tables II-1 and II-2; for information on unexpectedly large quantities of newsprint, see Laura Denman, "New York City's Curbside Recycling Program," *Resource Recycling*, January/February 1988, pp. 16–17, 48.
5. Franklin Associates, *Characterization of Municipal Solid Waste in the United States, 1960 to 2000 Final Report* (Washington, DC: EPA, Office of Waste Programs Enforcement, July 25, 1986), pp. 2-1 to 2-2.
6. For more information and views on waste reduction, see: Abt Associates, *Promoting Source Reduction and Recyclability in the Marketplace: A Study of Consumer and Industry Response to Promotion of Source Reduced, Recycled, and Recyclable Products and Packaging* (Washington, DC: EPA, Office of

Policy, Planning, and Evaluation, September, 1989); EPA, *Methods to Manage and Control Plastic Wastes—Report to Congress* (Washington, DC: EPA, Office of Solid Waste, 1990); Ellen Feldman, *Collision Course: Plastic Packaging vs. Solid Waste Solutions* (1989). Available for $12.95 from the Environmental Action Coalition, 625 Broadway, New York, NY 10012; "Special Report: Packaging Under Attack," *Packaging; The Cahners Magazine for Decision-Makers*, August 1989. Issue devoted to packaging and solid waste issues; Ordinance of the city of Minneapolis. 89-Or-060. Passed March 31, 1989. Restricts the retail sale of certain types of packaging; contact William Barnhart, Govt. Relations Representative, Office of City Coordinator, 325M City Hall, Minneapolis, MN 55415, for copies; Jeanne Wirka, *Wrapped in Plastics, The Environmental Case for Reducing Plastics Packaging* (1988). Available for $10.95 from the Environmental Action Foundation, 1525 New Hamshire Avenue, NW, Washington, DC 20036.

7. Environmental Task Force, "Waste Reduction," *RE:SOURCES* (Washington, DC: ETF, Summer 1986); and "Cost of Packaging Food Could Exceed Farm Net," *Journal of Commerce*, August 12, 1986. Both cited in Cynthia Pollock, *Mining Urban Wastes: The Potential for Recycling* (Washington, DC: Worldwatch Institute 1987 paper no. 76), p. 8.

8. For example: "Source reduction, which is at the top of the solid waste management hierarchy, is a concept easy to understand, but very difficult to put into practical application or to measure"; "The term 'source reduction' is used frequently, but is very difficult to define or apply universally since any concept, including source reduction, will be interpreted differently based on the needs and values of those concerned"; From: William Franklin and Warren Bird, "Source Reduction: A Working Definition," mimeographed (Washington, DC: Council on Plastics and Packaging in the Environment, December 29, 1989), p. ii, 3.

9. "Mobay to Eliminate Cadmium; Announces New Nylon 6 Resin," *Plastics News*, April 17, 1989, p. 22; "Du Pont Sets Environmental Agenda," *CMA News*, September 1989, p. 11.

10. "Wal-Mart throws 'green' gauntlet," *Advertising Age*, August 21, 1989, p. 1, 66; "Companies Make Products Kinder to Nature." *USA Today*, August 23, 1989, p. 1B, 2B; Seventh Generation Catalog, available from 10 Farrell Street, South Burlington, VT 05403. (800) 456-1177.

11. "Editor's Note: Guilty as Charged," *American Demographics*, February 1989, p. 2.

12. Tom Watson, "Product Labeling Efforts Are on the March Worldwide," *Resource Recycling*, October 1989, pp. 18–21.

13. Personal communication with Lorie Parker, Director of Recycling, Seattle Solid Waste Utility, August 1989; Lisa Skumatz and Cabell Breckinridge, "Volume-Based Rates in Solid Waste: Handbook for Solid Waste Officials" (1990). Available from the Seattle Solid Waste Utility, 710 Second Avenue, Seattle, WA 98104. (Draft versions only available as of January 1990.)

14. David Riggle, "Only Pay for What You Throw Away," *BioCycle*, February 1989, pp. 39–41; Kimberly Sproule and Jeanne Cosulich, "Higher Recovery Rates: The Answer's in the Bag," *Resource Recycling*, November/December 1988, pp. 20–21, 43–44; legislation signed in New Jersey on January 2, 1990, would enable municipalities throughout the state to enact volume-based rates.

15. See, for example, AB 8823-B introduced on January 27, 1988, in the New York State Legislature by Assemblyman Maurice D. Hinchey.

16. For information on emerging local and state regulation of packaging, and other issues, see *Plastics Recycling Update*, a newsletter published by Resource Recycling, Inc., P.O. Box 10540, Portland, OR 97210. (503) 277-1319.

17. General Assembly of North Carolina, 1989 Session, Chapter 784, Senate Bill 111, Sections 130A-309.10.

18. Minnesota Grocers Association and the Council for Solid Waste Solutions, "This Friday your Minneapolis City Council plans to vote on a ban that could hit you like a food tax," *Minneapolis Tribune*, March 29, 1989 full page ad, "Ad Campaign Defending Plastics Backfires," *Minneapolis/St. Paul Star Tribune*, March 30, 1989, pp. 1A, 10A.

19. See, for example, The Council for Solid Waste Solutions, "The Urgent Need to Recycle" (advertising insert to *Time* magazine), July 17, 1989, (Reportedly costing $750,000 to run, 13 pp.); In general, plastics recycling is both promising and problematic. On the one hand, properly processed, segregated plastics resins can be highly valuable. On the other, plastics collection costs are often very high, and some plastic items do not lend themselves to easy segregation by resin type because of multiple resin lamination or difficulty in identifying resin types. For more information on plastics recycling, see note 6 and Gretchen Brewer, *Plastics Recycling Action Plan for Massachusetts* (Boston: Mass. Dept. of Environmental Protection, 1988); "Little Hope Held by Texas Rescuers; Twenty-Two Workers Missing at Plant where 2 Died in Explosion and Fire," and "Reverberations for Industries but not for U.S. Households," *New York Times*, October 25, 1989, p. A18; Mt. Auburn Associates, *Plan for the Development of Connecticut Markets for Recovered Materials* (1989). Available from the Connecticut Department of Economic Development, 865 Brook Street, Rocky Hill, CT 06067; EDF is currently engaged in extensive research on plastics recycling and reduction. Look to the *EDF Letter* in the fall of 1990 for announcements of publications.

20. Franklin Associates, *Characterization of Products Containing Lead and Cadmium in Municipal Solid Waste in the United States, 1970 to 2000* (Washington, DC: EPA Office of Solid Waste, 1989.

21. Marie Steinwachs, "A Report on Household Hazardous Waste Management," *Resource Recycling*, September 1989, pp. 20–23, 59–60; Environmental Defense Fund, *Household Hazardous Products*, Environmental Information Exchange report (Washington, DC, 1990).

22. Connecticut General Assembly, Substitute House Bill no. 6641 (Public Act No. 89-385), Section 12.

23. Concern, Inc., *Household Waste: Issues and Opportunities* (Washington, DC, October 1989), p. 11.
24. EDF work on this proposal is in progress. For a general discussion of the use of economic incentives in environmental protection, see: Robert Stavins, *Project 88: Harnessing Market Forces to Protect Our Environment: Initiatives for the New President*, a public policy study sponsored by Senator Timothy Wirth and Senator John Heinz (Washington, DC, December 1988).
25. Richard Denison and Jeanne Wirka, *Degradable Plastics: The Wrong Answer to the Right Question* (Washington, DC: Environmental Defense Fund and Environmental Action Foundation, December 1989). Six national environmental organizations recently called for a consumer boycott of so-called degradable plastics.
26. Jim Glenn, "Degradables Tested in Compost Programs," *Biocycle*, October 1989, pp. 28–32.
27. The plastics recycler who no longer takes plastic bags because of the introduction of degradables is Appleget Mountain Polymers of Greensboro, North Carolina. Other major brokers of plastics in the Northeast report that buyers will not accept loads of recovered plastic film with even minute amounts of degradable plastic mixed in.

CHAPTER 2

Physical Capacity to Manage the Waste Stream

THIS CHAPTER ESTABLISHES the basis for our comparison of incineration and recycling as management methods for MSW. The discussion of each option begins with an overview of the various technologies or approaches in use, the scope of both current and potential use of each, the ability of each to manage various components of our waste, and the nature of residuals left behind or produced through the use of each option that must themselves be managed. The chapter concludes by addressing a critical component to the success of recycling as a large-scale option for solid waste management—the development of markets for recycled materials.

INCINERATION TECHNOLOGY, POTENTIALS, AND RESIDUALS

THE ANATOMY OF AN INCINERATOR: AN OVERVIEW

Modern incinerators, though simple in concept, are highly complex machines. The heart of any incinerator, of course, is the combustion chamber, where waste is burned. All waste that enters an incinerator's combustion chamber exits in one of four forms:

- as *combustion gases*, which exit via the stack except to the extent that some may be removed by air pollution control devices;
- as emissions of *particulate material*, which is composed of lightweight particles that are borne out of the combustion chamber along with the combustion gases and are small enough to escape the air pollution control devices;

- as *fly ash*, which is made up of particulate material light enough to be borne upward with the combustion gases but heavy enough to fall out as the gases cool before leaving the stack or large enough to be captured by the air pollution control devices;[1]
- as *bottom ash*, which is the solid material that passes through the combustion chamber on the grates, and is usually automatically conveyed to a water-filled pit for quenching.[2]

Depending on the composition of the waste that is burned, from 10 to 30 percent (by volume) of the input waste will typically remain as ash. Put another way, incineration reduces the volume of waste by 70 to 90 percent.

Table 2.1 lists the primary or most toxic constituents of each of these four types of combustion products.

Several basic varieties of MSW incinerators are currently in use. The most widely used, and frequently the largest, are mass-burn facilities, which are designed to burn MSW with virtually no processing. Figure 2.1 illustrates the basic design of a mass-burn incinerator. Modular incinerators are usually smaller-scale facilities that also burn unprocessed waste. Refuse-derived fuel (RDF) incinerators typically utilize a shredded waste

TABLE 2.1
Primary and Most-toxic Constituents of Incinerator By-products

Combustion Product	Primary Constituents	Toxic or Environmentally Harmful Constituents
Gases	Carbon dioxide (CO_2) Water (H_2O) Nitrogen oxides (NO_x) Sulfur dioxide (SO_2) Hydrochloric acid (HC1)	Nitrogen oxides (NO_x) Sulfur dioxide (SO_2) Hydrochloric acid (HC1)
Particulate emissions	Oxides or salts of silicon, aluminum, etc.	Heavy metals Products of incomplete combustion (PICs)
Fly ash	Oxides or salts of silicon, aluminum, etc.	Heavy metals Products of incomplete combustion (PICs)
Bottom ash	Uncombusted waste (e.g., glass, metal)	Heavy metals Uncombusted organic compounds

SOURCE: EDF.

FIGURE 2.1
Diagram of a Modern Mass-burn MSW Incinerator

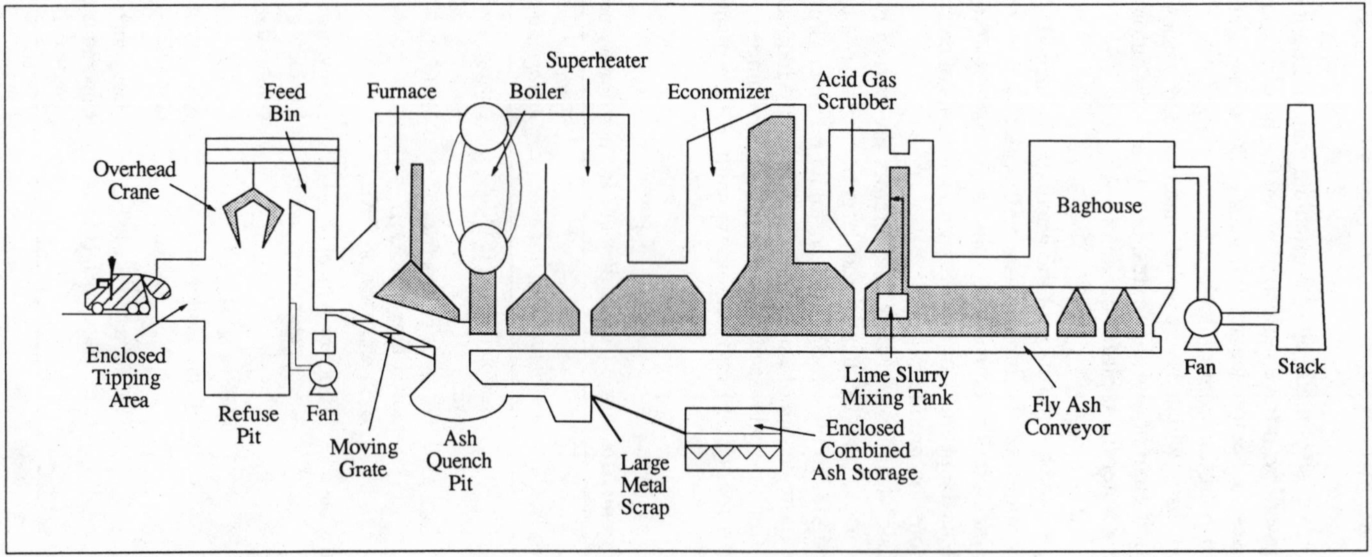

SOURCE: EDF, based on U.S. Environmental Protection Agency, *Municipal Waste Combustion Study: Report to Congress* (Washington, DC: Office of Solid Waste and Emergency Response, June 1987, EPA/530-SW-87-021a), p. 10.

60

from which heavier, noncombustible items such as glass and metal have been removed. Figure 2.2 illustrates the components of a typical RDF processing facility.

Other designs are also employed, though less commonly. Several fluidized-bed incinerators, which typically burn a waste stream that has undergone at least some preprocessing and may simultaneously burn other wastes such as sewage sludge, are in operation or under construction. RDF is frequently burned in standard or modified utility boilers, typically mixed with coal.

Most incinerators include an energy-recovery system. Such a system captures the heat released during combustion and converts it to steam or electricity, which serves as a source of revenue to partially offset the costs of the incinerator. Virtually all incinerators now being planned include energy-recovery systems, and about 100 of the more than 160 incinerators now in operation are so equipped.

Most modern incinerators are equipped with relatively sophisticated combustion control systems. Older facilities may be little more than enclosed fire pits with moveable grates, but newer incinerators rival the space shuttle in the number and complexity of computerized controls. These controls allow the operator to adjust, for example, the rate at which waste is fed into the incinerator and the amount of air in the combustion chamber. These parameters, in turn, influence the 3 Ts: temperature, time (how long the waste remains exposed to high temperature), and turbulence (the extent of mixing of the waste with air). By controlling these combustion conditions, incinerator operators can increase the efficiency of combustion, maximize volume reduction, and reduce the formation of products of incomplete combustion (PICs), such as dioxins.

Finally, incinerators are equipped with air pollution control devices of various types. Virtually all incinerators have particulate control devices, ranging from wet scrubbers to electrostatic precipitators to fabric filters. The newest generation of facilities also have acid-gas scrubbers to remove hydrochloric acid and sulfur dioxide and, in a few cases, nitrogen oxide controls as well. (Chapter 6 discusses these technologies at greater length.)

Solid Waste Volume Reductions as a Result of Incineration

The obvious and primary advantage of incineration as a technique for managing MSW is its ability to reduce volumes requiring disposal. Given the high organic content of solid waste, efficient combustion can accomplish up to an order-of-magnitude reduction in the volume of material introduced into an incinerator.

FIGURE 2.2

Diagram of a Refuse-derived Fuel (RDF) Processing System for MSW

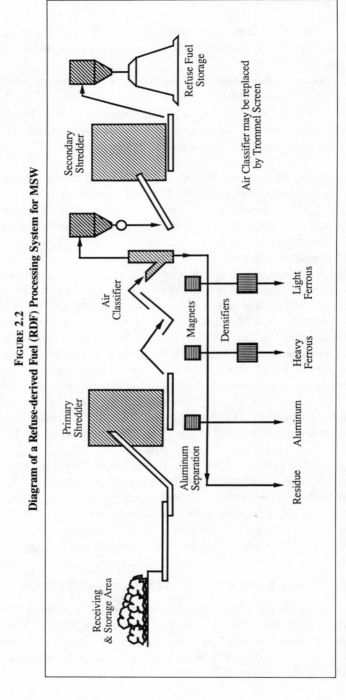

SOURCE: EDF; based on U.S. EPA, *Municipal Waste Combustion Study: Report to Congress* (Washington, DC: Office of Solid Waste and Emergency Response, June 1987, EPA/530-SW-87-021a), p. 13.

Actual volume reductions vary tremendously in practice. For efficient mass-burn systems, reasonable rule-of-thumb estimates are 80 to 90 percent by volume relative to the amount of waste received uncompacted. (The reduction in weight is smaller, typically in a range of 65 to 75 percent; weight reduction is often relevant, as tipping fees are frequently assessed on a per-ton basis.) Examples of much less impressive reductions are common, however, even for relatively modern incinerators. For example, a Tuscaloosa, Alabama, facility, built in 1984, is reported to achieve only about 50 percent volume reduction.

The degree of volume reduction depends on two factors—the technology employed and the nature of the waste received. Operational and design factors such as waste feed rate, temperature, residence time, and air turbulence affect combustion efficiency. Preprocessing of the waste stream can also drastically alter the degree of volume reduction achieved. Refuse-derived fuel (RDF) systems are designed to remove much of the noncombustible portion of the waste stream prior to burning. As a result, the relative quantity of ash is far less than for mass-burn systems. If the removed material, which can approach 40 percent by weight, were to be recycled rather than landfilled, overall volume reduction for the RDF system would greatly exceed that of a comparably sized mass-burn system.

Degree of volume reduction is best evaluated by comparing the physical volume of the incoming waste against the physical volume of the ash residue. Table 2.2 shows these volumes as a function of waste density, which varies substantially across different types of waste and ash.

Evaluating volume-reduction data thus requires knowing what types of figures are being compared. For example, the ranges for volume reduction

Table 2.2
Comparison of Typical Volume Measurements
for MSW and Incinerator Ashes
(Lbs/yd³)

MUNICIPAL SOLID WASTE:	
Uncompacted solid waste	250 lbs/yd³
Landfilled solid waste	800 lbs/yd³
Baled solid waste	1,600 lbs/yd³
INCINERATOR ASH RESIDUE:	
Fly ash/scrubber residue	3,000 lbs/yd³
Bottom ash	1,500 lbs/yd³
Combined ash	1,700–2,200 lbs/yd³

SOURCE: EDF calculations.

presented at the beginning of this section were based on a comparison of landfilled solid waste and ash. If, however, it is assumed that landfilled solid waste is first baled, these figures change considerably. Evaluating volume-reduction estimates for incineration should take into account two additional factors: (1) the amount of nonprocessible waste (e.g., construction debris, white goods such as refrigerators), which can account for as much as 25 percent of the waste delivered to an incinerator but cannot be processed in it;[3] and (2) the amount of bypass waste (i.e., waste that must be turned away during scheduled or unscheduled downtimes at the incinerator), which typically account for 10 to 15 percent or more of incinerator capacity.[4]

The National League of Cities recently assessed the impact of all these factors in a publication geared toward local decision makers, illustrating their major impact on the waste disposal needs of a typical community.[5] An excerpt from that publication is reproduced in the sidebar below.

Ash residues resulting from incineration include several distinct wastes. Bottom ash typically accounts for 75 to 95 percent (by weight) of the total ash residue. Fly ash and/or scrubber residues account for the remaining 5 to 25 percent. The relative amounts of fly and bottom ash vary considerably and depend on combustion-chamber turbulence, the nature of the waste burned, and the types of air pollution controls used. For example, mass-

---

An Assessment of Volume Reduction Achieved through Incineration

Consider a community that generates 400 tpd [tons per day] of MSW exclusive of source reduction and recycling programs. Some of this waste is "non-processible" material that cannot be incinerated, such as demolition waste and construction rubble, bulky items such as appliances ("white goods"), large tree stumps, etc. This kind of material typically amounts to 15 percent of the total waste stream (60 tpd in our example) and it absolutely must be landfilled. The remaining waste (340 tpd in our example) can be incinerated but there will be times when the incinerator is shut down for maintenance or repairs. Typically, shutdowns occur about 15 percent of the time over the life of the facility. When shutdowns occur, MSW must be taken (or "bypassed") to a landfill. Performing some quick calculations, note that 15 percent of the remaining 340 tpd equals an average of 51 tpd that must be landfilled due to periodic shutdowns at the facility. Therefore, taking into account nonprocessible and bypass waste, the average amount of MSW that this community can incinerate comes to a total of 289 tpd.

But this community's landfill needs do not end there. The residue remaining after incineration is typically 20 to 25 percent by weight of the MSW incinerated. Often, water is added to the residue ash when it is removed from the furnace in order to cool the ash down, increasing the overall percent by weight to about 30 percent of the MSW actually burned. In our example, this formula means the community burn incinerators generally produce a higher proportion of bottom ash because the initial waste contains glass, metal, and other noncombustible items; since those materials are at least partially removed from RDF waste, RDF incinerators yield less ash overall, but a higher proportion is fly ash. Use of scrubbers may substantially increase fly-ash volumes by adding excess lime and the salts produced from acid-gas neutralization.

Several liquid waste streams can be generated by incinerators, depending on their design and operation. Boilers and scrubbers may generate contaminated liquid effluents that are discharged with or without prior treatment. Quench water is the excess liquid used to cool the ash as it exits the furnace; because it comes into intimate contact with the ash, quench water may contain very high levels of salt and heavy metals dissolved from the ash (see chapter 5). With good design, the need to discharge these liquid waste streams can be avoided through "recycling": Scrubber effluents can be used to quench the ash; because the ash absorbs a considerable amount of water upon quenching, proper design and operation of the quench system can reduce or eliminate the need to discharge quench water. Although many newer facilities achieve zero discharge of these wastes, many operating facilities routinely discharge large amounts of contaminated wastewater, which is often not recognized as another incinerator emission.

---

would be left with 30 percent of 289 tpd, or 87 tpd, in ash. If this amount is added to the non-processible and bypass waste amounts, a total of 198 tpd out of 400 tpd MSW must be landfilled even after an incinerator is built.

There is one piece of good news in these figures which should not be overlooked. Because incinerator ash is significantly more dense than raw MSW (1,500 to 2,000 lbs/cubic yard compared to 1,000 lbs/cubic yard), one ton of ash occupies only one-half to two-thirds of the landfill space as the same weight of MSW. Nevertheless, the sample community's landfill needs are still significant. The bottom line is that once it builds a WTE [waste-to-energy] facility, the community still will need approximately 40 percent of the landfill volume it would have needed without incineration.

As the above example illustrates, local government officials need to be very wary of excessive claims regarding the volume reduction that can be accomplished through incineration. Often, the claim is made that "incineration reduces the volume of waste by 75 percent" or some other high percentage. This claim can only be supported by making some misleading comparisons between the volume and weight of a typical ton of MSW and volume and weight of a ton of incinerator ash. The claim cannot be supported when you consider the overall garbage disposal needs of the entire community. While there is a large reduction in volume due to incineration, this reduction does not translate into an equivalent reduction in the need for landfill space.[6]

FUTURE USE OF MSW INCINERATION IN THE UNITED STATES

A number of factors have been operating over the last several years to significantly expand the use of incineration in managing MSW. These include dwindling landfill capacity, especially in heavily urbanized areas of the Northeast, along with rising landfill costs and siting difficulties; an aggressive marketing campaign conducted by incinerator vendors; a perception, which is partially justified, that waste to energy is cleaner and more conserving of resources than landfilling; a perception that the one-stop-shopping approach that incineration offers is easier, albeit more expensive, to implement than are community-wide recycling programs; and a perception that incineration is the only so-called proven technology for managing MSW.

More recently, however, new factors have entered into the debate. Factors restraining the development of incineration include intense public opposition; unresolved risk issues surrounding air emissions and ash residues; uncertainty over regulatory requirements; major long-term economic risks, an initially high price tag, and frequent cost overruns; and growing concern over the effect that a long-term commitment to incineration may have on more preferred management approaches such as recycling.

These factors are having the effect of reducing the rate at which new incinerators are being built or planned. Numerous proposals have been canceled or put on hold. In 1987, Kidder, Peabody's annual survey found that new capacity coming on-line that year increased slightly over 1986 (about 21,000 tpd versus 18,000 tpd), but almost 36,000 tpd of capacity in previously ordered incinerators was canceled, and capacity in the planning stages was down 30 percent.[7] Another study found that between 1986 and 1988 the number of projects in advanced planning dropped 12.5 percent, although projects in the conceptual stage were reported to increase by 85 percent during the same period. The same study identified 21 projects in California alone that had been delayed or scratched since 1986.[8] EDF's compilation of U.S. incineration facilities identified more than 60 projects that had been delayed or canceled (see Appendix A).

Even the current use of incineration in the United States is difficult to estimate with any degree of precision for it constantly changes as new facilities come on-line or old ones are shut down. Similarly, projections of even near-future capacities are fraught with uncertainties (see tables 2.3 and 2.4 for the best estimates of current and projected numbers).

Current incineration capacity is estimated by EPA to represent about 10 percent of the total municipal waste stream in the United States, and incineration capacity is projected to rise toward 25 percent by the end of the

TABLE 2.3
Existing Municipal Waste Combustors

Type of Technology	Number of Facilities*	With Energy Recovery	Approximate Capacity
Mass burn	63	37	34,000 tpd
Modular	72	43	4,500 tpd
Refuse-derived fuel (RDF)	12	12	11,500 tpd†
Fluidized bed-burning RDF	3	3	—
RDF plus coal	7	4	—
TOTAL	157	99	50,000 tpd

SOURCES:

"1988 Refuse Incineration and Refuse-to-Energy Listings," *Waste Age,* 19, no. 1 (November 1988): 195–212.

Citizen's Clearinghouse for Hazardous Wastes, *Incineration Fact Pack* (Arlington, VA, January 5, 1989).

Radian Corporation Progress Center, *Final Report: Municipal Waste Combustion Industry Profile* (Research Triangle Park, NC, September 16, 1988).

Radian Corporation Progress Center, *Planned and Projected Municipal Waste Combustors Profile Update* (Research Triangle Park, NC, May 18, 1988).

The United States Conference of Mayors National Resource Recovery Association, *City Currents* 7, no. 4 (October 1988).

*Existing facilities operating as of April 1988.
† Includes capacity for fluidized-bed and RDF-plus-coal facilities.
tpd = tons of MSW per day.

century. More than 100 communities are reportedly in the early stages of project planning. An estimated 4 to 5 million tons of ash residue was estimated by EPA to have been produced in 1988.

The operating and planned facilities are not distributed evenly on a geographic basis, but rather are generally concentrated in areas of high-population density, particularly in the Northeast and industrialized Midwest. Figure 2.3 shows the distribution (by state and EPA Region) of 163 operating U.S. incinerators and the distribution of an additional 133 facilities that are either under construction (26) or planned (107). In addition, EDF's compilation revealed 63 additional incinerators that have been canceled or delayed, and at least 12 additional facilities that have been shut down recently. The individual facilities in each of these categories are listed by state in Appendix A. (The number and status of facilities in figure 2.3 does not correspond exactly to those in tables 2.3 and 2.4, because of differences in sources and status definitions used.)

TABLE 2.4
Planned Municipal Waste Combustors

Type of Technology	Number of Facilities*	Approximate Capacity
Mass burn	78	78,000 tpd
Modular	15	3,500 tpd
Refuse-derived fuel (RDF)	15	31,000 tpd
Fluidized bed-burning RDF	12	7,500 tpd
RDF plus coal	Unknown	Unknown
Total	120	120,000 tpd

SOURCES:

"1988 Refuse Incineration and Refuse-to-Energy Listings," *Waste Age,* 19, no. 1 (November 1988): 195–212.

Citizen's Clearinghouse for Hazardous Wastes, *Incineration Fact Pack* (Arlington, VA, January 5, 1989).

Radian Corporation Progress Center, *Final Report: Municipal Waste Combustion Industry Profile* (Research Triangle Park, NC, September 16, 1988).

Radian Corporation Progress Center, *Planned and Projected Municipal Waste Combustors Profile Update* (Research Triangle Park, NC, May 18, 1988).

The United States Conference of Mayors National Resource Recovery Association, *City Currents* 7, no. 4 (October 1988).

*Planned number of facilities not operating as of April 1988, but projected to begin construction by December 1989.
tpd = tons of MSW per day.

RECYCLING TECHNOLOGY, POTENTIALS, AND RESIDUALS

A community's solid waste is produced in a variety of forms by a variety of sources. Incineration generally entails feeding this mixed waste stream into a large, technologically complex facility. In contrast, recycling depends on segregating recyclable materials, usually where they are generated, and sending them, in differentiated streams, to industries that use them in manufacturing new products. If anything is complicated about large-scale recycling, it is that well-designed programs do not follow a single model for collection and processing, but combine a number of different program components, or modules, to facilitate source separation and collection of recyclable materials from different waste generators.

The first step in assessing the potential of large-scale recycling is to

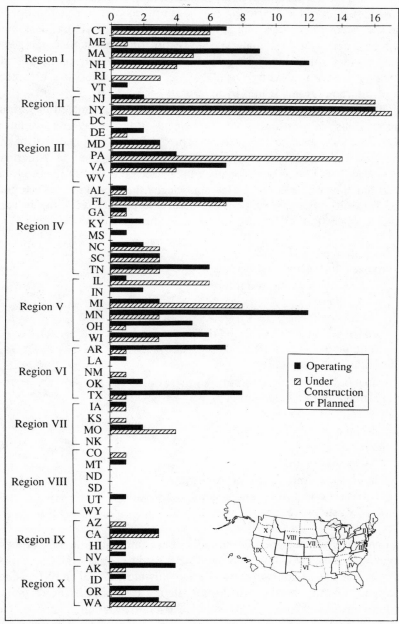

FIGURE 2.3
Distribution of MSW Incinerators in the United States,
Operating and Under Construction or Planned

SOURCE: See Table 2.3.

69

understand the composition of the waste stream as generated by specific sources, such as office districts or single-family residential neighborhoods. The next steps are designating specific materials for recycling, designing programs to recover those materials, and estimating the fraction of targeted materials that will actually be recovered. As reliable data on large-scale recycling become increasingly available, our ability to assess the full potential of future programs is improving rapidly.

Following are nine recycling modules that can be assembled in various combinations to constitute a comprehensive program. Where available, waste diversion data for representative programs are supplied. All of the programs described have been successfully implemented in American cities. New York City is occasionally emphasized because EDF has concentrated much of its research and local advocacy there, and to illustrate that even in a city where most people would assume that recycling is very difficult, opportunities for large-scale recycling abound.

1. drop-off centers
2. buyback and processing centers
3. commercial recycling programs
     office paper
     corrugated boxes
     construction and demolition debris
     bulk waste
     additional materials
4. residential curbside collection
5. apartment building collection
6. rural recycling programs
7. material recovery facilities
8. composting
     backyard composting
     large-scale composting in windrows
     in-vessel composting and anaerobic digestion
9. mixed waste processing

In any program designed for an individual community, the mix of these recycling modules will obviously vary; what works in Palo Alto, California, may not make sense for rural New Mexico, downtown Atlanta, or Lansing, Michigan. For this reason, we do not attempt to assemble the recycling modules presented into a representative overall program. Nor does the section attempt to systematically survey the current state of recycling or suggest that the programs described represent the best that can be achieved.

Because recycling is growing so rapidly, the section refers to journals, government agencies, industry sources, and nonprofit groups that provide up-to-date information on the state of recycling.

1. DROP-OFF CENTERS

Drop-off centers, which accept materials voluntarily collected and brought in by the public, are among the least expensive and most easily established types of recycling programs. Though drop-off centers will not achieve high recycling rates on their own, they can offer recycling options to neighborhoods where curbside or apartment collection programs may not be phased in for years. Drop-off centers are a good way to publicize recycling; they provide an immediate way for volunteers to get involved in running recycling operations and can help train future recycling professionals.

The design of drop-off centers can be tailored to specific local needs. For example, Vallejo, California, and communities in Ohio use a mobile system, where bins are moved from place to place on trailers.[9] Drop-off centers can also be sited in areas where materials like newspaper and beverage containers rapidly accumulate, including subways, airports, and train stations, shopping malls, and schools and universities.

2. BUY-BACK CENTERS

Buy-back centers pay people for materials they bring in, rather than relying on donations. For this reason, they usually collect greater tonnages than drop-off centers. Buy-back centers can accept materials from businesses as well as households, and can insist that materials be prepared according to certain specifications (e.g., no color-mixed glass), which reduces contamination and assists in marketing.

Buy-back centers range widely in size and scale. Some do relatively little processing of material, relying on private intermediaries for this function. For example, Many Happy Returns of San Francisco, a nonprofit company partially supported by the city of San Francisco, runs six small centers, each providing bins for different materials, a scale, and accounting equipment. Revenues from sales of materials from these centers are often donated to causes that benefit the local community, such as foundations providing support to AIDS victims, thereby providing further public benefit.

Other buy-back/processing centers are more like small factories, buying large varieties of material from the public, processing it on-site, and selling directly to manufacturers around the world. In the United States, probably the largest example of this type of operation is the R2B2 recycling company. R2B2 was founded in 1982 in the South Bronx, New York City, by the South Bronx 2000 Local Development Corporation, a nonprofit organization concerned with housing rehabilitation and stabilization, commercial revitalization, and job creation in the South Bronx and elsewhere. R2B2 is a for-profit company owned by its nonprofit originator. R2B2 stands for Recoverable Resources/Boro Bronx 2000 (R2B2), Inc. This innovative approach to urban recycling is described in the accompanying sidebar.

Aside from their substantial job creation and economic development benefits, inner-city buy-back and processing operations based on the R2B2 model can be set up quickly, and are substantially less expensive, on a per-ton basis, than most other types of urban residential collection programs. As R2B2 has shown, large buy-back and processing operations can also function as market development laboratories, providing manufacturers with samples of materials to test in their production machinery, and tailoring the processing of materials to the needs of specific buyers. Centers like R2B2 are in Philadelphia (National Temple Recycling), Newark (Orchard Street Recycling), Miami, and Chicago (The Resource Center).

Of course, the inner-city buy-back/processing operation is not the only successful variant on the buy-back model. The aluminum industry also runs its own extensive network of local buy-back operations. Under Assembly Bill (AB) 2020, California's experiment with container-deposit legisla-

---

An Innovative Approach to Urban Recycling

Recoverable Resources/Boro Bronx (R2B2) currently purchases, processes, and markets over 35 materials brought to the center by the public and businesses, including standard recyclables such as paper, glass bottles, and aluminum cans, as well as metal cans, corrugated boxes, wood pallets, books, window glass, and many plastics, which include shampoo bottles, antifreeze jugs, plastic film, manufacturing scrap, used swimming pool liners, commercial videotape cartridges, and window molding.[10]

Slightly less than half of the material processed at R2B2 is beverage-container glass accumulated by local grocery stores and small beverage distributors, which originate and redeem their own deposits under the New York State Returnable Container Law (RCL), but do not have access to recycling capacity. R2B2 is essentially a "recycler of last resort" for these small firms, and is not itself a deposit redemption center.

To support the purchase and processing of most non-RCL materials that R2B2 buys from the public, the New York City Department of Sanitation (DOS) pays R2B2 a processing fee of about $45 per ton. Relative to the combined cost of DOS waste collection and disposal, which is at least $140 a ton, the city's support for

---

tion, mobile buy-back centers have been established at about 2,400 sites near supermarkets, usually in parking lots. However, because of staffing requirements imposed by state law, these centers have been heavily subsidized, on the basis of tonnage collected.

3. COMMERCIAL SECTOR RECYCLING

In principle, private businesses face a strong economic incentive to recycle because what they cannot divert from their waste stream, they must pay private carters to haul away. In turn, private carters must pay landfill or incinerator operators for every ton they deliver for disposal; if paid a fixed fee by businesses for their carting services, the fewer tons a carter must tip, the more profit will be made. Municipal government, the third party in this relationship, usually regulates the private-carting industry, and also stands to benefit if private haulers and their clients act together to divert material from municipal disposal facilities.

Many businesses produce substantial quantities of recyclable material, often unmixed, more readily separable, or having fewer contaminants than household waste (see tables 1.3 and 1.4 in chapter 1). Those materials with the most-immediate potential for recycling are first discussed, followed by a brief description of other materials.

R2B2 is clearly a bargain. In one form or another, DOS has been providing financial support to R2B2 since late 1985, currently accounting for 20 to 25 percent of R2B2's gross income. Most important elements of R2B2's cash flow derive from the center's own marketing acumen.

As of early 1989, R2B2 was marketing about 60 tons of materials per day, roughly the quantity of waste generated by a municipality the size of Beverly Hills, California, or Poughkeepsie, New York. At this rate, the company now pays out about $20,000 per month to individual recyclers on a cash-for-trash basis, and through salaries and cash payout has an overall economic impact on the South Bronx of about $2 million per year. In late 1989, R2B2 began operations at a separate $1.5 million plastics-processing facility. The managers of Bronx 2000 have helped set up similar centers in Philadelphia, Newark, and Miami, and are working on additional projects in Brooklyn, the Monongahela Valley outside Pittsburgh, and Dublin, Ireland.

Through a separate program, Bronx 2000's managers broker material throughout the East. The managers of Bronx 2000 feel that New York City could easily support nine additional buy-back/processing centers of R2B2's size, with commensurate economic development, cost savings, and waste-diversion benefits for the city.

Office Paper and Corrugated Boxes

The financial districts of large cities produce enormous amounts of valuable high-grade office paper; a common rule of thumb is that the typical office worker generates about one-half pound of high-grade paper per day.[11] Many businesses generate substantial quantities of bulky corrugated boxes. Both of these materials enjoy a relatively steady demand by paper mills, which use them in the manufacture of new paper products, such as tissue paper produced for the commercial market (e.g., nonhome use), corrugating medium (the wavy material that comprises the middle section of corrugated boxboard), or certain types of paperboard (the gray material that makes up cereal boxes and backings of writing tablets). If the management of a company decides it is in its interest to recycle, high participation rates can be achieved with relative ease.

Evidence of private-sector paper recycling is all around us. On the loading docks behind most supermarkets, one can see large bales of corrugated boxes awaiting shipment to paper dealers or mills. In New York City, private carters have required owners of delicatessens, restaurants, and other businesses to flatten corrugated boxes and consolidate them in loose bales at the curb. These boxes are tossed into the large packer trucks that roam New York City streets at night collecting waste from commercial clients, and are later separated for recycling from the floors of private transfer stations or from conveyer belts built for the purpose. Some carters make separate runs to collect the corrugated material.

In the New York City area, even in good market conditions, the selling price of secondary corrugated fiber, $40 per cubic yard, represents a fraction of the current tipping fee of approximately $100 per ton at the city's Fresh Kills landfill. Thus, carters who recycle corrugated material gain much more from avoiding the tipping fee than from actual sales on secondary-paper markets. In combination, the market price of corrugated cardboard and the avoided tipping fee provide a powerful incentive to recycle.

Despite the prevalence of private-sector recycling, much more could be done. In many cities waste collection is provided to government agencies and nonprofit institutions for free; for example, in New York City about 1,600 tons per day of material, or 6 percent of the waste stream, is thus disposed of. In addition, private waste haulers have limited abilities to induce their clients to undertake full source-separation programs, which are the key to attaining the maximum potential of recycling. This situation creates an obvious entrée for government recycling officials, who, more so than private carters, can convince business leaders that recycling is a simple way of keeping the costs of doing business down while, at the same time, providing a service to the community. Government agencies can also help broker collection and sales agreements between office tenants and haulers, who often have their own relationships with paper brokers. The Seattle Solid Waste Utility has established a rate structure for private carters that rewards source separation and recycling.

In San Francisco, the Office of Recycling has extensively publicized the benefits of office-paper recycling. The city conducts over 100 office-paper-recycling workshops per year for local corporations, and has issued a how-to brochure that includes a work sheet allowing companies to calculate their potential savings on waste disposal costs if they recycle their waste paper. The city also provides desk-side bins that simplify separation of paper from other waste. The city's private waste-hauling company usually returns 70 to 100 percent of the revenue collected from paper sales to the participating corporations, which, in turn, often donate that money to high-visibility public charities such as the city's Adopt a School program.[12] The New York City DOS and a quasi-public agency, the Council on the Environment of New York City, provide recycling containers and instructions to over 425 corporations and nonprofit institutions in the city; both programs could be expanded.[13]

Primarily because of strong efforts in the private sector, San Francisco and Seattle, Washington, were each recycling about 25 percent of their waste *before* the cities began to put residential curbside collection programs in place. The equipment required for office-paper collection (desk-side bins, educational materials, and larger collection containers for back hallways or utility rooms) is relatively modest and inexpensive; this type of program can, in fact, be one of the least-expensive and easiest-to-install forms of recycling.[14]

Additional Materials

Of course, paper is not the only recyclable material produced by private and nonprofit firms. Office-paper-recycling programs can be a first step in providing the means to recycle beverage containers, newsprint, plastic, and even furniture discarded from businesses. And offices are not the only workplaces that generate recyclable waste materials.

In addition to an established network of paper dealers, most large American cities host companies that recycle construction and demolition debris, including mixed and segregated loads of bricks, metal, asphalt, wood, and concrete, into aggregate, new building materials, and inputs to steel mills and secondary metal smelters. The traditional auto-shredding, scrap metal, and materials-processing industries can also process bulk waste such as white goods—a machine that can shred a car can also shred a couch or washing machine. Wood from such operations is often used in cogeneration plants.

The amounts of materials processed by these firms can be substantial. In New York City, for example, Con-Agg crushes 500 to 800 tons of concrete rubble per day, producing new aggregate for use in making concrete and construction subbase material at its plant in the Bronx.[15] A Queens-based waste hauling firm, Allied Sanitation, is currently chipping 150 tons of wood waste per day. Another hauler, Star Recycling, segregates many tons per day of wood and paper waste from its collections. Several other private haulers have installed low-technology materials recovery operations at their transfer stations, in total processing 500 to 1,000 tons of material per day with 30 to 40 percent recovery rates. One of these firms, Lehigh Carting, is in the process of installing a conveyer-based hand-sorting and baling operation that will recover 150 tons per day of wood and paper.[16] In San Rafael, California, a model processing operation run by Marin Sanitary Systems runs up to 350 tons per day of wood, paper, yard wastes, and metal through its facility, and even includes a small farm where pigs are fed food waste from local restaurants.[17]

The tonnages processed in private recycling/carting operations are heavily influenced by tipping fees charged at available landfills, transportation costs, the market value of the material after it has been processed, and the costs of processing. Since the benefits of recycling to the general public (e.g., lengthened life of a local landfill) may be greater than current tipping fees, municipal governments can affect this equation and increase the level of recycling by existing businesses by delivering materials to private processors, paying for additional recycling, or both. For example, the New York City DOS directly collects about 700 tons per day of bulk waste from residential neighborhoods. Proposals to put this material out to bid and deliver it to processors rather than to the landfill are now being developed by DOS; the department projects that it can deliver 635 tons per day of this material by 1991.[18]

Municipal governments can also install their own processing equipment for materials they collect in quantity. For example, the New York City DOS has also proposed to install concrete crushing and screening equipment at the Fresh Kills landfill on Staten Island. The equipment would be used to transform incoming rubble from construction projects run by the city and private companies into material usable as landfill cover, which DOS now buys for about $12 per ton, or as aggregate for roadbeds around the landfill. Some incoming material is already used for this purpose, but the proposed machinery would allow more to be used. DOS estimates that 150,000 cubic yards of material amenable to crushing and screening are produced every year from government-contracted construction projects alone. Other estimates have put the total amount of construction and demolition debris accepted at the landfill at 1 million cubic yards per year, or 455,000 tons.[19]

Because bulk waste and construction and demolition debris are not accepted at incinerators, recycling this material will not directly alter the size of a proposed incinerator. However, recycling nonburnables will lengthen the life of a local landfill, usually at a lower cost per ton than incinerating other partially combustible waste. Under the principle that the least-expensive waste management options should be pursued first, and that overall reduction of dependence on landfilling is the basis for comparing recycling and incineration, aggressive recycling of nonburnable waste should be considered in any survey of solid waste management options.

4. RESIDENTIAL CURBSIDE COLLECTION

The most common image associated with recycling is probably collection of newspaper, cans, and bottles picked up from the curbside in moderate-density city and suburban neighborhoods. With over 1,000 communities now operating some kind of curbside collection program in the United States, the broad formulas for successful curbside recycling in most locales have become clearly defined.[20] Curbside programs often work best if the sponsoring municipality or its private contractor offer large, brightly colored containers for separating recyclable items in households that choose to participate. When these containers are in use, it is easy to see who on the block is participating and who is not; neighborhood peer pressure can thus work to promote recycling. Such containers can also contain recycled plastic content.

Mandatory recycling ordinances also increase participation, primarily because the enactment of a mandatory law generates a lot of publicity and shows that local elected officials are serious about recycling. The typical means of enforcing mandatory source-separation ordinances—fines or refusal to pick up the garbage for households that ignore several prior warnings—are useful in getting the last 10 to 30 percent of local households to participate. This has been the case in smaller towns like Hamburg, New York, and Woodbury, New Jersey, which claim participation rates of 95 to 98 percent.[21]

Participation appears to be higher if households are required to separate their waste into only two or three categories, and if recyclables are picked up the same day as the regular trash. For example, all types of bottles and cans can be placed in one container, and then sorted at a truckside or at a central processing plant. These plants, known as material recovery facilities (MRFs), are described below.

The periodicals *Resource Recycling* and *BioCycle*, which are devoted to recycling and composting, and *Waste Age*, which covers all aspects of the waste management industry, feature a continuing stream of articles on large-scale curbside recycling programs and advertisements for equipment used in recycling.[22] Examples of successful curbside collection programs in large cities and small towns across the United States appear in table 2.5, which also gives data on the fraction of the local residential waste stream diverted by such programs.

Curbside recycling alone will not achieve high recycling rates across an entire community. For example, in reaching its 60 percent recycling goal, Seattle plans on implementing a wide range of programs in the commercial and residential sector (see chapter 4). Newark, New Jersey, reports reaching a 41 percent recycling rate through a combination of programs.[23]

Savings in Conventional Refuse Collection Costs as a Result of Recycling

Curbside collection of residential recyclables can be quite expensive if it means adding a duplicate collection system to existing collection systems for regular refuse. However, one often overlooked aspect of recycling in general, and curbside recycling in particular, is its potential ability to substantially reduce the costs of conventional garbage collection. By definition, the more material that is collected for recycling, the less will have to be picked up by regular garbage packer trucks. Where a well-established recycling program is diverting a significant quantity of material, regular trash collection trucks should be able to travel longer routes, make more stops, and require less maintenance. If sanitation engineers adjust their routing systems to account for the effect of recycling (route optimization is, after all, a major part of their responsibility), fewer conventional garbage collection trucks are required.

At first, especially if small fractions of material are diverted for recycling, conventional cost savings may not be especially great; routes may not be reconfigured, and costs like garages and administrative staff remain fixed over the short term. As more and more materials are collected, and as time goes on, savings in conventional collection costs should grow. In the first year of a program in San Jose, California, city officials estimated that for every two tons of recyclables collected, the cost of picking up one ton of regular garbage is saved.[24] Other cities have experienced higher offsets after longer periods of time.[25] In densely populated cities, garbage collection takes place not once but two to four times each week. Under these conditions, substantial recycling might eliminate the need for an entire collection run, achieving close to a one-to-one cost savings.[26]

Another factor that has a significant effect on the costs of curbside collection is the design and use of collection vehicles. Some of the most widely publicized curbside recycling programs are notable for their fleets of shiny new recycling trucks, but buying specialized vehicles for separate collection of recyclables is not always necessary. Smaller cities may be able to use existing vehicles not fully employed by the local public works department to tow trailers with bins for separated recyclables. Other cities have tried a variety of approaches, including using regular packer trucks to pull recycling trailers, mounting bins underneath packer-truck bodies to collect newspaper, or adapting beer trucks or other vehicles to recycling. Small towns can also pool resources to buy a fleet of recycling vehicles that they share.

Even when using new, specialized recycling trucks, the design of the truck itself and the way it is used can have major cost ramifications. For example, when the New York City DOS began its pilot curbside collection program for newsprint in 1986, it purchased a fleet of 28 trucks with a fairly small capacity for carrying collected materials, about 12 cubic yards. Because the city lacked recent waste composition data, it underestimated the amount of available newsprint by twofold. In moderate-density neighborhoods like Greenwich Village, the new trucks filled up with newspaper in about three hours; in less-dense areas such as Staten Island, the trucks filled up in five hours. By the time the trucks were full, street traffic was heavy; without nearby intermediate processing centers (IPCs) or recycling transfer stations, operating costs mounted as the trucks sat in DOS garages, waiting for another shift of drivers to take them to paper dealers in Brooklyn.

This situation could be avoided with the construction of recycling mini-transfer stations or IPCs that would allow trucks to make two collection runs per shift or by buying trucks with greater capacity. DOS is now experimenting with a 40-cubic-yard recycling truck and, for the last two years, has been using a comparably large front-loading EZ Pack compactor truck to collect newspaper from high-rise apartment buildings. Many more innovations in truck design and routing can be expected as the recycling industry continues to grow.

Many other factors, such as labor costs, union rules, topography, housing density, and real estate values, influence the costs of residential recycling collection. However, these factors tend to affect the costs of regular garbage

TABLE 2.5
Summary of Data on 20 Curbside Recycling Collection Programs

City	Estimated Population Served	Waste Diversion (%)	Partici- pation (%)	Estimated Lbs. Recovered/ Capita/Year	Start Date	Mandatory	Materials Collected
Wilton, NH	8,500	44[a]	65	600	1979	Yes	All
Madison, WI	143,000	6	75	50	1968	Yes	NP, AP, YW
Prarie du Sac, WI	2,300	30–50	95	250	N/A	Yes	All
Montclair, NJ	38,000	23	75–80	235	1971	Yes	NP, AL, GL, YW, AP
Islip, NY	300,000	6	50	N/A	1980	Yes	All
Mecklenburg Cty, NC	22,500	N/A	70	115	1984	No	NP, YW, MO, OP, GL, AL, CC
Marin County, CA	255,000	22	60	190	1981	No	NP, AL, GL, MM, MO, CB
Somerset County, NJ	81,000	23	N/A	N/A	N/A	N/A	N/A
Essex County, NJ	850,000	15–20	N/A	235	N/A	Yes	AL, GL, YW, AP, NP
San Jose, CA	400,000	5	58	115	1985	No	GL, AL, YW, NP
Kitchener, Ontario	250,000	12[b]	84	100	1983	No	GL, AL, MM, MO, AP, NP
Santa Monica, CA	90,000	N/A	28	45	1985	No	GL, AZ, MM, MO, NP, CC
Austin, TX	115,000	4	20–25	550	1982	No	GL, AZ, MM, NP
Minneapolis, MN	270,000	11	20–25	55	1982	No	GL, AL, NP
Ann Arbor, MI	54,000	10[b]	25–50	95	1978	No	AL, GL, MO, NP

Naperville, IL	39,000	N/A	35–40	N/A	N/A	No	GL, AL, PL, NP
Omaha, NE	250,000	N/A	N/A	N/A	1988	No	GL, NP
Portland, OR	450,000	24	20	75	1987	Yes	All
Champaign, IL	31,000	N/A	65	130	1986	No	GL, AL, NP
Urbana, IL	10,300	N/A	65	110	1986	No	GL, AL, NP

SOURCE: P. Grogan and A. Peters, "Community Recycling; What Is Working Best," *BioCycle*, May/June 1988, pp. 32–36.

a Percent of waste collected at transfer station diverted.
b Residential waste stream only.

Key:
NP	= newspaper	PL	= plastics
GL	= glass	MO	= motor oil
AL	= aluminum	MM	= mixed metals
CC	= corrugated cardboard	AP	= appliances (white goods)
OP	= office paper	AB	= auto batteries
YW	= yard waste—leaves		
MP	= mixed paper	All	= all of the above

collection in the same way, making savings in conventional collection costs all the more important. In addition to a growing number of consulting firms, several publications and computer models are now available to help recycling planners evaluate the costs of different types of collection in their communities.[27]

5. APARTMENT-BUILDING COLLECTION

Those unfamiliar with recycling often assume that because apartment dwellers have less space than suburbanites, and because it is difficult to tell who is not recycling in apartment buildings, apartment collection of recyclable materials is not workable. But many apartment dwellers already have built-in systems for disposing of their trash; the key is to design recycling systems that match them. For many buildings, well-designed and promoted apartment recycling programs may cost substantially less per ton than curbside collection. In addition, many local ordinances currently require apartment maintenance staff to place trash at the curb for pickup in a specified way; these ordinances can be adapted to recycling.

One successful approach to apartment recycling has been pioneered by the Environmental Action Coalition (EAC), a nonprofit group in New York City that began installing recycling collection systems in New York apartment buildings in 1984. Under EAC's approach, recyclable materials are not stored in individual apartments. Instead, they are stacked or placed in special containers in places where people would ordinarily dispose of their trash: in trash-chute rooms, next to chutes, and in laundry rooms (for plastic bottles). Recycling does not increase the overall amount of waste the maintenance staff and dwellers in buildings have to handle, but simply separates it into different categories; it also reduces the chances of staff cutting themselves on broken glass buried in plastic bags when handling the regular trash. For different sizes of buildings, different types of storage and collection systems are used.

The New York City DOS has organized its own apartment recycling programs. Because materials accumulate quickly in high-rise apartment buildings, they can often be handled in large containers that can be picked up and emptied by automated collection vehicles. Such a system is far more efficient than repeatedly stopping to pick up smaller bins at the curb in a low-density suburb. By 1989, DOS and EAC had made recycling available to several hundred thousand apartment units in New York City. Similar plans or programs are underway in Minneapolis/St. Paul, Los Angeles, San Francisco, Seattle, and Philadelphia, to name a few.

6. RURAL RECYCLING

In large cities, space for garages and processing plants is at a premium, costs are high, and logistics are difficult, but materials accumulate very rapidly. In contrast, recycling in rural areas requires efficient transportation and storage systems to concentrate materials collected over sparsely populated areas. In many rural areas, separate collection can be provided by residents themselves, who already routinely haul their trash to a local landfill, by outfitting the landfill with bins for recyclable materials. Wellesley, Massachusetts, which has no regular garbage collection service, and the New Hampshire towns of Peterborough and Wilton are notable examples of this approach.[28] Wellesley's parklike recycling center has reportedly become a social meeting place, and even includes a book exchange. Combined with its composting program, Wellesley is now diverting over 40 percent of its waste through recycling.[29]

The New Hampshire Resource Recovery Association, a nonprofit group supported by a state grant and member dues, assists recyclers throughout the state in marketing materials and routing trucks for efficient collection.[30] Athens County, in south-central Ohio, employs central collection points that are convenient to stores and churches, in addition to operating a program that cleans up roadside dumps.[31]

In more remote territory, Montana Recycling, a private business, relies on a network of six collection warehouses to accumulate materials collected in Montana, Wyoming, Idaho, and North Dakota. A central dispatching office identifies trucks that would otherwise leave the region empty, and routes them to the warehouses, allowing the company to profitably ship 15,000 tons of material a year to buyers hundreds of miles away.[32]

As rural recyclers continue to innovate, various nonprofit organizations have begun to track successful programs and disseminate information about good program design.[33] And, of course, many people in rural areas already compost a large fraction of their organic waste.

7. MATERIAL RECOVERY FACILITIES

As collected directly from homes, apartments, and businesses, materials are not ready for marketing. Glass, aluminum, tin, plastic, and bimetal containers may be commingled and contaminated by other materials. In addition, it is expensive to ship loads of whole, loose bottles and other relatively low-density materials. For these reasons, it is becoming common to process recyclables soon after they are collected at material recovery facilities (MRFs), also known as intermediate processing centers (IPCs).

MRFs and IPCs employ hand-sorting and various types of machinery, such as air classifiers, magnets, cyclones, trommels, crushers, grinders, and balers, to produce clean, segregated loads of recyclable materials in large quantities. MRFs are thus a kind of market development tool, providing manufacturers with the consistent, reliable supplies needed to justify building new plants or retooling existing facilities to use more secondary materials. Innovations in MRF design and capacity are regularly featured in the recycling press.[34] Starting from plants that could handle up to 40 tons of material per day (tpd), (the Resource Recovery Systems [RRS] plant in Groton, Connecticut, opened in 1982), MRFs now commonly handle 250 to 500 tpd (e.g., Rabanco's Recycle Seattle plant can process 500 tpd, Marin Recycling's plant in San Rafael can process 350 tpd, and a new RRS plant in Springfield can handle 240 tpd).

Not all material received at MRFs is recyclable; some is regular garbage, and some may be materials the MRF is not equipped to handle. For example, New York City's East Harlem IPC operated by Resource Recovery Systems was initially designed to process only newspaper, aluminum, tin and bimetal cans, and glass containers, the materials collected in DOS's curbside and apartment collection programs. In fact, the plant now also handles large quantities of plastic, bales of aluminum foil and pie plates, and miscellaneous household metal items, such as pots and pans, appliances, bicycle frames, etc. Crushed ceramics, pyrex, stones, and contaminated color-mixed glass that cannot be sent to glass manufacturers are shipped to New York City's municipal asphalt plant for use in making asphalt. Municipalities served by Resource Recovery Systems's MRF in Camden County, New Jersey, specifically ask for ceramics and pyrex, to keep the material out of the county incinerator.[35]

8. COMPOSTING

According to recent waste composition estimates, Americans dispose of 28.3 million tons of yard waste—leaves, tree trimmings, and grass—annually, accounting for about 20 percent of the municipal waste stream.[36] In many suburban areas, yard waste is the first- or second-largest component of the residential waste stream; for example, yard waste accounts for more than 30 percent of the residential waste stream in Los Angeles, and is produced year-round.[37] If major contamination from other nonorganic waste materials is avoided, yard waste can easily be composted, taking advantage of natural microbial decomposition processes to produce a useful soil amendment.

Yard-waste Collection Systems

The first step in transforming yard waste from a disposal burden to a marketable product is to collect it separately from plastics, metals, and other noncompostible materials. As with other types of recycling, different sources of yard waste are best addressed by varying collection and composting methods. Some yard waste need not be collected at all. For example, grass clippings can be left where they are cut, working their way back into the soil and producing a healthier lawn. Seattle's composting program emphasizes this approach. Seattle also encourages backyard composting, which can include vegetative food waste, to reduce municipal refuse collection costs and at the same time, reward composters with a high-quality soil amendment for their gardens. The Master Composter program used in Seattle trains volunteers to show other households how to compost in their neighborhood.

Yard waste can also be collected by municipalities for composting in large-scale centralized facilities; there are now over 650 such operations nationwide.[38] With one collection technique, citizens place their leaves and branches in piles next to the curb on pickup dates. The piles are then picked up by a highly mobile front-end loader that carries a claw attachment for scooping them up and placing them in a conventional packer truck. The front-end loader/packer truck combination operates very quickly because no one has to get out of the truck, and can remove material from the curbside faster than conventional refuse collection crews. This system has been used in Davis, California, since 1972, and has been adopted in many other cities.[39]

Some cities already use what are essentially giant vacuums mounted on trucks to collect leaves that drop into the street in the fall; this material can be taken directly to composting centers. Leaves placed by homeowners in paper or plastic bags can be diverted to the composting center, where the bags are mechanically ripped open and removed. Paper bags may be shredded and composted along with the leaves. Large quantities of compostible materials are also collected by municipal landscape gardeners, who deliver it directly to transfer stations or landfills where they usually pay a fee to get rid of it. A survey of 48 landscape gardeners in Brooklyn found they would gladly deliver yard waste to compost transfer stations in return for a lower tipping fee, and would be interested in buying back the resulting compost.[40] City parks also produce substantial amounts of source-separated yard waste, and city and state parks and public works projects can be the first users of new compost, demonstrating the viability of the product, and reducing the municipalities' need to identify other markets.

A number of states have passed laws that require or facilitate the diversion of yard waste from landfills. Seven states have banned specified types of yard waste, typically leaves, from landfills and incinerators, though most of these bans actually go into effect in 1990 to 1992.[41]

Windrow Composting

A commonly used method of large-scale composting is windrow composting, where materials are shredded to a fairly uniform size and assembled in long piles up to eight feet high. The windrows can be aerated by forcing air through the piles by means of pipes and pumps or by turning the rows mechanically. Relying on naturally occurring bacteria and fungi to promote aerobic decomposition, this method takes 3 to 18 months to produce a finished product and is moderately land intensive. Composting time can be reduced by adding nitrogen sources, such as grass clippings, to the piles. Composting yard waste substantially reduces the volume of the original material composted, from 50 to 85 percent. Table 2.6 gives an overview of the size and operating parameters of several yard-waste composting facilities in the United States.

Technically speaking, the elements of a good composting system—odor and leachate control, marketing, reduction of contaminants, and the like—are well understood, and are the subject of a growing body of scientific literature and research by state agencies and private consultants.[42]

In-vessel Composting and Anaerobic Digestion

Yard waste may be the most obvious target for composting, but other organic materials, such as household food waste, commercial food processing/preparation waste, food-contaminated paper, and animal manure, can be bacterially decomposed as well. Americans discard about 12.5 million tons of food waste annually, or about 9 percent of the waste stream. Though these materials can be composted by combining the windrow method with special preprocessing, faster results and better control of odors and pests can be achieved with systems that regulate temperature and

TABLE 2.6
Data from Selected Yard-waste Composting Programs

City, State	Households Served	Household Partici-pation Rate (%)	Collection Method	Start-up Date	Municipal Solid Waste Generation (Tons/Yr)	Total Yard Waste Composted (Tons/Yr)	Fraction of Total Waste Stream Composted (%)
Columbia, SC	29,000	95	Curbside pickup—claw/packer truck	1950s	87,000	35,000	40
Huntington Woods, MI	2,500	50	Curbside pickup—30-gal. bin/packer truck	5/89	5,000	1,000	20
Islip, NY	78,000	N/A	Curbside pickup—misc. containers/packer truck	9/88	390,000	75–80,000	19–20
Modesto, CA	35–40,000	N/A	Curbside pickup—claw/packer truck	1/89	120,000	6,000	5
Sacramento	100,000	85–90	Curbside pickup—claw/packer truck	1950s	250,000	66,000	26
Urbana, IL	7,500	30–35	Curbside pickup—biodegradable plastic bags	1988	40,000	2,000	5

SOURCE: J. Glenn, "Taking a Bite Out of Yard Waste," *BioCycle*, September 1989, pp. 31–35.

moisture in large, enclosed steel vessels or special buildings. Such composting systems can rely on aerobic decomposition, as does regular composting, which produces carbon dioxide and water vapor, or anaerobic decomposition, which relies on different, fast-acting bacteria that thrive at relatively higher temperatures. Anaerobic decomposition occurs in the absence of oxygen and produces methane and water vapor as primary by-products. Most anaerobic systems are designed to capture methane for generating energy. Volume reduction by this method can be 70 percent or greater.[43]

A variety of Japanese, European, and American advanced composting or digestion technologies are currently available in the United States.[44] Such systems have been most thoroughly developed for composting sewage sludge—over 125 operating facilities in the United States—but are rapidly being adapted for processing mixed solid waste, food waste, and other materials.[45]

Though the individual features of these systems vary, most rely on a few generic processing steps. First, material is preprocessed: Nonorganic contaminants are mechanically removed, the material is reduced to a consistent size, and the moisture level is adjusted to optimal conditions. Next, the material is composted or digested in a special container or building, a process that lasts from 10 to 30 days, and produces a dark, rich soillike material. During this period, the material is mechanically aerated and moistened. In a third step, the compost product is cured, or stored in piles to achieve complete stabilization, which can take another 20 to 30 days. Finally, the material may be screened again, to remove remaining plastics, glass, and metals. If high quantities of food waste are used, the end product will be valuable fertilizer-grade compost. If a high level of contamination is present, which may be the case if raw, mixed garbage is processed, the resulting low-grade compost may be mixed with dirt and used as landfill cover, which many cities otherwise pay for.

In-vessel systems are more expensive than windrow composting but work faster with a wider range of materials, and require much less land. For this reason, they are particularly well suited to handling food waste produced by restaurants and commercial food processors, and possibly yard waste, in large cities. Collection of such material by private carters might be promoted by using a discounted tipping fee for loads of organic-rich material brought to digestion centers. Solely for volume reduction and production of landfill cover, in-vessel systems may also be useful as an adjunct or final element in a large-scale recycling system.

As of mid-1989, there were 14 mixed solid waste composting plants in the United States in pilot or operating stages with another 75 in construction or planning. Existing plants can compost 9 to 300 tons per day; 800 tpd plants are planned in Florida.[46] A number of additional facilities exist to compost commercial food-processing waste, such as fish cleaning, cranberry- and apple-processing wastes.[47] In general, this is a technology with enormous waste management potential when applied to organic waste streams, and would make an ideal target for accelerated R&D programs.

9. MIXED-WASTE PROCESSING

As cities search for waste management alternatives, a number of systems for recovering recyclable materials from mixed solid waste have been proposed. Many of these are quite similar to the preprocessing equipment employed with RDF incinerators, but are used in combination with systems to compost or digest, rather than burn, the organic fraction of processed waste.

The advantage of these mixed-waste processing systems is that they require little modification in existing solid waste collection patterns. A major disadvantage is that when materials are mixed and compressed in compactor trucks, major contamination occurs—newsprint that is splattered with spaghetti sauce and embedded with cat litter may be compostible, but is clearly not a good candidate for reuse as newspaper. (As noted previously, some types of commercial waste may be more amenable to picking operations.) A few mixed-waste processing systems involve hand-sorting of residential garbage, which poses employee health and safety problems.

Despite these shortcomings, R&D on mixed-waste processing is continuing, and there are a few operating plants in the United States.[48] Ultimately, these systems are unlikely to replace the need for aggressive waste reduction and recycling, but may serve as an adjunct to achieve further volume reduction and material recovery after maximum source separation has occurred.

RECYCLING RESIDUALS

Recycling operations produce various types of residuals that must be disposed of at some cost. In addition, overall recycling systems are subject to the same laws of physics and chemistry as incinerators. For example, if material collected for composting is contaminated with heavy metals, the metals will pose management problems for the final product.

In some cases, recycling operations produce concentrated toxic by-products, particularly in the final stages of preparing a material for reuse. This is true, for example, in detinning operations where a caustic chemical solution is used to strip tin from tin-coated steel cans producing a sludge that requires handling as hazardous waste.

Recycling must be held to strict environmental safeguards. However, in considering the environmental impacts of recycling, another factor must be taken into account: the energy and resources saved and pollution avoided by (1) substituting recycled materials for ones made from virgin products and (2) obviating the need for disposal of those products once discarded. Taking into account the full cycle of raw-material processing, use, and disposal, several studies have suggested that recycling is by far environmentally preferable to production from virgin resources. Though incineration with energy-recovery conserves energy resources, compared to landfilling, recycling most materials conserves more energy than burning them, especially as materials are recycled again and again.[49]

DEVELOPING MARKETS FOR SECONDARY MATERIALS

Recycling collection and processing programs are only the first steps in the process of recycling. Equally important is the function of markets for secondary materials, which transform materials diverted from solid waste into useful products that reenter the economy. The final step in the recycling process is actual use of recycled products by consumers. These steps make up the three chasing arrows in the traditional recycling symbol.

If public agencies intend to collect materials for recycling, they must make sure that markets are available to absorb these new supplies. For some materials, markets will naturally grow as new materials become available. For others, the public and private sectors should work together to promote growth in industries that can rely on secondary materials in their production processes. Initial recycling programs can also be designed with some flexibility to avoid problem materials. For example, if the regional market for secondary newsprint (about 8 percent of the waste stream) is weak, collection programs first can concentrate on other materials, such as yard waste (about 20 percent of the waste stream) or materials in the commercial sector.

A wide range of public and private policy instruments are available to promote secondary-materials markets. The main question is which are the most cost-effective in a given situation, and whether the public sector is willing to commit resources to making market development programs work. A number of detailed analyses completed on this topic are synthesized here briefly.[50]

Markets for secondary materials vary by material and by region. Markets for aluminum, ferrous metals, glass, polyethylene terephthalate (PET) and high-density polyethylene (HDPE) plastic, and certain grades of paper, including computer, ledger, and corrugated stock, are expected to remain strong, assuming the material meets or is processed to meet industry specifications. Prices for secondary HDPE, which is used to manufacture plastic milk jugs, containers, bags, and other products, weakened significantly in mid-1989, but then rose sharply in the aftermath of a fire at a virgin HDPE plant that eliminated almost 20 percent of domestic supplies.[51] For most of these materials, markets have grown to absorb available supplies, especially for aluminum and for PET soda bottles collected in states with container deposit laws. Markets for compost vary depending on the quality of the material, and tend to be strong in the many areas of the country where regular topsoil sells at a premium.

Paper markets in the United States tend to be strongest on the West Coast because of the proximity of Asian countries that import large amounts of waste paper and domestic mills that consume recycled fiber and in the Southeast because of a large number of domestic recycling mills (e.g., Southeast Paper's newsprint plant in Dublin, Georgia).

The performance of markets can be measured in terms of prices offered, which will fluctuate like prices for all commodities, and in terms of the size of the total market, for example, how much material is being moved. For good reasons, solid waste managers should be much more concerned with the security of a market—whether the market will always be there to absorb materials—than with extracting the highest market price from every transaction. (After all, the main benefit of a landfill is that it will always be able to receive garbage—until it fills up.) This distinction is often missed by media reports on the topic, however.[52]

COLLAPSE AND RECOVERY IN SECONDARY-NEWSPRINT PRICES

Since late 1988, prices on the historically shifting secondary-newsprint market have been very low, especially in the Northeast. As of late 1989, prices were recovering, but during the worst part of the slump, in a few places, material could not be sold at all. The collapse of prices in the secondary-newsprint market reflects the new economics of solid waste management. Commodity markets that once served paper-stock brokers, who make their profits buying, processing, and selling recovered paper, have been flooded by municipalities and private waste haulers, who are not overly concerned with commodity prices, as long as materials can be moved, because they are recycling to avoid high tipping fees. In the Northeast, in 1989, cities commonly paid private paper-stock dealers $5 to

$30 per ton to take their old newsprint, but also paid waste haulers up to five times as much to take their garbage. In these cases of negative pricing, private paper dealers are simply covering their costs of processing—removing contaminants and baling loose material—and transportation. Prices paid to the processors by mills and export buyers are rarely negative.

A review of basic statistics on newsprint consumption and recycling offers insights into this price collapse and its remedies. According to the American Paper Institute, in 1987, the U.S. consumption of newsprint from foreign and domestic sources equaled 13,582,000 tons, about 4,494,000 tons of which (33 percent) were recycled domestically or through exports. In 1988, 4,765,000 tons of newsprint were recycled; in 1989, 4,520,000 tons, the decline coming from an unusual drop in export buying. (These figures reflect mill capacity and exports, rather than collections; mill inventories grew substantially during this period. In 1989, about 27 million tons of all grades of paper were recycled).[53] In other words, a modest increase in recycling from 1987 to 1988, combined with export fluctuations and labor difficulties at two major newsprint recycling mills in Oregon, precipitated a drop in prices of over 100 percent in the Northeast. These basic statistics confirm the obvious: Commodity prices are highly sensitive to relatively slight changes in supply.

The uses of recovered newsprint in 1988 were as follows: manufacture of new newsprint (32 percent), paperboard and other paper products (e.g., cereal boxes) (29 percent), exports (22 percent), construction paper (6 percent), sanitary tissue (5 percent), and uses such as cellulose insulation, animal bedding, molded pulp products (e.g., egg cartons and packaging materials) (6 percent).[54]

Opportunities for Increased Use of Secondary Newsprint

From the standpoint of businesses that consume secondary newsprint, the demonstrated availability of this low-priced raw material represents an opportunity for expansion, especially when combined with prospective pressure from state legislatures on newspaper publishers to use more recycled fiber. In fact, because some investments in plants that use secondary newsprint (e.g., de-inking mills) are very expensive, it is unlikely that paper companies would even consider expansion or retooling without being certain that raw material supplies are available.

New demand for secondary newsprint may come from several areas, each with its own timing and investment parameters. First, as of January 1990, several paper companies are considering building world-class newsprint mills in the Northeast. One such mill would consume over 200,000 tons of old newsprint per year, cost about $300 to $400 million, and take about three years to construct. The most prominent of these companies is probably the Jefferson Smurfit Corporation, which owns two large recycled-newsprint mills in Oregon.

Other paper manufacturers have already announced plans to retrofit existing newsprint mills with de-inking equipment to allow them to blend virgin and secondary fiber. Abitibi-Price will convert two machines in Augusta, Georgia, at a cost of $27 million each to handle a total of 500 tons of secondary fiber per day. The first conversion is scheduled for completion in late 1990, the second in 1992. Canadian Pacific Forest Products announced in late 1989 that it would invest $175 million to convert mills in Thunder Bay, Ontario, and Gatineau, Quebec. These conversions will require increased consumption of secondary newsprint and magazines of 275 and 500 tons per day at the two mills, respectively, and be completed in mid-1991.[55] (Canadian mills supply slightly less than 60 percent of the newsprint consumed in America.) The North Pacific Paper Corporation, a subsidiary of Weyerhauser and Jujo Paper Company of Japan, is adding de-inking equipment and a new papermaking machine to its Longview, Washington, newsprint mill, at a cost of $300 million.

Adding de-inking equipment to existing mills costs less and requires less construction time than building new mills, and does not increase the total supply of finished newsprint on the market. Newsprint de-inking mills also hold several environmental advantages over virgin pulp mills. Since mills are already shipping finished newsprint by rail and truck to urban centers, back hauls can be used to bring recovered newsprint to the mills.

By late 1989, reports of additional new mill construction or conversions that would increase consumption of secondary newsprint were circulating widely in the paper industry. These involved major producers such as Bowater Southern Paper Company in Tennessee, Champion International in Texas, Daishowa in Washington State and Quebec, Donohue in Montreal and Quebec, Newstech Recycling in British Columbia, Cascades at a mill in Quebec or Niagara Falls, New York, in a joint venture with Steinbeis, a German manufacturer of recycled office forms and computer paper, Mac-Millan Bloedel in British Columbia, and several others. Including expansions by the Southeast Paper Company, which started up a new machine in Dublin, Georgia, in September 1989, and Atlantic Packaging, which will buy additional newsprint for mills in Ontario in 1990, it is possible that over 1.5 million tons of new de-inking capacity per year will be added in mills in North America between 1989 and 1992. This compares to a total capacity in North American newsprint mills to accept roughly 2 million tons per year of secondary fiber in 1988.[56]

New flotation/washing de-inking technology will work best when magazines are blended with recovered newsprint, substantially improving market prices for magazines. Because of the international character of secondary-newsprint markets, with prices led on both coasts by export buying, new capacity in one region can affect prices in others. Ironically, these new investments in recycling will come at a time when the market for finished newsprint in North America is itself glutted because of recent expansions in capacity at a number of virgin mills whose owners apparently did not foresee the increased supplies of secondary fiber.[57]

As suggested previously, solid waste managers are highly concerned with the security of markets that will serve recycling collection programs. As mills make multimillion-dollar investments in new recycling capacity, the reliability of supplies obviously becomes a major concern, as does the assurance that incoming materials will be substantially free of contaminants. This situation creates common ground for negotiating long-term supply contracts of five years or more with prices that could be set under a number of different terms. Such arrangements are already being made between private parties, such as Waste Management and Jefferson Smurfit and Laidlaw and Canadian Pacific, and municipalities or states, or their representatives, may soon find ways to do the same.[58]

In addition to news-to-news, a number of other markets for secondary newsprint could conceivably expand in the near or long term, including smaller-volume specialty groundwood papers, such as business and computer forms. Growth in other, less-conventional markets may be possible, such as molded pulp products (e.g., trays, protective shipping material, cardboard egg cartons, and other substitutes for polystyrene foam, which are actually recycled newsprint). Many of these alternative uses require low capital investment, may work in rural areas as well as urban markets, and become profitable as the price of newsprint falls.[59]

The U.S. Department of Agriculture's (USDA) Forest Products Lab in Wisconsin is researching new technologies for utilizing recycled fiber that may have important impacts on markets in the long term. One product, called "spaceboard," uses 100 percent recycled newsprint in two laminated layers of waffle-pattern paperboard to form a corrugated board that is reportedly 30 to 200 percent stronger than conventional corrugated board made from kraft fiber. Research is also underway on a damp-paper forming technology that would allow the economical manufacture of newsprint in minimills to produce 50,000 tons per year of newsprint, achieving economies of scale at one-fifth the size of current state-of-the-art newsprint mills. The minimill would use less water and land area, would rely on local collection of secondary fiber, and would sell to local markets, minimizing transportation costs. This technology would thus be ideal for large urban areas.[60]

MARKET-DEVELOPMENT INSTRUMENTS

The existence of potential business opportunities does not mean that companies will follow through on them; this depends on a number of factors that reside in both the private and public sectors. Government agencies in many cases can help bring projects to fruition. One of the most important roles that public officials can have in market development is ensuring that collected materials meet industry specifications, and conveying information about the timing and availability of new supplies.

Increasingly, market development for secondary materials is becoming a task for economic-development specialists. For example, for large projects, state economic-development agencies can assist companies in finding sites, arranging favorable financing, and meeting environmental compliance standards. For smaller projects, low-interest loans, grants, loan guarantees, and other forms of direct financial assistance may be appropriate.

A wide range of market-development tools are, in fact, available to public and private entities concerned with recycling. A number of these are listed below; more information is available from the sources listed in note 50.

INSTRUMENTS FOR DEVELOPING SECONDARY-MATERIALS MARKETS

Public Initiatives

- preferential government procurement of products containing recycled content;
- investment tax credits for purchases of equipment related to industrial expansion;
- secondary-materials-use tax credits (tax credits that award consumers of products containing secondary content);
- direct-commodity price supports (e.g., California's AB 2020);
- material-recovery facilities (as a means of providing high-quality supplies);

- packaging taxes (aimed at improving the competitive price advantage of products with recycled content).

Cooperative Public-Private Action

- direct negotiations with individual firms over the terms of public assistance (e.g., site selection, financial assistance, water treatment facilities, permit review procedures);
- economic development/financial assistance programs (e.g., low-interest loans, loan guarantees, direct grants, industrial development bonds);
- state RFPs for development of post-MRF processing capacity (e.g., for production of pelletized secondary-plastic resins) or direct end-user expansion;
- long-term contracts with end users;
- information-based strategies (e.g., industry or government clearing-houses, public-private university research programs, industry R&D consortia);
- loans from international development banks (World Bank, International Monetary Fund) for construction of overseas facilities that would consume American waste paper or wood;
- infrastructure investments enhancing the ability of ports to export secondary materials.

Initiatives That Could be Undertaken by Public or Private Concerns Separately or in Concert

- cooperative marketing (e.g., New Hampshire Resource Recovery Association, Montgomery County, Pennsylvania, Montana Recycling);
- investments in transportation improvements (e.g., consolidation points for rail shipment);
- labeling of materials containing secondary content by manufacturers;
- coding of plastic containers by resin type either voluntarily or through regulation;
- intensive overseas promotion of secondary-materials exports by private firms or public agencies at the port authority, state economic development department, or federal Department of Commerce/state department level.

NOTES

1. At most U.S. facilities, fly ash is conveyed, either manually or automatically, to the ash pit or to the same trucks used for bottom ash. Thus, combined ash is the most common form actually disposed of. Because fly ash and bottom ash are generated in distinct locations in the incinerator, however, separate management could be accomplished by reconfiguring the conveyor system or similar modification. The fly ash from facilities possessing acid-gas scrubbers (see chapter 5) will include unreacted lime and neutralized acid salts contributed by the scrubber, as well as particulate material.

2. Quench water can appropriately be considered an additional incinerator waste product, and can be significantly contaminated with suspended ash or dissolved heavy metals or salts.

3. R.W. Beck and Associates, *The Nation's Public Works: Report on Solid Waste* (Washington, DC: National Council on Public Works Improvement, 1987), p. 21.

4. Downtimes for incinerators, which vary considerably, can exceed the typical 10 to 15 percent range cited here. The following table compares design capacities and actual throughputs for five Connecticut incinerators, documenting an average downtime of more than 20 percent.

Location	Name-plate Capacity (tpd)	Annual Throughput (tpy)	Avg. Daily Throughput (tpd)	% of Design Capacity Utilized
Hartford	2,000	576,000	1,578	78
Bridgeport	2,250	657,000	1,800	80
Bristol	650	169,000	463	71
Wallingford	420	120,000	329	78
Windham	130	26,000	71	55
Total	5,450	1,548,000	4,241	78

SOURCE: Connecticut DEP, *State of Connecticut Proposed Solid Waste Management Plan* (Hartford, CT, September 1988), p. 15.

5. As explained in note 4, the percentages for bulk waste and incinerator downtimes may well be higher than assumed by the National League of Cities.

6. *Municipal Incinerators: 50 Questions Every Local Government Should Ask* (Washington, DC: National League of Cities, December 1988).

7. Kidder, Peabody, and Co., "Resource Recovery as of December 31, 1987," Industry Comment Series, April 29, 1988.

8. Governmental Advisory Associates, *1988–89 Resource Recovery Yearbook*, New York, NY, 1989, as reported in R.N. Gould, "Refuse-to-Energy Is Not Dead!" *Waste Age*, November 1988, pp. 61–66.

9. Dan Cotter, "Taking It to the Streets," *Resource Recycling*, July 1987, pp. 28–29; Benjamin Pedigo, "Successful Recycling in Rural Ohio," *Resource Recycling*, January/February 1988, pp. 34–35, 53; Jim Glenn, " 'New Age' Drop-off Programs," *BioCycle*, February 1989, pp. 42–45.

10. For more information on R2B2 write Phyllis Atwater, President, R2B2, 1809 Carter Avenue, Bronx, NY 10457

11. San Francisco Recycling Program, "Your Office Paper Recycling Guide" (1987), p. 1. Available from San Francisco Recycling Program, Room 271, City Hall, San Francisco, CA 94102.

12. Personal communication with Amy Perlmutter, Director, San Francisco Recycling Program, City and County of San Francisco, 1987.

13. Personal communications with staff members Charles Redman and Anne Marie Alonso from the Office of Recycling, New York City Department of Sanitation and Council on the Environment of New York City, respectively, October 1989.

14. For information on starting your own office paper recycling program, see: Tamra Peters, *Working with Nature: How to Start a Paper Recycling Program at Your Company* (1989). Available from Working with Nature, 12 Oak Knoll Avenue, San Anselmo, CA 94960.

15. Joseph Robertson, "Mid-Town Recycling Plant Focuses on Market, Quality," *Rock Products*, February 1983.

16. James Cook, "Not in Anybody's Backyard," *Forbes*, November 28, 1988, p. 180; Personal communication with Gordon Boyd, President, Schillinger, Salerni and Boyd (recycling and waste management consultants), Albany, New York, 1989.

17. Skip Lacaze, "Martin Resource Recovery Center," *Resource Recycling*, July 1987, pp. 12–15.

18. New York City Department of Sanitation, *White Paper—New York City Recycling Strategy* (New York City: DOS, January 1988), Appendix B.

19. Agapito Diaz (Director for Administration, Bureau of Waste Disposal, NYC Dept. of Sanitation), "FY 88 Budget Request for Purchase of Screening Equipment," internal DOS memorandum, June 18, 1987, p. 2; New York City, Mayor's Office of Construction, Construction Waste Disposal Task Force, "Progress Report," mimeographed, June 15, 1987.

20. Jim Glenn and David Riggle, "Where Does the Waste Go?" *BioCycle*, April 1989, pp. 34–39; Marian Chertow, *Garbage Solutions: A Public Official's Guide to Recycling and Alternative Solid Waste Management Technologies* (1989). Available from National Resource Recovery Association/U.S. Conference of Mayors, 1620 Eye Street, NW, Washington, DC 20006, $14; Richard Garrison, "Curbside Collection Service: Estimating Equipment Needs," *Re-*

source Recycling, August 1988, pp. 30–32; Christy Grove, "Demystifying the Curbside Plan," *BioCycle*, June 1989, pp. 45–47.

21. Environmental Defense Fund; *Coming Full Circle: Successful Recycling Today* (New York: EDF, January 1988), pp. 47–54; Joe Salimondo, "A Tale of Two Towns (Woodbury and Berlin, New Jersey)," *Waste Age*, June 1989, pp. 84–88.

22. *Resource Recycling*, P.O. Box 10540, Portland, OR 97210. (503) 227-1319. Also publishes *Plastics Recycling Update and Bottle and Can Recycling Update; BioCycle*, Box 351, Emmaus, PA 18049. (215) 967-4135; *Waste Age*, 17230 Rhode Island Avenue, NW, Washington, DC 20036, a publication of the National Solid Wastes Management Association. (202) 861-0708. Also publishes *Recycling Times; The Newspaper of Recycling Markets.*

23. Frank Sudol, "Newark, New Jersey Recycles," mimeographed. Available from Frank Sudol, Manager, Division of Engineering, Room 410, City Hall, 920 Broad Street, Newark, NJ 07102.

24. Personal communication with Richard Gertman, (Former) Director of Recycling, Office of Environmental Management, San Jose, California, 1988. Currently with R.W. Beck and Associates. The city's estimate of cost savings was not necessarily shared by its private waste collection contractor.

25. Environmental Defense Fund, *To Burn or Not to Burn: The Economic Advantages of Recycling Over Garbage Incineration for New York City* (New York: EDF, 1985), Appendix C.

26. New York City DOS, *White Paper—New York City Recycling Strategy*, Appendix B.

27. For example, the Tellus Institute (formerly the Energy Systems Research Group) now offers a model called "WastePlan." Available at 89 Broad Street, Boston, MA 02110; Peter Andersen, of New Paths, Inc., offers "RecycleWare," a program that reportedly optimizes recycling efficiency. Available at 2701 Packers Avenue, Madison, WI 53704; Jeffery Morris, an economist at Sound Resources Management Group, also offers maximum recycling and optimization services. Available at 7220 Ledriot Court, Seattle, WA 98136; for older models and commentary, see: EDF, *Coming Full Circle*, Appendix D.

28. Peterborough, New Hampshire, recycles 43 percent of its waste. See David Morris and Brenda Platt, *Garbage Disposal Economics: A Statistical Snapshot* (Washington, DC: Institute for Local Self-Reliance, February 1989), pp. 87–88; the recycling center/solid waste transfer station in Wilton, New Hampshire, recycles 45 percent of the material brought to it. See Patricia Moore, "[Wilton, New Hampshire:] Success is 45% Recycling," *BioCycle*, May/June 1987, pp. 23–26.

29. Personal communication with George Barry, Director, Wellesley Department of Public Works, 1989.

30. For more information, write New Hampshire Resource Recovery Association, P.O. Box 721, Concord, NH 03302.

31. For more information, write Southeastern Ohio Recycling Terminal, P.O. Box 5736, Athens, OH 45701.

32. Personal communication with Doug Stewart, President of Montana Recycling, Missoula, Montana, 1987. See: EDF, *Coming Full Circle*, pp. 108–109.

33. Susan Schmidt, *Case Studies in Rural Solid Waste Recycling* (November 1987). Available for $8 from the Minnesota Project, 2222 Elm Street SE, Minneapolis, MN 55414; Lowell Shaw and William Park, *The Economic Feasibility of Rural Recycling: Three Case Studies*, (Knoxville: Agricultural Experiment Station, University of Tennessee, August 1989/research report 89–15; National Association of Towns and Townships, *Why Waste A Second Chance?: A Small Town Guide to Recycling* (1989). Available from NATT, 1522 K Street, NW, Suite 730, Washington, DC 20005; For information on rural recycling market development, write Margaret Gainer, Gainer & Associates, 928 H Street, Arcata, CA 95521.

34. Jim Glenn, "Material Recovery Facilities: A Guide to Technologies and Vendors," *BioCycle*, January 1988, pp. 24–27; John Roderique, "Four MRFs in Action," *BioCycle*, October 1989. pp. 54–59; Jerry Powell, "Rabanco Opens Innovative Facility," *Resource Recycling*, September/October 1988, pp. 33–35.

35. Joe Salimondo, "MRF of the Month (New York's Laboratory in Harlem)," *Waste Age*, June 1989, pp. 100–106.

36. Franklin Associates, *Characterization of Municipal Solid Waste in the United States, 1960 to 2000 (Update 1988) Final Report*. (Washington, DC: EPA, Office of Solid Waste and Emergency Response, March 30, 1988), p. 7.

37. Resource Integration Systems/Resource Conservations Consultants et al., *City of Los Angeles Recycling Implementation Plan, Final Report* (Los Angeles: City of Los Angeles, Department of Public Works, Bureau of Sanitation, 1989, p. 2–1.

38. Jim Glenn and David Riggle, "Where Does the Waste Go?," pp. 34–39.

39. Mark Selby, "Yard Waste Collection," *BioCycle* June 1989, pp. 52–54.

40. Maarten van de Kamp, *Feasibility Study for a Brooklyn Landscape Wastes Composting Project* (Brooklyn: Cornell University, Cooperative Extension, 1986).

41. Jim Glenn, "Regulating Yard Waste Composting," *BioCycle*, December 1989, pp. 38–41.

42. Peter Strom and Melvin Finstein, *Leaf Composting Manual for New Jersey Municipalities* (1989, rev.). Available from New Jersey DEP, Div. of Solid Waste Mgmt., Office of Recycling, 401 State Street, CN 414, Trenton, NJ 08625; BioCycle staff, eds., *The BioCycle Guide to Composting Municipal Wastes* (Emmaus, PA: The JG Press, 1989); California Waste Management Board, "Municipal Composting Handbook for Park, Yard and Landscaping Plant Wastes," mimeographed (Sacramento, CA, 1983); Richard Kashmanian and Alison Taylor, "Cost of Composting Yard Wastes vs. Landfilling," *BioCycle*, October 1989, pp. 60–63. (Full study available from EPA, Office of Policy, Planning, and Evaluation [PM-223], 401 M Street, SW Washington, DC 20460.)

43. We appreciate the assistance of Michael Simpson, associate scientist at the Tellus Institute, 89 Broad Street, Boston, MA 02110, for supplying much of the information in this section.

44. BioCycle staff, eds., *The BioCycle Guide to In-Vessel Composting* (Emmaus, PA: The JG Press, 1986).

45. Nora Goldstein, "A Guide to Solid Waste Composting Systems," *BioCycle*, January 1989, pp. 38–47.

46. Nora Goldstein, "Solid Waste Composting in the U.S.," *BioCycle*, November 1989, pp. 32–37.

47. James Cato, "Putting Crab Wastes to Use," *BioCycle*, November 1989, p. 38.

48. Marian Chertow, "Hybrid Systems Process Mixed Wastes," *BioCycle*, October 1989, pp. 36–39.

49. See: Barry Commoner, et al., *Development and Pilot Test of an Intensive Municipal Solid Waste Recycling System for the Town of East Hampton.* (Flushing, NY: Center for the Biology of Natural Systems, Queens College, CUNY, Net Environmental Impact of Intensive Recycling 1987), pp. III-81 to III-107. (See additional references to EPA publications on pollution impacts of virgin manufacturing technologies.); Howard Edde, *Environmental Control for Pulp and Paper Mills* (Park Ridge, NJ: Noyes Publications, 1984); Paul Ehrlich, Anne Ehrlich, and John Holdren, *Ecoscience; Population, Resources, Environment* (San Francisco: W.H. Freeman and Company, 1977), table 8-34, p. 494; Robert Letcher and Mary Sheil, "Source Separation and Citizen Recycling," in *The Solid Waste Handbook: A Practical Guide*, ed. William Robinson (New York: John Wiley & Sons, 1986), table 10.1, p. 220; U.S. Congress, Office of Technology Assessment, *Facing America's Trash: What Next for Municipal Solid Waste* (Washington, DC: U.S. Government Printing Office, 1989/OTA-0-424), pp. 190–94; Talbot Page, *Conservation and Economic Efficiency* (Baltimore: The Johns Hopkins University Press, 1977); Radian Corporation, *Plastics Processing: Technology and Health Effects* (Park Ridge, NJ: Noyes Data Corporation, 1986); Roberta Forsell Stauffer, "Energy Savings from Recycling," *Resource Recycling*, January/February 1989, pp. 24–25.

50. EDF, *Coming Full Circle: Successful Recycling Today*, chapter 7; Robert C. Anderson, and Roger C. Dower, *An Analysis of Scrap Futures Markets for Stimulating Resource Recovery* (Washington, DC: U.S. Department of Commerce, National Technical Information Service, 1978); Mt. Auburn Associates, *Plan for the Development of Connecticut Markets for Recovered Materials* (1989). Available from the Connecticut Department of Economic Development, 865 Brook Street, Rocky Hill, CT 06067; Resource Conservation Consultants, *Pennsylvania Recyclable Materials Market Development Study* (1988). Available from Pennsylvania Department of Environmental Resources, Bureau of Waste Management, P.O. Box 2063, Harrisburg, PA 17120; Recoup, *American Recycling Market 1989 Directory/Reference Manual* (Ogdensburg, NY: Recoup Publishing Limited, 1989).

51. "Little Hope Held by Texas Rescuers; Twenty-Two Workers Missing at Plant where 2 Died in Explosion and Fire," and "Reverberations for Industries but Not for U.S. Households," *New York Times*, October 25, 1989, p. A18.

52. Consider, for example this inaccurate report from the *New York Times*:

> The city turned to recycling because it is running out of space in dumps to hold all its waste. But now it is in danger of running out of outlets for the trash it wants to recycle. Buyers for recycled newpaper, glass and plastics are proving difficult to find . . . Despite the mountain of trash, recycling does not pay. City Hall does not expect its fledgling recycling program to break even. "Recycling is not a moneymaker," [Sanitation Commissioner] Mr. Sexton declared. So far, the city has had the most success with glass, which it sells for $50 a ton . . ."

(From "Now the Recyclable Trash is Overwhelming New York," December 12, 1989).

53. American Paper Institute (Newsprint Division), "Newsprint Key Recycling Statistics," mimeographed (New York: API, September 7, 1989). Preliminary 1989 figures calculated by taking API capacity survey data and adjusting for exports and other uses of paper using Bureau of the Census and American Newspaper Publisher's Association data.

54. American Paper Institute data, cited in Mt. Auburn Associates, *Plan for the Development of Connecticut Markets for Recovered Materials.* pp. 1–42.

55. "Abitibi-Price Announces Recycling Facility," Abitibi-Price press release, December 19, 1989; "Canadian Pacific Forest Products Announces $175 Million Investment for Two Recycling Facilities. Laidlaw to Supply Waste Paper for Recycling," Canadian Pacific press release, December 20, 1989; Personal communication with Ed. Sparks, Manager of Secondary Fiber Procurement for Abitibi-Price, December 1989.

56. John Ruston, "Deinking Capacity Additions Requiring Increased Consumption of Secondary Fiber at United States and Canadian Newsprint Mills— Expansions Announced or Under Study." list compiled by EDF, available from the New York office, February 1990; Fred Iannazzi, "The Economics Are Right for U.S. Mills to Recycle Old Newspapers," *Resource Recycling*, July 1989, pp. 34–37; Ed Sparks, "Dynamics Affecting Future Waste Paper Markets," *Resource Recycling*, January 1990. pp. 20–21, 65.

57. For more information on the paper industry, see: *1989 Lockwood-Post's Directory of the Pulp, Paper and Allied Trades* (San Francisco: Miller Freeman Publications, Inc., 1989); Willard Mies, et al., eds. *Pulp & Paper 1988 Factbook* (San Francisco: Miller Freeman Publications, Inc., 1988); NY Newspaper Publishers Assn., NYS Dept. of Economic Development, NYS Department of Environmental Conservation, *Final Report of the New York State Newspaper Recycling Task Force*, December 12, 1989.

58. "Waste Management to Form Venture with Smurfit on Paper for Recycling," *Wall Street Journal*, January 1, 1990.

59. Jerry Powell, "Molded Pulp: A Paper Recycling Market on the Rebound," *Resource Recycling*, January 1990, pp. 42–43, 70; EDF is researching mar-

kets for secondary newsprint in molded pulp, cellulose insulation, shipping materials, animal bedding, kitty litter, hydro-seeding mulch, and other products. Publication of any reports produced will be announced in the *EDF Letter.*

60. Mt. Auburn Associates, *Plan for the Development of Connecticut Markets for Recovered Materials*, pp 1–42.

CHAPTER 3

Economic Comparisons

IF ANYTHING IS CLEAR about the future of solid waste disposal in the United States, it is that new ways of dealing with our trash are going to be much more expensive. Though incinerators were once promoted as an inexpensive substitute for landfills ("from tipping fee to tipping free" was a slogan heard in New York a decade ago), these facilities have turned out to be enormously expensive. In large cities, proposed expenditures on incineration represent investments comparable in scale to major infrastructure and public works projects, such as mass transit improvements, sewage treatment plants, and bridge and freeway repairs. In medium-sized cities or collections of suburban counties, incinerators may be the most expensive public investments proposed in local history.

Recycling programs also have their costs, and are usually new items in municipal budgets. Unless recycling is given a dedicated source of funding, new programs will have to compete with municipal services like sanitation, police, fire, and education for start-up funding. Although the public health hazards of improper waste disposal clearly entail their own economic impacts, this chapter and the next present economic considerations that are of even more immediate relevance. In an era of limits on government spending, nearly everyone can relate to the impact that garbage disposal will have on local taxes, the cost of running a business, or our ability to obtain other important public services.

Our discussion of economic comparisons begins with a fundamental economic fact: Though individual companies may profit from building incinerators, operating landfills, or running recycling programs, on the whole, waste disposal is something that society must pay for. Solid waste can be burned to produce electricity or steam for sale, but energy revenues alone will not nearly cover the full costs of building and operating an incinerator and disposing of ash. Similarly, although sales may cover collec-

104

tion costs for a few materials, like aluminum and computer paper, revenues from the sales of a broad range of recovered materials generally will not recoup the costs of running a large-scale recycling program.

This state of affairs is nothing new. Traditionally, private and some public landfill operators have imposed a tipping fee upon individuals and businesses for the privilege of dumping waste at their facilities. This fee helped cover operating costs and provided profits at private facilities; other public landfills have historically charged little or no fee, recovering costs through tax revenues. Incinerator operators also charge a tipping fee, often called a "service charge," to cover operating expenses and generate profits.

Unfortunately, some debates on solid waste management still are predicated on the assumption that although incinerators should be able to charge a tipping fee, recycling must be entirely self-supporting from the sale of reclaimed materials before it can qualify as a legitimate waste management option. This double standard is plainly absurd; if incinerators can enjoy a subsidy in the form of tipping fees, recycling operations should be granted the same level of support in some comparable form. However obvious it is, this basic concept—that recycling programs should be funded on an equivalent basis with incinerators and landfills—is very powerful. As discussed in chapter 4, allowing recycling and incineration to compete on a level playing field could increase the cost-effectiveness of government solid waste spending, foster entrepreneurial activity, and allow market forces to play a greater role in solid waste management decisions.

To compare the net economic costs of incineration and recycling involves comparing the required tipping fee, or its equivalent, for each option. This means determining the extent to which sales of the products of each system—energy and, in some cases, ferrous metals from incinerators and various materials from recycling—fall short of covering each system's full costs of construction and long-term operation. As this chapter shows, the economic concepts and calculations required to undertake such a comparison, or to review a comparison conducted by a government agency, are not so complex as to be inaccessible to the public. In fact, the opposite is true; it is the public's money that will be spent on future solid waste programs, and taxpayers deserve to know whether they are getting the best deal for their dollars.

This chapter sets out the basic economic concepts required to compare the long-term costs of recycling and incineration, and works through sample calculations for each option. These long-term comparisons are based on projections of future costs for a whole range of goods, which naturally brings a variety of uncertainties into the picture. Important uncertainties in the case of incineration include expected revenues from the sale of energy, unanticipated technical problems, and ash disposal costs. Uncertainties about the future operation of recycling programs include prevailing commodity prices and the availability of markets for selling recovered materials. To some extent, these uncertainties can be accounted for by comparing the costs of each option under favorable and unfavorable scenarios.

LIFE-CYCLE COST COMPARISONS: BASIC CONCEPTS

In this section, basic economic concepts are introduced one by one, as we step through a comparison of the costs of waste management services offered by two imaginary companies. Our hypothetical comparison starts very spare, and adds details until we have a basic model that can be used for evaluating real waste management options.

LIFE-CYCLE ANALYSIS

Incineration and recycling programs involve two distinct types of costs: recurring costs that are paid as they arise, and capital costs that are too large to be paid off as they arise but rather are recouped over many years. Operation and maintenance costs are in the former category: major construction costs are in the latter. For incineration, capital expenditures include constructing the incinerator itself, its air pollution control equipment, and the ash disposal facility; for recycling, capital expenditures include material-processing centers. Both incineration and recycling systems can entail other capital costs, such as trucks purchased to haul solid waste, ash, or separated materials to their respective facilities.

For a variety of reasons, incinerators tend to incur a higher proportion of their costs up-front as capital expenditures, with a relatively lower level of ongoing costs, than do recycling programs. As a result, incinerator vendors sometimes claim that incineration is cheaper than recycling in the long run, even though the start-up costs for incineration are substantially greater. To evaluate this type of claim, economists use a method called life-cycle analysis, which takes into account all the revenues and expenditures that come into play over the lifetime of a project.

"All of the revenues and expenditures that come into play over the lifetime of a project" can encompass a number of items. Major construction costs are incurred at the outset of the project, and are typically repaid in equal annual installments, similar to the way a mortgage on a house is paid off. On the other hand, operating expenses are incurred continually or periodically, over the life of the project, and fluctuate from year to year. In total, operating costs depend on the combined performance of a number of different factors, such as revenues from sales of materials or energy, the technical performance of the facility, changing regulatory requirements, and the individual costs of labor, fuel, insurance, and residue disposal.

In the first year of full operation of an enterprise such as a waste management complex, total costs, or the required tipping fee if expressed on a per-ton basis, are simply expenses minus revenues. Thanks to the ever-present fact of inflation, in future years of operation, the costs of different components of the total revenue/expenditure picture are expected to rise, with some costs perhaps inflating more rapidly than others. To illustrate this point, table 3.1 begins our economic comparison of two hypothetical waste management companies, Waste Saviours, and Miracle Technologies (Tech). At the moment, we are not concerned about what these companies actually do or the costs of the individual items that are in sum responsible for the overall portrait of revenues and expenditures.

It is evident from table 3.1 that each company plans to begin full operations in 1990, and expects to offer the same basic service for 20 years; we will assume they are processing the same tonnage each year. Revenues for the first company, Waste Saviours are expected to start at $25 per ton in 1990, and rise at a rate of 1 percent a year until 2005, when they suddenly begin to rise at 10 percent annually. In contrast, expenditures at Waste Saviours start at $38 per ton, and rise at 6 percent per year for the whole period.

For the second option, Miracle Technologies, revenues start out at $7 per ton, and remain at that level until 2001, when they jump to $24 per ton and rise at 7 percent a year thereafter. (This might occur if, for example, a low-cost local landfill competing with Miracle Tech is expected to close in 2000, allowing Miracle Tech to raise its rates). Miracle Tech's expenditures, on the other hand, start at $19 per ton, rise at 3 percent per year until 1998, and then rise at 7 percent per year. For both companies, the total cost in any given year is equal to expenditures less revenues.

INFLATION, DISCOUNTING, AND PRESENT VALUE

All of the costs in table 3.1 are expressed in current terms; they represent the number of dollars that are actually spent in each year as shown. It is also possible to present future costs in real terms, which takes into account the general effect of inflation in reducing the power of money to purchase goods and services. Thus, if the rate of inflation is expected to average 6 percent

TABLE 3.1
Hypothetical Life-cycle Cost Comparison
(costs expressed on a per-ton basis)

| Year | WASTE SAVIOURS, INC. (OPTION A) | | | MIRACLE TECHNOLOGIES (OPTION B) | | |
	Revenues	Expenditures	Total Cost	Revenues	Expenditures	Total Cost
1990	$25.00	$ 38.00	$13.00	$ 7.00	$26.00	$19.00
1991	25.25	40.28	15.03	7.00	26.78	19.78
1992	25.50	42.70	17.19	7.00	27.58	20.58
1993	25.76	45.26	19.50	7.00	28.41	21.41
1994	26.02	47.97	21.96	7.00	29.26	22.26
1995	26.28	50.85	24.58	7.00	30.14	23.14
1996	26.54	53.90	27.37	7.00	31.05	24.05
1997	26.80	57.14	30.33	7.00	31.98	24.98
1998	27.07	60.57	33.49	7.00	34.22	27.22
1999	27.34	64.20	36.86	7.00	36.61	29.61
2000	27.62	68.05	40.44	7.00	39.17	32.17
2001	27.89	72.14	44.24	24.00	41.91	17.91
2002	28.17	76.46	48.29	25.68	44.85	19.17
2003	28.45	81.05	52.60	27.48	47.99	20.51
2004	28.74	85.91	57.18	29.40	51.35	21.95
2005	31.61	91.07	59.46	31.46	54.94	23.48
2006	34.77	96.53	61.76	33.66	58.79	25.13
2007	38.25	102.33	64.08	36.02	62.90	26.89
2008	42.07	108.46	66.39	38.54	67.31	28.77
2009	46.28	114.97	68.69	41.24	72.02	30.78

SOURCE: EDF calculations.

over the next 20 years, and landfill tipping fees are projected to rise an average of 10 percent per year over the same period, in real terms, tipping fees are rising at 4 percent a year (e.g., 4 percent faster than general inflation). This type of cost increase is of interest to municipal officials because it signifies that if future tax revenues rise at the rate of general inflation, everything else being equal, waste disposal will cost more as a proportion of the budget than it does now. In contrast, if commodity market prices for mixed waste paper have not changed in the last five years, this means that in real terms, they have declined, since the relative price of most everything else has gone up.

The projected per-ton costs of the processes offered by our two companies are graphed in figure 3.1. As you can see, the Waste Saviours

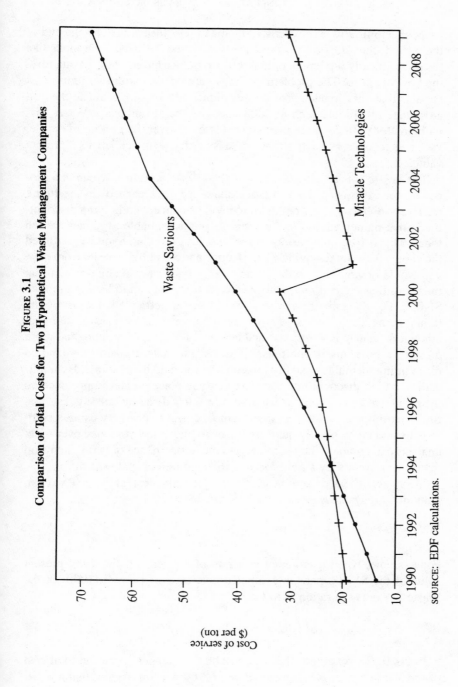

FIGURE 3.1

Comparison of Total Costs for Two Hypothetical Waste Management Companies

Waste Saviours

Miracle Technologies

Cost of service
($ per ton)

70
60
50
40
30
20
10

1990   1992   1994   1996   1998   2000   2002   2004   2006   2008

SOURCE: EDF calculations.

proposal is initially less expensive than Miracle Tech's, but, by the end of the period, the situation is dramatically reversed. Miracle Tech looks like the economically preferable option, but, so far, we have no way of quantifying how much so. The problem is that we are dealing with two future cost streams that vary in each year. For example, how can we evaluate the cost advantage of Miracle Tech in 2008 vis-à-vis the advantage of Waste Saviours in 1990? To compare the two cost streams over their entire life cycle, we need to express each stream as a singular term, called its "present value."

The key to this transformation is called "discounting," which is a procedure for expressing the value of dollars spent, or earned, in the future relative to dollars spent, or earned, today. The concept underlying discounting is that money earned in the future is not as valuable as money earned today. This is true for a variety of reasons; for example, if you were offered the choice between receiving $1,000 today and $1,000 five years from now, you would obviously take the money today, because you could invest it at the prevailing interest rate, and five years later you would have more than $1,000. For the same reason, you would prefer getting $1,000 in 5 years rather than 20. In terms of your perspective today, the same nominal amount of money is worth less and less as it is available in more and more distant years. (This is one reason the discount rate used in the standard discounting formula is usually linked to a projected interest rate. By implication, a high discount rate suggests that you place greater importance on the near term and less on the distant future; a low discount rate suggests that future earnings are nearly as important as current ones.) By using a common formula to explicitly quantify the changing value of money over time, analysts can compare the overall economic performance of two systems no matter what year they start in or how their future cost patterns differ.

In any given year, assuming a discount rate r, the present value (PV) of an amount S_n, payable N years from now is:

$$PV = S_n / (1 + r)^N$$

For example, when discounted at a rate of 10 percent, the 1989 present value of the $13.00 per ton estimated cost in the first year (1990) of the Waste Saviours operation is $11.82:

$$\$11.82 = \$13.00 / (1 + .10)^1$$

In 2009, 20 years into the future, table 3.1 suggests that the total cost of the Waste Saviours process will be $68.69 per ton. Again, using a discount rate of 10 percent, the 1989 present value of this figure is just $10.21:

$$\$10.21 = \$68.69 / (1 + .10)^{20}$$

Since results of the last two calculations are both expressed in 1989 dollars, we can add them—and the discounted values of all the other costs in the 20-year stream—to obtain a single present value figure. This is done for each option in table 3.2.

TABLE 3.2
**Annual Costs of Hypothetical Waste Management Proposals
(in current and discounted dollars)**

Year	Waste Saviours, Inc. (Option A) Current Dollars	Discounted to 1989 Dollars	Miracle Technologies (Option B) Current Dollars	Discounted to 1989 Dollars
1990	$13.00	$ 11.82	$19.00	$ 17.27
1991	15.03	12.42	19.78	16.35
1992	17.19	12.92	20.58	15.46
1993	19.50	13.32	21.41	14.62
1994	21.96	13.63	22.26	13.82
1995	24.58	13.87	23.14	13.06
1996	27.37	14.04	24.05	12.34
1997	30.33	14.15	24.98	11.65
1998	33.49	14.21	27.22	11.54
1999	36.86	14.21	29.61	11.42
2000	40.44	14.17	32.17	11.28
2001	44.24	14.10	17.91	5.71
2002	48.29	13.99	19.17	5.55
2003	52.60	13.85	20.51	5.40
2004	57.18	13.69	21.95	5.25
2005	59.46	12.94	23.48	5.11
2006	61.76	12.22	25.13	4.97
2007	64.08	11.52	26.89	4.84
2008	66.39	10.86	28.77	4.70
2009	68.69	10.21	30.78	4.58
Present value (in 1989 dollars)		262.14		194.93

Assumes discount rate of 10%

SOURCE: EDF calculations.

From table 3.2, the present value of the Waste Saviours proposal is thus $262.14; the present value of Miracle Tech's is $194.93. In other words, over the full life cycle of the project, the present value of Miracle Tech's proposal is 26 percent less than Waste Saviours'; this is our quantitative basis for the cost comparison.

In fact, it is unnecessary to discount the costs for each year individually and then sum the whole discounted stream. Calculating present values is one of the most basic functions of computer spread-sheet programs and calculators designed for business applications. Typically, one can give a computerized spread sheet a stream of payments that occur at regular intervals (e.g., months or years), set the discount rate, and let the program calculate the present value of the entire stream. The present value is usually calculated for the year previous to the first year in the cost stream in question. For example, if the stream of payments starts in 1993 and ends in 2009, the spread sheet will calculate the present value for 1992. This present value figure can then be further discounted with the standard formula to give present value of the 1993 to 2009 stream in 1989 dollars.

Levelization

When a stream of annual costs is discounted and summed to its present value, the units that define the annual costs (e.g., cost per ton) no longer apply. For example, from table 3.2, we can see that the present value of the 20-year stream of per-ton costs for the Waste Saviours proposal is $262.14, but this clearly does not mean the present value of this stream is $262.14 per ton (and simply dividing $262.14 by 20 is not suitable either). To give present-value expressions an annual dimension, it is common to compute a levelized value, which is, in essence, an annual cost figure that reflects the present value of the original, varying stream of income and expenditures.

There are two ways to levelize present-value calculations. For each waste management option, table 3.3 presents three cost streams, each having exactly the same present value. The streams in columns A and D are the costs of each proposal in dollars as spent, the same as originally shown in table 3.1. The remaining columns show the original cost streams as transformed by the two different levelization techniques.

Columns B and E give the present value of the two cost streams as levelized in constant terms. In this case, the present value of the Waste Saviours proposal is $30.79 per ton; the present value of the Miracle Tech proposal is $22.90 per ton. In other words, if we were to spend $30.79 per ton on the Waste Saviours process in every year, the present value of this constant stream of expenditures would be equivalent to the present value of the original, varying stream of expenditures. Given a discount rate r, the formula for an initial year value, v of a stream that remains constant over N years and has a given present value (PV), is:

$$v = (PV) \frac{r}{1 - \left(\frac{1}{1+r}\right)^N}$$

As this formula is applied in table 3.2, the present value (PV) of the 20-year stream is expressed in 1989 dollars. The resulting levelized present value is thus expressed in 1989 dollars as well.

Columns C and F levelize the present values of the original two cost streams in real terms. That is, if we paid $20.04 per ton for Waste Saviours' services in 1990, and the cost of this payment rose over future years at the 6 percent rate of general inflation, the present value of this steadily inflating cost stream would be the same as the present value of the original, varying stream of expenditures. The initial 1989 value of such a steadily inflating stream is $18.90 (i.e., 6 percent less than in 1990). The formula for this type of levelization simply incorporates the rate of inflation into the formula given above. Thus, the formula for the initial-year value v of a stream that rises at the rate of inflation, i over N years and has a given present value (PV), is:

$$v = (PV) \frac{r - i}{(1 + i) \left[1 - \left(\frac{1 + i}{1 + r}\right)^N \right]}$$

The ratio between the present value of the Waste Saviours proposal and the present value of the Miracle Tech proposal is the same, regardless of how the present-value terms are levelized or whether or not they are levelized at all. In other words, if you were trying to explain this comparison in a hurry—for example, on the phone to a reporter—you could say that, considering the cost of each project over its life span, the estimated present value of Miracle Tech's proposal is 26 percent less than the present value of Waste Saviours' proposal.

Though the distinctions between constant and real levelization may seem like devices to maintain the obscurity of the economists' dialect, each approach does have its benefits. Though less widely used and perhaps more difficult to explain, the method of levelizing in real terms offers some advantages over levelizing in constant terms. First, although both levelization methods shown in table 3.3 can be stated correctly to represent present values in 1989 dollars, present-value estimates produced by levelizing in

TABLE 3.3
Levelized Present Value Cost Comparisons
(cost per ton)

Year	WASTE SAVIOURS, INC. (OPTION A)			MIRACLE TECHNOLOGIES (OPTION B)		
	Current Dollars A	Levelized in Constant Terms B	Levelized in Real Terms C	Current Dollars D	Levelized in Constant Terms E	Levelized in Real Terms F
1990	$ 13.00	$ 30.79	$ 20.04	$ 19.00	$ 22.90	$ 14.90
1991	15.03	30.79	21.24	19.78	22.90	15.79
1992	17.19	30.79	22.52	20.58	22.90	16.74
1993	19.50	30.79	23.87	21.41	22.90	17.75
1994	21.96	30.79	25.30	22.26	22.90	18.81
1995	24.58	30.79	26.82	23.14	22.90	19.94
1996	27.37	30.79	28.42	24.05	22.90	21.14
1997	30.33	30.79	30.13	24.98	22.90	22.41
1998	33.49	30.79	31.94	27.22	22.90	23.75
1999	36.86	30.79	33.85	29.61	22.90	25.17
2000	40.44	30.79	35.89	32.17	22.90	26.69
2001	44.24	30.79	38.04	17.91	22.90	28.29
2002	48.29	30.79	40.32	19.17	22.90	29.98
2003	52.60	30.79	42.74	20.51	22.90	31.78
2004	57.18	30.79	45.31	21.95	22.90	33.69
2005	59.46	30.79	48.02	23.48	22.90	35.71
2006	61.76	30.79	50.90	25.13	22.90	37.85

2007	64.08	30.79	53.96	26.89	22.90	40.12
2008	66.39	30.79	57.20	28.77	22.90	42.53
2009	68.69	30.79	60.63	30.78	22.90	45.08
Present value, 1989	262.14	262.14	262.14	194.93	194.93	194.93
1989 Levelized cost		30.79	18.90		22.90	14.06

Assumptions

Discount rate 10%

Inflation rate 6%

SOURCE: EDF calculations.

115

real terms can be compared directly to other 1989 expenditures on municipal services, presuming one uses appropriate discount and inflation rates.
This allows a more intuitive appraisal of the present value of the costs of a
proposal, and can simplify some procedures in a complicated analysis. On
the other hand, it is more common, and in some ways more straightforward,
to levelize in constant terms because one need not account for the effect of
inflation. At any rate, what matters is that cost figures for all compared
options are expressed in the same terms. For the sake of simplicity, we will
levelize in constant terms in the following comparisons.

SELECTING THE APPROPRIATE INFLATION AND DISCOUNT RATES

By now, you probably sense that present-value calculations are very sensitive to which discount and inflation rates are used. Choosing the appropriate discount rate is not a clear-cut task; the calculations in the latter part of
this chapter employ the 10 percent rate typically used by incinerator vendors, even though doing so may tend to be unduly favorable to incineration.
The bias comes about in this case because a 10 percent discount rate is fairly
low compared to discount rates used in most business decisions. That is,
most people and businesses tend to pay more attention to near-term costs
and less attention to long-term costs than a 10 percent discount rate implies.
This circumstance, coupled with the fact that incinerators are most expensive in the near term, leads to a more favorable evaluation of incineration in
comparison with recycling than would be the case with a higher, perhaps
more realistic, discount rate. With a higher discount rate, the higher, up-
front costs of incineration would receive more relative emphasis. In conducting a full-fledged comparison, it is important to use the same discount
and inflation rates throughout. If certain assumptions are unduly favorable
to one option or another, they can be changed in a sensitivity analysis,
which involves systematically changing the values of important variables to
test the impact on the final result. (An example of the sensitivity of the cost
of recycling programs to changes in the price of secondary materials
appears in chapter 2.)

LIFE-CYCLE COSTS OF INCINERATION

This section works through the calculation of the cost per ton of incinerating
solid waste for a typical incinerator. Life-cycle costs are calculated to
account for the variety of cost and revenue items that vary over time.

THE INCINERATOR TIPPING FEE

Although there can be a number of additional complications in calculating a life-cycle incineraₜor tipping fee, such as revenue-sharing agreements between the municipality and the owner and/or operator of the incinerator, the basic requirements for calculating the tipping fee are:

- the projected construction cost of the incinerator or, alternatively, the size of the projected bond issue;
- the projected cost of operation and maintenance;
- the projected cost of disposing remaining ash;
- the projected price at which electricity will be sold; and
- economic assumptions about projected inflation rates, interest rates, and discount rates.

These assumptions are used to calculate year-by-year costs and revenues as they would occur while the incinerator operates. The annual expenses of paying back the construction cost of the incinerator and of operating the incinerator less the annual revenues from electricity sales result in a net annual cost of operation. This net annual cost is charged to waste haulers as a tipping fee to make the project economically viable. Profits resulting from tipping fees in excess of net annual costs are assumed not to exist in this analysis or to have already been included in the annual operation and maintenance cost estimates.

Once the year-by-year costs and revenues have been estimated, the various present-value and levelization methods are used to calculate life-cycle cost-per-ton tipping fees, which can be directly compared with alternative waste management options.

The first estimated annual expenses are the repayment of the construction cost of the incinerator. A preliminary calculation must determine the size of the bond issue necessary to pay for the construction of the incinerator. Table 3.4 shows this calculation. The construction cost is $250 million in 1990 dollars.[2] This is the hypothetical cost of building the incinerator if all materials and labor were bought instantaneously in 1990. In fact, the projected construction period is three years, from 1991 through 1993. Inflation in materials and labor costs is expected over that period. Table 3.4 estimates the effects of inflation by allocating one-third of the construction cost to each of the three years of the construction period and applying the inflation rate to these estimated costs. The total construction cost after accounting for inflation is $281 million.

Bonds must be issued at the beginning of the construction period to cover

TABLE 3.4
Incinerator Construction Costs
(in 1,000s of dollars)

Assumptions
Construction cost $250,000 (1990 dollars)
Inflation rate   6% per year
Interest rate   10% per year
Bond issuance cost   4% of bond issue

Year	Total Construction Cost	Fraction Each Year	Construction Cost Each Year	Construction Cost After Inflation
1990	$250,000			
1991		0.33	$83,333	$ 88,333
1992		0.33	83,333	93,633
1993		0.33	83,333	99,251
Total construction				$281,218
Net interest during construction				42,183
Bond issuance costs				13,475
Bond issue (beginning of year 1991)				$336,876

SOURCE: EDF calculations.

these construction costs. There is another expense, however, that the bond issue must cover. This expense is the interest that must be paid to the bond holders during the construction period. The incinerator will not produce revenues until it is operating. The bond holders, however, will require interest payments (generally on a semiannual basis) as soon as the bonds are issued. Thus, the size of the bond issue must be increased to pay for interest during construction. An offsetting factor must also be taken into account: The construction expenditures do not all occur at the beginning of the construction period. As a result, the proceeds from the bond issue can be placed in interest-earning accounts until the construction expenditures occur. (A loophole in the federal tax codes that has since been closed allowed the proceeds from tax-exempt bonds to be reinvested at taxable interest rates, which are higher than the interest rates on tax-exempt bonds. Project proponents could thus earn a profit even from an incinerator that was never built.) Table 3.4 estimates the effects of these factors by calculating net interest during construction equal to one and one-half year's interest on the total construction cost after inflation. In our example, this net interest during construction is $42 million.

Finally, there are various fees that must be paid to the financial institutions that arrange and complete the bond transactions. Table 3.4 estimates these to be 4 percent of the total bond issuance.[3] The bond issuance costs of $13 million bring the total bond issuance to $337 million.

Table 3.5 calculates annual costs. Bond issues are generally arranged so that principal and interest payments over the operating period of the project are approximately equal each year. Table 3.5 calculates the construction-cost repayment assuming equal annual installments.[4] This results in annual bond payments of $39,569,000, assuming an interest rate of 10 percent and a payment period of 20 years. The annual bond payments are shown in the first column of table 3.5.

The next column shows operation and maintenance expenses. These are $12 million per year at 1990 prices, and are assumed to go up each year at the rate of inflation.

The third column shows the expense for ash disposal. The amount of ash depends on the amount of garbage actually burned, which depends on how much garbage the plant is designed to process—2,000 tons per day maximum throughput—and the assumption that the plant will operate 85 percent of the time on average. The average throughput is 620,500 tons per year. The amount of ash also depends on how much ash is generated for each ton of garbage burned. The fraction used here is 30 percent by weight, in the mid-range of typical estimates that ash is between 25 percent and 35 percent by weight of incinerated garbage. This weight fraction is greater than the typical 10 to 20 percent estimated remaining ash by volume. The 30 percent by-weight figure will be appropriate in situations where transportation is involved—where costs are usually charged per ton—and where landfills charge on a per-ton basis. In cases where landfills charge on a volume basis, the calculations will be nominally correct; however, it is unlikely that a landfill would accept incinerator ash for the same price per cubic yard as other refuse. This is because ordinary refuse can be counted on to decompose and compress over the long term to a significantly smaller volume than ash. It is that ultimate volume that determines the life of a landfill. Thus, on a volume basis, ash will cause a landfill to fill up faster than other refuse. One would expect a landfill operator to charge a higher price to compensate for this difference.

Finally, table 3.5 calculates ash disposal costs based on the amount of ash generated and the cost per ton for dumping ash at the landfill, which includes the costs of transporting ash to the landfill. Here, the cost of disposing ash, including transportation, is assumed to be $40 per ton in 1990. The costs of ash disposal are assumed to increase each year at the rate of inflation.

Revenues from the sale of electricity depend on the price of electricity

TABLE 3.5
Incinerator Life-cycle Costs
(in 1,000s of dollars)

Assumptions	
Bond issue	$336,876
Interest rate	10.0% per year
Incinerator life	20 years
Operation and maint.	$12,000 per year (1990 dollars)
Inflation rate	6.0% per year
Ash disposal cost	$40.00 ton ash (1990 dollars)
Incinerator size	2,000 tons per day
Capacity factor	85%
Ash fraction	30% (by weight)
Electricity price	$0.040 per kilowatt-hour (1990 dollars)
Elect. price inflatn.	6.0% per year
Net elect. generation	466 kilowatt-hour per ton
Discount rate	10.0% per year

	Bond Payments	Operation & Maint.	Ash Disposal	Electricity Sales	Total Net Cost	Throughput (tons/year)	Tipping Fee ($/ton)
1994	$ 39,569	$ 15,150	$ 9,400	$ 14,602	$ 49,517	620,500	$ 79.80
1995	39,569	16,059	9,964	15,478	50,114	620,500	80.76
1996	39,569	17,022	10,562	16,407	50,747	620,500	81.78
1997	39,569	18,044	11,196	17,391	51,418	620,500	82.87
1998	39,569	19,126	11,868	18,435	52,129	620,500	84.01
1999	39,569	20,274	12,580	19,541	52,882	620,500	85.23
2000	39,569	21,490	13,335	20,713	53,681	620,500	86.51

2001	39,569	22,780	14,135	21,956	54,528	620,500	87.88
2002	39,569	24,146	14,983	23,273	55,425	620,500	89.32
2003	39,569	25,595	15,882	24,670	56,377	620,500	90.86
2004	39,569	27,131	16,835	26,150	57,385	620,500	92.48
2005	39,569	28,759	17,845	27,719	58,454	620,500	94.20
2006	39,569	30,484	18,915	29,382	59,587	620,500	96.03
2007	39,569	32,313	20,050	31,145	60,788	620,500	97.97
2008	39,569	34,252	21,253	33,014	62,061	620,500	100.02
2009	39,569	36,307	22,529	34,994	63,411	620,500	102.19
2010	39,569	38,486	23,880	37,094	64,841	620,500	104.50
2011	39,569	40,795	25,313	39,320	66,357	620,500	106.94
2012	39,569	43,242	26,832	41,679	67,965	620,500	109.53
2013	39,569	45,837	28,442	44,180	69,668	620,500	112.28
Present value, 1993	$336,876	$198,189	$122,976	$191,023	$467,018		$752.65
In 1990 $	$282,848	$166,403	$103,253	$160,386	$392,117		$631.94
1990 Levelized cost (in constant terms):							
	$ 33,223	$ 19,546	$ 12,128	$ 18,839	$ 46,058		$ 74.23

SOURCE: EDF calculations.

and the amount of electricity available for sale, which, in turn, depends on how much electricity can be produced from each ton of garbage burned. The price at which an electric utility company will buy electricity generated by incinerators is generally set by state regulatory agencies to reflect utility avoided costs, that is, the price reflects what the utility company would otherwise have to spend to generate the electricity itself. Such avoided-cost prices vary with time of day; for example, the daytime on-peak price will be greater than the nighttime off-peak price. Incinerators generally operate on around-the-clock schedules and, therefore, realize a price that is an average of on-peak and off-peak avoided costs.

In addition to variation by time of day and season, avoided costs also vary from year to year. Short-run avoided costs are usually the price the utility company is willing to pay for a short-term purchase of electricity. These short-run avoided costs can be expected to increase each year with, for example, increases in fuel prices. In addition, avoided costs may be expected to increase over time as the utility company experiences growth in the total amounts of electricity it sells, and perhaps comes to need new sources of electricity generation. Long-run avoided costs are usually an average of forecasted short-run avoided costs. Sometimes utility companies are willing to buy electricity from incinerators at a long-run price. Such a price is expected to be higher than short-run avoided cost in the near term, but lower in the long term. Utility companies are willing to enter such agreements only under the assumption that the incinerator will operate over its full expected life.

Avoided costs also vary from utility to utility. These variations in electricity prices can be crucial to the economics of incinerators. In locations where utilities have built excess generating capacity that has low operating costs—such as coal-fired generating plants—avoided costs will be low since the costs of building that capacity have already been incurred. The only cost that is avoided by the production of incinerator-generated electricity, in such a case, is the cost of coal fuel. A representative short-run avoided cost may be about two cents per kilowatt-hour in this case. On the other hand, a utility that needs generating capacity and relies on high-priced oil and natural gas fuels will have significantly higher avoided costs. Representative short-run avoided costs may be 10 to 12 cents per kilowatt-hour in this case.

The issue of avoided-cost payments for incinerator-generated electricity was an important element in the bankruptcy of the Vicon Recovery Systems incinerator in Vermont in 1988. The state regulatory agency did not approve a contract for electricity payments based on long-run avoided costs because the agency did not have sufficient assurance that the incinerator would operate long enough to justify the long-term electricity rate.[5] In another case, threatened bankruptcy of several Florida incinerators was only avoided when the state legislature superseded the authority of the state regulatory agency and mandated that the utilities make payments greater than avoided cost.[6] In effect, electricity users subsidize incineration in this case.

The figures in table 3.5 reflect an assumption that 466 kilowatt-hours of net electricity generation occurs for each ton of garbage incinerated.[7] The price of electricity is assumed to be four cents per kilowatt-hour in 1990 and to increase every year at the rate of inflation.

Total net costs are thus construction-cost repayments, plus operation and maintenance expenses, plus ash disposal, less electricity sales revenues. This figure is divided by the tons per year throughput to calculate the annual tipping fee. This figure is $79.80 per ton in 1994, and increases over time to $112.28 in 2013. The present value of per-ton tipping fees (that is, the 1993 value of tipping one ton of garbage every year for the 20 years between 1994 and 2013) is $752.65 in 1993 dollars. This value is $631.94 per ton in 1990, taking into account inflation only.

Levelization methods can be used to determine annual per-ton tipping fees that have the same present value. If the present value is levelized in constant terms, that is, the tipping fee is the same every year, the constant tipping fee would be $74.23 per ton. If the present value is levelized in real terms, that is, the tipping fee goes up every year at the rate of inflation, the 1990 tipping fee would be $45.57 per ton.

POTENTIAL COST VARIABLES OF INCINERATION

The formulas for calculating incinerator costs represented in table 3.5 allow simple what-if analyses of potential increases in incinerator tipping fees. For example, if the price of electricity is not as high as originally projected, electricity sales revenues will decrease and the incinerator tipping fee must increase to offset the sales loss. Similarly, if incinerator ash must be handled in a more stringent manner than simply landfilling the ash with ordinary municipal refuse, incinerator tipping fees must increase to cover the increased expense. Finally, an additional what-if analysis considers a potential cost *decreasing* factor: What if the operating life of the incinerator is increased from 20 years to 30 years? In our analysis, the effects on projected tipping fees of several factors are examined one at a time. The combined effects of several such factors occurring together are not considered.

The assumption in table 3.5 was that electricity prices would increase at the rate of inflation every year through the life of the incinerator. Recently, however, the prices at which utilities will purchase electricity from independent producers, such as incinerators, typically have not been increasing at all. An alternative assumption is that electricity prices remain constant, in nominal terms, for several years, and then begin to increase. Under the assumption that electricity prices remain unchanged through 1995 and begin growing at the rate of inflation thereafter, the equivalent 1990 tipping fee is $81.80 per ton, compared to the calculation above of $74.23 per ton.

The assumption was also made in table 3.5 that ash disposal would cost $40.00 per ton in 1990 dollars. This figure is typical of disposal costs for ordinary municipal waste. If more stringent disposal methods are required, this figure could increase substantially with subsequent effect on the incinerator tipping fee. For example, a doubling of ash disposal costs to $80.00 per ton causes the equivalent incinerator tipping fee to increase to $93.77 per ton from the earlier calculation of $74.23 per ton.

Another assumption made in table 3.5 was that the incinerator would have a capacity factor of 85 percent. That is, the incinerator would operate at 85 percent of its maximum feasible capacity—24 hours a day, 365 days a year—assuming no unanticipated maintenance or other outages. If the incinerator operates at a lower capacity factor, less garbage is burned. Less electricity is generated for sale as fixed costs—the costs of building the incinerator itself—remain unchanged. Assuming a capacity factor of 75 percent leads to higher costs of $85.56 per ton for the 1990 equivalent tipping fee.[8]

Finally, a 20-year incinerator life was assumed in table 3.5. Life-cycle costs should decrease if the incinerator actually operates for 30 years. A simple what-if analysis assumes that there are no additional repair or reconstruction costs. With a 30-year incinerator life, the 1990 equivalent tipping fee that reflects the life-cycle costs of the incinerator is $62.45 per ton, compared to $74.23 per ton in the 20-year case. Thus, a 50 percent increase in the useful life of the facility leads to only a 16 percent decrease in life-cycle costs. There are two main reasons for this. First, the main effect of increased life is to decrease capital costs. These are saved, in essence, because we do not have to build a new incinerator at the end of 20 years in this case. Capital costs, however, are only one part of the costs of incineration. Ash disposal costs and operation and maintenance costs continue to increase every year. Second, the benefits of saved capital costs only occur after 20 years. The use of discounting in life-cycle analyses means that such distant future benefits receive relatively little economic weight.

LIFE-CYCLE COSTS OF RECYCLING

In this section a typical residential curbside recycling program illustrates the calculation of the life-cycle costs for a recycling program.[9] The same basic approach can be used to calculate life-cycle costs of other recycling programs, such as buy-back centers or yard-waste composting.

A residential curbside recycling program has a number of elements, such as containers used by households for storing and setting out recyclables, collection and processing of recyclable materials, sale of recovered materials, and promotion and administration of the recycling program. Most of these elements involve both capital expenditures, for items like recycling trucks and processing equipment, and on-going operating expenses, for items such as the salaries of truck drivers and processing-line workers.

Tables 3.6 through 3.9 show the costs of each curbside-recycling-program element in some detail. This detail is quite a bit greater than that shown for the capital and operating costs of a typical incinerator. One reason is that total capital and operating costs for an incinerator are usually simply provided by the vendor. Some recycling vendors have begun to offer package deals (e.g., in San Jose and Seattle), but this is usually not the case. It is also interesting to see what the element-by-element costs of a recycling program are so that these may be re-estimated under changing local circumstances.

RECYCLABLES AVAILABLE

Table 3.6 shows the amounts of recyclable materials—not counting yard waste—which are available in the residential waste stream, estimated separately for single-family and multiple-family dwellings. Participation rates indicate the fraction of households that will be collecting and setting out each of the recyclable materials. The efficiency factor estimates the fraction of the available materials that each participating household actually sets aside. Thus, for newspaper, 75 percent of single-family households are estimated to participate, but on average these households recycle only 90 percent of their newspaper (i.e., even participating households are assumed to throw away in their regular garbage 10 percent of their newspaper).

Table 3.6 calculates that total recyclables collected each year are 63,916 tons, which is 27 percent of the residential waste stream. Table 3.6 also calculates the expected revenue per year from sale of recycled materials. The calculation assumes that a fraction of the materials collected—8 percent—cannot be processed and sold. This fraction is discarded during processing and must itself be landfilled. The revenues in table 3.6—a total of $3,769,538 per year—reflect the fact that a fraction of the materials cannot be sold. The cost of disposing these rejects is considered a cost of processing, which is shown in table 3.11. A disposal cost of $40 per ton is used, the same as for ash.

TABLE 3.6

Materials Collected Through Residential Recycling Programs

Single-Family Houses
Total tons/year   175,000

	Fraction	Tons Available	Partici- pation	Efficiency	Tons Recovered	Revenue Per Ton	Total Revenue
Newspaper	5.3%	9,275	75%	90%	6,261	$ 25	$ 156,516
Glass	9.9%	17,325	75%	90%	11,694	35	409,303
Ferrous cans	2.3%	4,025	75%	85%	2,566	20	51,319
Aluminum cans	1.0%	1,750	75%	90%	1,181	1,400	1,653,750
Mixed paper	19.6%	34,300	60%	85%	17,493	0	0
Corrugated	5.3%	9,275	60%	85%	4,730	20	94,605
High-grade paper	1.4%	2,450	60%	85%	1,250	50	62,475
PET bottles	1.0%	1,750	60%	90%	945	100	94,500
Ferrous metals	2.6%	4,550	50%	80%	1,820	20	36,400
Nonferrous metals	0.3%	525	50%	80%	210	30	6,300
HDPE	2.0%	3,500	50%	80%	1,400	250	350,000
Other	49.3%						
Total	100.0%	88,725			49,550		$2,915,168

Multiple-Family Dwellings

Total tons/year   60,000

	Fraction	Tons Available	Partici- pation	Efficiency	Tons Recovered	Revenue Per Ton	Total Revenue
Newspaper	5.3%	3,180	65%	90%	1,860	$ 25	$ 46,508
Glass	9.9%	5,940	65%	90%	3,475	35	121,622
Ferrous cans	2.3%	1,380	65%	85%	762	20	15,249
Aluminum cans	1.0%	600	65%	90%	351	1,400	491,400
Mixed paper	19.6%	11,760	50%	85%	4,998	0	0
Corrugated	5.3%	3,180	50%	85%	1,352	20	27,030
High-grade paper	1.4%	840	50%	85%	357	50	17,850
PET bottles	1.0%	600	50%	90%	270	100	27,000
Ferrous metals	2.6%	1,560	40%	80%	499	20	9,984
Nonferrous metals	0.3%	180	40%	80%	58	30	1,728
HDPE	2.0%	1,200	40%	80%	384	250	96,000
Other	49.3%						
Total	100.0%	30,420			14,366		$ 854,370
Total single family and multifamily					63,916		$3,769,538

SOURCE: EDF calculations.

CURBSIDE COLLECTION

The residential curbside collection program uses special recycling trucks and crews, which will collect recyclables separately from regular garbage collection. This is assumed as a less-than-optimal scenario, since participation can be made simpler if recycling collection is coordinated with regular collection, that is, if recyclables are picked up on the same day as regular garbage for each household.

Table 3.7 estimates the number of recycling trucks necessary for the program. Two important factors in the calculation are the number of households that will participate each week, which allows calculation of the number of recycling pickups that need to be made each day, and the number of pickups that a truck can make in a day. Table 3.7 estimates that 65 percent of single-family households will participate each week. This figure is lower than the 75 percent overall participation rate in table 3.6 because not all participating households will set out recyclables every week. Table 3.7 also estimates that multifamily participation each week is 95 percent—a figure greater than the 65 percent overall multifamily participation rate in table 3.6. The higher figure (95 percent) accounts for pickups necessary even when only a fraction of the households in a multiunit building set out recyclables in any given week. Even if not all the households in a building set out recyclables every week, chances are that at least one household in the building will, thus involving a pickup.

Table 3.7 estimates that a recycling truck can make 550 pickups from single-family households in a day, or service 50 multifamily buildings in a

TABLE 3.7
Truck Requirements for Residential Collection Programs

Truck Needs	Single Family	Multifamily
Number of pickup points	145,000	4,500
Participation rate per week[a]	70%	95%
Number of pickups	101,500	4,275
Pickups per day[b]	20,300	855
Pickups per truck per day	550	50
Trucks required	34	17
Backup trucks at 10%	3	2
Total truck requirement	37	19

SOURCE: EDF calculations.

[a] Not all participating households will have a setout each week.
[b] Weekly pickup, 5 days per week.

day. This figure is derived from a judgment that considers a number of factors: the size of the truck; the volume of materials to be picked up; the amount of time for each pickup; the travel time between pickups; the number of trips each day for unloading the truck; and the travel time to the unloading point.

Finally, table 3.7 estimates that additional trucks will be required to provide backup, since some portion of trucks will require maintenance or repair at any particular time. Backup requirements are estimated at 10 percent.

Tables 3.8 and 3.9 estimate the year-by-year capital and operating costs of curbside collection. Table 3.8 shows the various capital expenditures necessary in the initial year of the program for recycling trucks and con-

TABLE 3.8
Residential Curbside Collection—Equipment and Labor Costs

	Single-family	145,000 households
	Single-family participation	75%
	Multifamily units	80,000 households
		4,444 buildings
	Multifamily participation	65% of households
		95% of buildings

	1990 Unit Cost	Number	Total Cost	Useful Life (years)
Capital costs				
Trucks	$75,000	56	$4,200,000	7
Containers[a]	12	160,750	1,929,000	10
90-gallon carts[b]	45	6,333	285,000	10
300-gallon carts[c]	180	929	167,200	10
3-cubic-yard bins[d]	300	127	38,000	10
Operating costs per year				
Truck O&M and fuel[e]	$ 7,660	51	$ 390,660	—
Drivers[f]	31,200	68	$2,121,600	—

SOURCE: EDF calculations.

[a] One set for each participating single-family and multifamily household.
[b] 75% of multifamily buildings get two each.
[c] 22% of multifamily buildings get one each.
[d] 3% of multifamily buildings get one each.
[e] Cost per operating truck.
[f] One driver per truck plus 33% backup.

TABLE 3.9

Residential Curbside Collection—Life-cycle Costs

Inflation rate	6.0% per year
Interest rate	10.0% per year
Discount rate	10.0% per year
Recyclables collected	58,803 tons per year

		Capital Costs			Amortized Capital Expenditures			Operating Costs		Total Annual Costs	Cost Per Ton ($)
		Trucks	Initial Containers	Bins, Carts[a]	Trucks	Initial Contain.	Bins, Carts	Drivers, Truck O&M	Replacmnt. Containers[b]		
Useful life (years)		7	10	10	7	10	10				
Expenditure/year ($1,000)	1990	$4,202	$1,929	$490	$ 863	$ 314	$ 80	$ 2,512		$ 3,769	$ 64.09
	1991				863	314	80	2,663	$ 204	4,124	70.13
	1992				863	314	80	2,822	217	4,296	73.06
	1993				863	314	80	2,992	230	4,478	76.16
	1994				863	314	80	3,171	244	4,672	79.45
	1995				863	314	80	3,362	258	4,877	82.93
	1996				863	314	80	3,563	274	5,094	86.62
	1997	$6,318			1,298	314	80	3,777	290	5,759	97.93
	1998				1,298	314	80	4,004	307	6,003	102.08
	1999				1,298	314	80	4,244	326	6,261	106.48
	2000			$878	1,298		143	4,499	345	6,285	106.88
	2001				1,298		143	4,769	366	6,575	111.82
	2002				1,298		143	5,055	388	6,883	117.06
	2003				1,298		143	5,358	411	7,210	122.61

Year							
2004	$9,500	1,951	143	5,679	436	8,210	139.62
2005		1,951	143	6,020	462	8,577	145.86
2006		1,951	143	6,381	490	8,966	152.47
2007		1,951	143	6,764	519	9,378	159.48
2008		1,951	143	7,170	551	9,815	166.91
2009		1,951	143	7,600	584	10,278	174.79
Present value, 1989		$ 9,682	$828	$32,862	$2,583	$47,650	$810.33
In 1990 $		$10,263	$878	$34,834	$2,738	$50,509	$858.95
1990 Levelized cost ($1,000/yr): (in constant terms)		$ 1,206	$103	$ 4,092	$ 322	$ 5,933	$100.89

Present value, 1989 also: $1,929
In 1990 $ also: $2,045
1990 Levelized cost also: $ 240

SOURCE: EDF calculations.

[a] See Table 3.8.
[b] 10% replaced each year after first.

tainers for recyclables to be provided to participants. Table 3.8 also indicates how long these items are expected to last. In addition, table 3.8 shows annual labor costs in the initial year. Table 3.9 calculates life-cycle costs of curbside collection by estimating annual costs each year that the curbside program operates over a 20-year period. The 20-year period is chosen for the sake of comparing life-cycle recycling costs with the 20-year life cycle of the typical incineration plant.

Table 3.9 calculates the year-by-year costs to cover capital outlays—labeled "amortized capital expenditures"—assuming payment for each item in equal annual installments over the life of the item. Table 3.9 includes the costs of replacing equipment at the end of its useful life. For example, recycling trucks are assumed to be replaced every seven years. Containers provided to each household are a special case—10 percent of these are assumed to be lost or broken each year, although the costs of the initial distribution of containers are amortized over the first ten years in equal annual installments.

Although table 3.9 gives considerable detail about the year-by-year costs of curbside collection, a few simplifying assumptions should be noted. First, the program is not assumed to grow over time. This makes the cost comparison with incineration alternatives a little easier to make. Second, all costs are assumed to go up equally each year at a constant rate of inflation. Though this will doubtless turn out to be untrue, it is probably the best estimate that can be made, and is consistent with estimates typically made for incinerators. A more detailed analysis would also break out employee benefits, maintenance labor, licensing, taxes, contingency, and other costs in more detail.

Finally, table 3.9 calculates the 1989 present value of the annual recycling collection expenditures, and uses levelization methods to determine levelized annual costs, which have the same present value. When the present value is levelized in constant terms (i.e., collection costs are the same every year), the constant recycling collection cost is $100.89 per ton.

One factor not included in table 3.9 is cost savings in regular garbage collection as a result of recycling. The curbside recycling program diverts material that would otherwise have to be picked up by the regular collection service. Cost savings result because the regular trucks do not have to be unloaded as frequently, and regular collection routes consequently can be rearranged for greater efficiency. (This important cost factor is discussed at length in chapter 2.)

When recycling diversions are larger, cost savings are likely to be higher. For example, if curbside collection of recyclables, along with other recycling programs such as collection of yard waste and buy-back centers, reduced conventional collection by half or more, there are greater possibilities for savings. If twice-weekly conventional collection were reduced to weekly service, or weekly service were reduced to biweekly, one would expect one-for-one savings, in operating costs (e.g., nonadministrative): Cutting garbage in half means half as many trucks are needed, half as many workers, and so forth. Lesser reductions in garbage probably mean that savings per ton diverted are not as great. For example, a 30 percent reduction in garbage might not mean a 30 percent reduction in costs, because it might not be possible to rearrange routes to take full advantage of the change. If a 30 percent reduction in garbage led to a 15 percent reduction in collection costs, savings on regular garbage collection can be said to be 50 percent for each ton diverted.

It is reasonable to estimate savings in conventional collection to be 50 percent for each ton diverted. Thus, assuming conventional collection costs average approximately $65 per ton, each ton of recycling saves $32.50 of the cost of conventional collection. These savings will be incorporated into the curbside-recycling program results presented in table 3.13.

PROCESSING

Tables 3.10 and 3.11 estimate the year-by-year costs of processing recyclables after they have been collected. Typical processing steps are the separation of different metals and colors of glass from mixed bottles and containers, and the separation of different grades of paper. Processing also includes discarding unusable materials, and preparing separated materials for market by removing contaminants and densifying the materials (e.g., by crushing, grinding, or baling).

Table 3.10 shows the equipment and labor requirements for the processing center, including site preparation and land costs. Equipment needs are based on a formula that indicates that equipment costs $30 for every ton of recyclables expected to be processed per year. (This is equivalent to $7,500-per-ton-per-day capacity, assuming 250 operating days per year. The processing facility to handle 63,916 tons per year of recyclables will have a capacity of 256 tons per day.) Labor costs generally reflect the experience of operating MRFs in the United States (see chapter 2).

Table 3.11 calculates the year-by-year capital and operating costs of the processing facility. Capital costs are taken from table 3.10 and paid for in equal annual installments over the useful life of the capital equipment. This calculation is straightforward and shows the annual costs in a manner close to the way these costs will actually be incurred, but it only approximates life-cycle costs in this case. For example, the actual 30-year useful life of

TABLE 3.10
Processing Center—Equipment and Labor Costs

Recyclables collected	58,803 tons per year		

Capital costs
Site preparation	$ 750,000
Equipment[a]	1,764,090
Land[b]	1,500,000

Operating costs per year

	Unit Cost	Number	Total Cost
Material handlers	$19,000	15	$285,000
Equipment operators	33,300	6	199,800
Maintenance staff	33,300	1	33,300
Managers	53,000	2	106,000
Clerical	25,000	2	50,000
Equipment repair and maintenance			37,840
Fuel			38,000
Plant supplies			37,840
Utilities			37,840
Insurance			58,333
Total operating costs per year			$883,953

SOURCE: EDF calculations.
[a] Based on $30 per annual ton processed.
[b] Three acres at $500,000 per acre.

site-preparation expenditures is greater than the 20-year period over which life-cycle costs are calculated. Thus, at the end of the 20-year life of the processing center, there will still be 10 years of useful life remaining.

The annual cost of the land for the processing facility is a special case. A simple economic assumption is that land will rent for a fraction of its value each year. The economically correct fraction is the real interest rate (net of inflation).[10] The life-cycle results of these rent calculations are equivalent to the life-cycle costs of buying the land outright at the beginning of the period, assuming the land appreciates at the rate of inflation each year, and then selling the land at the end of the 20-year period.

Annual operating costs in 1990 for the processing facility are taken from table 3.10, and are assumed to increase each year at the rate of inflation.

Finally, table 3.11 also includes the cost of disposing materials that are rejected during the processing step. Discards are assumed to be 8 percent by weight of the material brought to the processing center and are disposed of by landfilling at a cost of $40 per ton. This cost estimate is likely to be too high, since many materials, such as ceramics, plastics, and pyrex, which are rejected as unsuitable for conventional processing, may be useful in other applications, such as asphalt additives.

Life-cycle costs are calculated as before by taking the present value of the annual expenditures over the 20-year life of the processing facility. Table 3.11 shows levelized values in constant terms and indicates a total capital and operating cost of $37.50 per ton in 1990.

PROMOTION AND ADMINISTRATION

Table 3.12 estimates costs related to promotion and administration of the residential curbside recycling program. Table 3.12 shows the various cost categories, and how the number of people or needed materials change from year to year. In general, start-up costs during the first four years are assumed to be significantly greater than annual operating costs thereafter. In addition, start-up costs begin in the year before the recycling program starts.

NET LIFE-CYCLE COSTS

Table 3.13 brings together the year-by-year costs and revenues associated with the residential curbside recycling program. Costs include collection, processing and residual disposal, and administration and promotion. Revenues from the sale of recycled materials are included as an offset to program costs. Finally, savings in regular garbage collection costs are also included as an offset to program costs.

Table 3.13 calculates life-cycle costs for each of these cost and revenue streams. On a per-ton basis, levelized in constant terms, the net cost of the curbside recycling program is $36.33 per ton in 1990.

SOLID WASTE MANAGEMENT AS PUBLIC WORKS

In a methodical and perhaps even unexiting way, this chapter has worked through some of the basic methods of analyzing the financial performance of investments in solid waste management. As the chapter shows, these methods can be applied to both incineration and recycling. As detailed, long-term performance data on recycling programs become widely available, anaylses far more complicated than the sketches offered here will

TABLE 3.11
Processing Center—Life-cycle Costs

Inflation rate	6.0% per year
Interest rate	10.0% per year
Discount rate	10.0% per year
Recyclables collected	58,803 tons per year
Reject rate	8%
Reject disposal cost	$40 per ton

| | Capital Costs | | | Amortized Capital Expenditures | | | Operating Costs[b] | Reject Costs | Total Annual Costs | Cost Per ton ($) |
	Site Prep.	Equipment	Land (Per Acre)	Site Prep.	Equipment	Land[a]				
Useful life (years)	30	15		30	15					
Expenditure/year ($1,000)	$750	$1,764	$1,500							
1990				$ 80	$ 232	$ 57	$ 884	$ 188	$ 1,440	$ 24.49
1991				80	232	60	937	199	1,508	25.64
1992				80	232	64	993	211	1,580	26.87
1993				80	232	67	1,053	224	1,656	28.16
1994				80	232	71	1,116	238	1,737	29.53
1995				80	232	76	1,183	252	1,822	30.99
1996				80	232	80	1,254	267	1,913	32.53
1997				80	232	85	1,329	283	2,009	34.16
1998				80	232	90	1,409	300	2,111	35.89
1999				80	232	96	1,493	318	2,219	37.73
2000				80	232	101	1,583	337	2,333	39.67

2001	80	232	107	1,678	357	2,454	41.74
2002	80	232	114	1,779	379	2,583	43.92
2003	80	232	121	1,886	401	2,719	46.24
2004	80	232	128	1,999	425	2,864	48.70
2005	80	556	136	2,119	451	3,341	56.81
2006	80	556	144	2,246	478	3,503	59.57
2007	80	556	152	2,380	507	3,675	62.50
2008	80	556	162	2,523	537	3,857	65.60
2009	80	556	171	2,675	569	4,051	68.88
Present value, 1989	$677	$2,269	$740	$11,564	$2,462	$17,712	$301.22
In 1990 $	$718	$2,405	$785	$12,258	$2,609	$18,775	$319.29
1990 Levelized cost ($1,000/yr): (in constant terms)	$ 84	$ 282	$ 92	$ 1,440	$ 306	$ 2,205	$ 37.50

$4,228

SOURCE: EDF calculations.

a Annual rent based on real interest rate and land value increasing at inflation rate.

b See table 3.10.

TABLE 3.12
Recycling Program Administrative, Promotion, and Enforcement Costs

Inflation rate 6.0% per year
Single-family units 145,000
Discount rate 10.0% per year

	Information Staff $15/hr.		Director $52,000	Delivery $5/hr.		Mailing $0.50/piece		Promo. Material	Adver- tising	Administration Manager $52,000	Clerical $25,000	Enforce- ment $100,000	Total Cost
1990 cost			$52,000							$52,000	$25,000	$100,000	
Number of people			1							6	8		
Expenditure/year ($1,000)	Hours	Cost		Hours	Cost	Pieces	Cost						
1989	8,320	$ 118	$ 49	6,000	$ 28	580,000	$ 274	$ 142	$ 142	$ 294	$ 189		$ 1,235
1990	8,320	125	52	1,500	8	580,000	290	150	150	312	$ 200	$ 100	1,386
1991	4,160	66	55	1,500	8	290,000	154	106	106	331	212	106	1,144
1992	4,160	70	58	1,500	8	290,000	163	112	112	351	225	112	1,212
1993	4,160	74	62	1,500	9	145,000	86	60	89	372	238	119	1,109
1994	4,160	79	66	1,500	9	145,000	92	63	95	394	252	126	1,176
1995	4,160	84	70	1,500	10	145,000	97	67	100	418	268	134	1,246
1996	4,160	89	74	1,500	11	145,000	103	71	106	443	284	142	1,321
1997	4,160	94	78	1,500	11	145,000	109	75	113	469	301	150	1,400
1998	4,160	99	83	1,500	12	145,000	116	80	120	497	319	159	1,485
1999	4,160	105	88	1,500	13	145,000	122	84	127	527	338	169	1,574
2000	4,160	112	93	1,500	13	145,000	130	90	134	559	358	179	1,668
2001	4,160	118	99	1,500	14	145,000	138	95	142	592	380	190	1,768
2002	4,160	126	105	1,500	15	145,000	146	101	151	628	402	201	1,874
2003	4,160	133	111	1,500	16	145,000	155	107	160	665	427	213	1,987
2004	4,160	141	118	1,500	17	145,000	164	113	170	705	452	226	2,106

2005	4,160	150	125	1,500	18	145,000	174	120	180	748	479	240	2,232
2006	4,160	159	132	1,500	19	145,000	184	127	191	793	508	254	2,366
2007	4,160	168	140	1,500	20	145,000	195	135	202	840	539	269	2,508
2008	4,160	178	148	1,500	21	145,000	207	143	214	891	571	285	2,659
2009	4,160	189	157	1,500	23	145,000	219	151	227	944	605	303	2,818
Present value, 1989	$ 991	$729	$126				$1,544	$ 973	$1,234	$4,376	$ 2,805	$ 1,308	$14,087
In 1990 $	$1,050	$773	$134				$1,637	$1,031	$1,308	$4,638	$ 2,973	$ 1,387	$14,932
1990 Levelized cost ($1,000/yr):													
(in constant terms)	$ 123	$ 91	$ 16				$ 192	$ 121	$ 154	$ 545	$ 349	$ 163	$ 1,754

SOURCE: EDF calculations.

TABLE 3.13
Total Recycling Program Life-cycle Costs
(in 1,000s of dollars)

Assumptions

Inflation rate	6%	per year
Discount rate	10%	per year
Recyclables collected	58,803	tons per year
Regular garbage collection costs	$65	per ton
Regular/recycling collection savings factor	50%	
Years before savings	5	

	Collection	Processing	Administration	Revenues	Regular Collection Savings	Net Costs	Net Costs Per Ton
1989			$ 1,235			$ 1,235	
1990	$ 3,769	$ 1,440	1,386	$ 3,468	$ 0	3,127	$ 53.18
1991	4,124	1,508	1,144	3,676	0	3,100	52.71
1992	4,296	1,580	1,212	3,897	0	3,191	54.27
1993	4,478	1,656	1,109	4,130	0	3,113	52.94
1994	4,672	1,737	1,176	4,378	0	3,206	54.52
1995	4,877	1,822	1,246	4,641	2,557	747	12.70
1996	5,094	1,913	1,321	4,919	2,711	697	11.86
1997	5,759	2,009	1,400	5,215	2,874	1,080	18.36
1998	6,003	2,111	1,485	5,527	3,046	1,024	17.42

1999	6,261	2,219	1,574	5,859	3,229	966	16.42
2000	6,285	2,333	1,668	6,211	3,422	653	11.10
2001	6,575	2,454	1,768	6,583	3,628	587	9.97
2002	6,883	2,583	1,874	6,978	3,846	517	8.79
2003	7,210	2,719	1,987	7,397	4,076	442	7.52
2004	8,210	2,864	2,106	7,841	4,321	1,018	17.30
2005	8,577	3,341	2,232	8,311	4,580	1,258	21.40
2006	8,966	3,503	2,366	8,810	4,855	1,170	19.89
2007	9,378	3,675	2,508	9,338	5,146	1,076	18.30
2008	9,815	3,857	2,659	9,899	5,455	977	16.62
2009	10,278	4,051	2,818	10,493	5,782	872	14.83
Present value, 1989	$47,650	$17,712	$14,087	$45,368	$16,923	$17,157	$291.78
In 1990 $	$50,509	$18,775	$14,932	$48,090	$17,939	$18,187	$309.28
1990 Levelized cost: (in constant terms)	$ 5,933	$ 2,205	$ 1,754	$ 5,649	$ 2,107	$ 2,136	$ 36.33

SOURCE: EDF calculations.

become commonplace in the offerings of engineering and financial consulting firms and in the work of MSW and budgeting offices. However, the real point of this chapter is not to demonstrate how arcane and detailed costs comparisons can become, but to make the more simple point that recycling and incineration are both types of public works projects. As such, we can estimate and compare the costs, financial risks, and delivery of solid waste management services offered by each type of solid waste management program. Although this practice is not common now, by the mid-1990s, we predict that it will become much more so. The implications of this trend are discussed in chapter 4.

NOTES

1. For more information on present value calculations, discount rates, inflation, and so on, see: Donald M. McAllister, *Evaluation in Environmental Planning; Assessing Environmental, Social, Economic and Political Trade-offs* (Cambridge, MA: MIT Press, 1980), chapter 8; Edith Stokey and Richard Zeckhauser, *A Primer for Policy Analysis*. (New York: W.H. Norton and Co, 1978), chapter 10.

2. The construction cost of $250 million in 1990 dollars for a 2,000 tpd incinerator is roughly representative of typical incinerator construction costs. The New York Department of Sanitation estimated that a 2,000 tpd incinerator without scrubbers to control emissions that cause acid rain would have a $163 million construction cost in 1984 dollars. "The Waste Disposal Problem in New York City: A Proposal for Action" (New York: Department of Sanitation, April 1984), table 3.2-6. Scrubbers were estimated to increase costs approximately 23 percent on the proposed 3,000 tpd Brooklyn Navy Yard facility. See EDF, "To Burn or Not to Burn," (New York: EDF, 1985), tables A-1 and A-2. Applying this increase leads to a 1984 cost of $200 million. Construction cost inflation of 5 percent per year through 1990 results in a 1990 construction cost of $269 million; the proposed 3,000 tpd Bay Area Resource Recovery Project was estimated to have a $305 million construction cost in 1985 dollars. Goldman, Sachs & Co., "Financial Projection Model Capital Cost and Service Fee Calculation" (New York, November 25, 1985). Assuming that a 2,000 tpd facility could be built at two-thirds that cost, and assuming construction cost escalation of 5 percent per year through 1990 results in a 1990 construction cost of $260 million; Seattle estimated a 1,000 tpd facility would have a construction cost of $128 million in 1988 dollars. Seattle Engineering Department, Solid Waste Utility, "Waste Reduction, Recycling and Disposal Alternatives" (July 1988), Appendix F estimates issuance costs of 3.5 percent.

Assuming a 2,000 tpd facility would cost twice that amount, and assuming construction cost escalation of 5 percent per year through 1990 results in a 1990 construction cost of $282 million.

3. Goldman, Sachs & Co. estimated issuance costs, which include cost of issuance, underwriter's discount, and issuer fee, at 4 percent of the total bond issue for the proposed Bay Area Resource Recovery Project. The Seattle Solid Waste Utility estimated issuance costs at 3.5 percent.

4. The formula for calculating the repayment of an initial cost in equal annual installments at an interest rate r per period over n periods is:

$$\frac{r}{1 - 1/(1 + r)^n}$$

5. "What's Ahead? Vicon Looks for Alternatives," *Rutland Daily Herald*, December 18, 1987, p. 1; and "Send Ash to Pittsfield Now; Take Theirs Later, Mayor Says," *Rutland Daily Herald*, December 19, 1987, p. 1.

6. "Florida Waste Incinerators Lobby for Higher kWh Rate," *Solid Waste and Power*, April 1988, pp. 36–40.

7. The New York DOS estimated 480 kWh per ton without scrubbers. Scrubbers are estimated to reduce net generation by 3 percent. The Bay Area Resource Recovery Project estimated 606 kWh per ton for the San Francisco waste stream and 547 kWh per ton for other communities. Seattle estimated 500 kWh per ton.

8. See chapter 2, note 4.

9. We use "typical" numbers for recycling programs; they do not represent any specific city. Many of the basic numbers used are abstracted from Seattle's economic studies of recycling.

10. The nominal interest rate can be thought to be approximately the sum of two parts—a "real" (net of inflation) interest rate plus the inflation rate. Thus, in the case where the nominal interest rate is 10 percent, and the inflation rate is 6 percent, the real interest rate must be 4 percent. In a more precise calculation, the effects are multiplicative rather than additive:

$$(1+i)\,(1+r_r) = r$$

where

i = the inflation rate;
r_r = the real interest rate; and
r = the nominal interest rate.

In this case, the real interest rate can be calculated to be 3.77 percent.

CHAPTER 4

Lessons from Comparisons

CHAPTER 2 SHOWED that a wide range of recycling and incineration strategies are available for managing various fractions of the municipal solid waste stream; chapter 3 showed how to make direct comparisons of the costs and uncertainties associated with these strategies. This chapter explains what this ability to conduct comparative analyses means, in practical terms, for citizens, businesses, and public officials now making decisions about their solid waste management future.

This chapter begins by summarizing the results of comparisons of recycling and incineration proposals that have been conducted in three distinctly different locales of the United States: Seattle, Washington, New York City, and North Hempstead, Long Island, New York. These studies, conducted by consulting firms, city agencies, and nonprofit organizations, served different purposes in the local waste management planning process. However, each provides quantitative support for the consensus that recycling, on a ton-for-ton or system-wide basis, is substantially less expensive than solid waste incineration. A number of less-detailed studies for other cities have led to the same conclusion.[1] The primary advantage of recycling comes from avoiding the enormous capital and operating costs of a facility designed to burn large quantities of very heterogeneous material at high temperature.

The remainder of this chapter draws and illustrates two overall lessons from the evidence presented in Part I. First, no incinerator should be constructed without an open, comprehensive analysis of the waste management potential of recycling and waste reduction. Depending on local conditions, this analysis might suggest that an incinerator is entirely unnecessary, that an incinerator should be delayed until recycling can establish and prove itself, or that an incinerator should be downsized. Of course, environmental issues will also enter into this judgment.

144

Good waste management decisions are based on good information about a range of options, information that has frequently been unavailable to local governments that are focused on incinerator proposals. The best pro forma studies of local large-scale recycling programs will draw upon data generated in local pilot programs, as well as data in similar cities or regions. One type of pilot-project concept that can help provide these data is an intensive recycling zone that is designed to test the feasibility of maximum recycling within a particular, representative part of a city or region. This concept is discussed later in this chapter.

EDF's second and most fundamental recommendation is that recycling and incineration should be allowed to compete for public and private funding on a "level playing field." Currently, a wide and generous variety of public measures to reduce financial risks and reward private investment are applicable to incineration projects. In contrast, funding opportunities for recycling are usually limited to whatever can be squeezed out of the annual state and local budget cycles. One recent survey of 18 states in the Northeast and Midwest found that planned state spending on incineration from 1989 to 1995 is eight to ten times higher than that for recycling. The same survey found that public financing instruments for incineration were much more supportive of private vendors than for recycling.[2]

In practice, this combination adds up to a fiscal policy that reverses the waste management hierarchy. Ambitious recycling goals can inspire citizens and local leaders, but are meaningless without the funding and political commitment that is needed to support innovation and success. Thus, this chapter concludes by describing a range of fiscal policies that can provide the foundation for recycling to reach its full potential.

SEATTLE'S RECYCLING POTENTIAL ASSESSMENT

In the early 1980s, the city of Seattle's two old and badly leaking municipal landfills were put on the EPA's National Priorities List and later closed. As a result of major groundwater contamination problems caused by the two landfills, cleanup, monitoring, and closure costs are estimated to be as high as $90 million. In 1986, the residential refuse collection rates of the Seattle Solid Waste Utility increased by 60 percent in order to develop a fund that is being used to remediate the two landfills.

Like many cities, in the mid-1980s Seattle began seriously to consider building a mass-burn incinerator, of 750 to 1,000 tpd capacity (initially, 1,800 tpd was proposed), to provide for future solid waste disposal. (Since the closure of its two landfills, Seattle has been relying primarily on the landfill belonging to surrounding King County. Under a contractual agreement between the city and the county, Seattle was legally obligated to define the terms of its future relationship with the county by October 1988.)

After the city had spent $1.2 million on consulting contracts for incinerator siting and design studies, including a $700,000 sole-source offering for one study, the Seattle City Council became concerned about the environmental effects and costs of incinerator ash disposal. To better understand its alternatives, in the fall of 1987, the city council authorized the Solid Waste Utility to conduct a feasibility and cost study of the potential for maximum recycling in Seattle, that is, to determine how much recycling the city could achieve if funds to be allocated to the proposed, full-sized incinerator were instead spent on recycling.

Conducted by Solid Waste Utility staff, with the assistance of two economists and a conservation planner for Seattle City Light, the city's public utility, and $70,000 worth of consulting time, the utility completed in five months the single best pro forma analysis of large-scale recycling to date. The study estimated that recycling levels of 50 to 78 percent are feasible in Seattle, and that, on a life-cycle, cost-per-ton basis, even very high rates of recycling would be less expensive than any level of incineration. After the study was concluded, the mayor and city council decided to table the incinerator proposal, and instead set the city on a path of achieving 40 percent recycling by 1992, 50 percent by 1993, and 60 percent by 1998. (Starting with a strong base in commercial recycling, Seattle is above 30 percent recycling already.)[3]

The analytical core of Seattle's Recycling Potential Assessment has two major parts. First, city staff developed an econometric model that forecast waste generation in the residential and commercial sectors (by economic subsector on the commercial side) and the response of private recyclers to projected increases in disposal fees; as disposal costs increased, the model predicted more recycling and less disposal demand. Second, the Solid Waste Utility staff developed a list of 21 individual recycling collection and processing modules, similar to those described in chapter 2. Different combinations of these modules were used to create six prospective recycling scenarios, which accounted for projected recycling levels of 50 to 78 percent.

For each recycling scenario, the utility staff estimated life-cycle cost of individual recycling modules, aggregated them for each scenario, and then combined recycling costs with projected costs for incineration or landfilling of residual solid waste, thereby producing a total system cost. The system cost also incorporated collection, transfer, and long-haul costs. In Seattle, the city's residential solid waste collection fees are set to pay for the total cost, to the city, of managing MSW. Hence, in the recycling assessment, the total system cost was plugged back into the econometric model in the form of increased collection rates and disposal fees, new disposal demand estimates were generated, and an equilibrium system cost per ton was calculated.

The main recycling program and cost elements of the study and Seattle's current recycling programs are described in tables 4.1 and 4.2, and in figure 4.1. Seattle's experience clearly shows that successful recycling depends on implementing a wide variety of different programs, each targeted to different parts of the waste stream. As figure 4.1 shows, curbside recycling is not the single most important part of Seattle's program; this role is assumed by commercial recycling. Seattle's current long-range recycling and solid waste disposal plans are described in its *Integrated Solid Waste Management Plan*, released in draft form in March of 1989, and approved by the city council in August.[4]

A FIRST-PHASE RECYCLING PROGRAM
FOR NEW YORK CITY

SETTING THE SCENE: A MASSIVE NEW INVESTMENT
IN WASTE DISPOSAL

For virtually all of its disposal needs, the New York City Department of Sanitation (DOS), along with most of New York City's private carters, relies on Staten Island's Fresh Kills landfill, the largest such facility in the world. Around the turn of the century, the DOS will have to find a substitute for Fresh Kills, which now accepts close to 25,000 tons of waste per day. In response to this epic planning and investment problem, since the late 1970s, DOS has proferred a plan to build five to eight mass-burn incinerators. Initially, one plant would be sited in each of New York's five boroughs, a political compromise achieved by the mayor's office in the early 1980s to ease potential interborough conflict over where the plants would be sited. If all eight plants are eventually built, they will burn about 17,850 tons of trash per day.[5]

The first incinerator in the DOS plan is a 3,000-ton-per-day plant proposed for construction at the Brooklyn Navy Yard (BNY). The proposed plant would be built by a subsidiary of Wheelabrator Technologies and would be privately owned and operated under contract with the city.

EDF has been concerned about the public health effects and enormous expense of the city's incineration plans since 1983 and, in 1984, undertook one of the first attempts to compare incineration and large-scale recycling

TABLE 4.1

Elements and Estimated System Costs of Recycling Scenarios Considered in Seattle's Recycling Potential Assessment (annual system performance projected for year 2000, expressed in 1988 dollars)

Recycling Scenario/Elements	ELEMENTS OF TOTAL SOLID WASTE SYSTEM COSTS ($1,000)				Total System Cost	Recycling Program Cost/Ton	System Cost/Ton
	Recycling Programs	Collection, Transfer, Transport	Landfill Tipping Fees	Admin., Closure, Haz. Waste			
Scenario 1 (45% recycling)	8,123	30,397	13,228	20,172	71,921	$31.73	$126.44
Backyard composting							
Voluntary yard-waste collection							
Voluntary separation of self-haul yard waste							
Expanded voluntary curbside collection							
Voluntary apartment source separation							
Self-haul dump/pick line							
Scenario 2 (55% recycling)	12,660	22,016	10,794	19,024	64,493	$40.47	$112.73
Backyard composting							
Voluntary yard-waste collection							
Voluntary separation of self-haul yard waste							
Expanded voluntary curbside source separation							
Voluntary apartment source separation							
Self-haul dump/pick line							
Voluntary expanded commercial source separation							
Processing of commercial waste							
Scenario 3 (74% recycling)	22,437	27,432	6,036	20,775	76,680	$53.30	$137.91
Existing curbside-collection program							
Mixed waste processing/recovery, followed by:							
DANO mixed waste composting							

148

Scenario 4 (61% recycling)	14,382	21,784	9,506	19,130	64,802	$41.45	$109.94
Backyard composting							
Mandatory yard-waste collection							
Mandatory separation of self-haul yard waste							
Mandatory commercial source separation							
Mandatory residential source separation (1993)							
Scenario 5 (78% recycling)	30,537	4,463	5,244	18,107	58,350	$68.83	$102.92
Backyard composting							
Mandatory yard-waste collection							
Mandatory separation of self-haul yard waste							
Mandatory commercial source separation with in-vessel food-waste composting (1990)							
Mandatory residential source separation (including food waste; 1996)							
In-vessel composting of food waste							
Material recovery line for dry residential trash							
Scenario 6 (64% recycling)	12,889	20,058	10,060	18,450	61,457	$35.41	$104.67
Waste reduction							
Backyard composting							
Voluntary separation of self-haul yard waste							
Voluntary expanded curbside source separation							
Voluntary food-waste separation/in-vessel composting							
Voluntary commercial source separation							
Processing/recovery of high-grade commercial loads							
Predisposal materials processing							

SOURCE: Seattle Solid Waste Utility, *Final Environmental Impact Statement: Waste Reduction, Recycling and Disposal Alternatives*, vol. 1 (July 1988), table I-1 and Appendix E.

Assumes total residential waste generation of 748,803 tons per year; after economically induced commercial recycling, 568,815 tons per year remain for disposal/recycling.

Tipping fee contractually set at county landfill, assumes "Cedar Hills low rate" of $35.77/ton by 2000.

TABLE 4.2

Comparative Solid Waste Management System Configuration and Costs, from Seattle's Recycling Potential Assessment (year 2000 performance levels, costs in 1988 dollars)*

Disposal Option/Combination	Annual System Cost (Million $)	System Cost/Ton ($)
Scenario 3 (74% recycling)	$141	$77.1
Scenario 2 (55% recycling) 1,000 tpd RDF plant	143	73.5
Scenario 1 (45% recycling)	130	72.6
Scenario 2 (55% recycling) 700 tpd mass-burn plant	127	69.1
Scenario 2 (55% recycling) 1,000 tpd mass-burn plant	125	68.5
Scenario 6 (64% recycling) 700 tpd mass-burn plant	123	67.4
Scenario 2 (55% recycling) 1,000 tpd mass-burn plant without energy recovery	123	67.1
Scenario 2 (55% recycling) 1,600 tpd mass-burn plant	121	66.0
Scenario 2 (55% recycling)	120	67.1
Scenario 4 (61% recycling) 700 tpd mass-burn plant	118	67.3
Scenario 6 (64% recycling)	114	65.4
Scenario 5 (78% recycling)	114	62.6

SOURCE: Seattle Solid Waste Utility, *Final Environmental Impact Statement Waste Reduction, Recycling and Disposal Alternatives,* vol. 1 (July 1988), table I-2.

* Same assumptions as table 4.1.

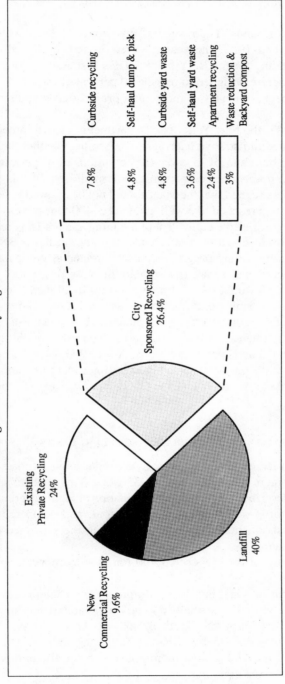

FIGURE 4.1

Seattle Solid Waste Management Plan: 60% Recycling and 40% Distant Landfill in 1998

7.8%	Curbside recycling
4.8%	Self-haul dump & pick
4.8%	Curbside yard waste
3.6%	Self-haul yard waste
2.4%	Apartment recycling
3%	Waste reduction & Backyard compost

City Sponsored Recycling 26.4%

Existing Private Recycling 24%

New Commercial Recycling 9.6%

Landfill 40%

SOURCE: Seattle Solid Waste Utility, *On the Road to Recovery: Seattle's Integrated Solid Waste Management Plan* (Seattle, WA: 1989).

on economic grounds. The results of this work, *To Burn or Not to Burn*, were released in 1985, the year the New York City Board of Estimate approved funding for the BNY plant. EDF's first study suggested that the costs of a program designed to recycle 40 percent of the city's waste would most likely be less than a five-incinerator project that would burn the same quantity.[6]

In July 1987, the New York State Department of Environmental Conservation began administrative hearings to determine whether the BNY facility should be built and, if so, what the conditions of its permits governing construction, operation, and air emissions should be. In this proceeding, EDF and others argued that the plant should not be allowed to burn garbage until the city had reached a recycling rate of 3,400 tons per day from DOS-sponsored programs, the equivalent of attaining about a 15 percent increase in recycling in close to three years. Under this approach, the BNY plant and the first-phase recycling program would be treated as comparable demonstration projects, and future investments in New York City's solid waste disposal projects would be conditioned on empirical data from each. EDF also proposed permit conditions for state-of-the-art controls and strict monitoring of air emissions from the plant, and stringent ash handling and disposal requirements, including a double-lined ash monofill to be identified before the plant is permitted. As of April 1990, New York City, which has responsibility for ash disposal, had still not identified an ash disposal site acceptable to the state, and the plant's permits were still being held in abeyance.

EDF's Estimates of First-phase Recycling Costs

In support of its recycling position, EDF produced an estimate of the costs of recycling more detailed than its 1985 work. This analysis, published in May 1988, described one possible combination of eight programs that could meet EDF's proposed 3,400-ton-per-day goal, and compared the per-ton life-cycle costs of these recycling programs to the projected costs of the BNY incinerator.[7]

The elements of the proposed 3,400-ton-per-day recycling program are:

- Nine multimaterial buy-back and processing centers. This buy-back-center network is essentially a large, fully capitalized expansion of the R2B2 operation in the South Bronx (see An Innovative Approach to Urban Recycling sidebar, Chapter 2), buying and marketing both conventional recyclables and more unusual materials, like plastics, window glass, and ceramics.

- Apartment and curbside collection programs limited to newspaper, beverage containers, and ferrous cans, and recovering 20 percent of the available supply of these materials in the residential waste stream. More materials would be added as the program is substantially expanded after 1991.
- A 500-ton-per-day-capacity material-recovery facility (MRF) to process and market materials collected in the residential apartment and curbside collection programs. The MRF would run on double shifts during the first years of the program, assuming additional facilities will be built as the city's recycling program expands.
- A moderately sized yard- and park-waste composting program utilizing city and commercial collection, with transfer to a composting site most likely located outside the city.
- A program to provide equipment, regulations, and incentives to cause greater recycling of commercial, institutional, and governmental wastepaper. Though a many-fold expansion over the DOS's current office-paper recycling programs, this program would target less than half the current office-paper waste stream.
- A program establishing contracts with existing processors of scrap metal, construction debris, and wood for the recycling of bulk items, like stoves and refrigerators, collected by DOS.
- Installation of material screening and crushing equipment at Fresh Kills to transform construction and demolition debris into material suitable for landfill cover or reuse as aggregate.
- A pilot program to test the feasibility of a New York City in-vessel anaerobic digestion facility for producing compost from yard waste, food waste, or mixed solid waste.
- An experimental intensive recycling zone, designed to test the full potential of maximum recycling in New York City.
- A network of 59 voluntary drop-off centers—one in each community district—in public facilities such as government office buildings, subway stations and schools, or locations that experience heavy public use, like supermarket parking lots.
- An additional annual budget of $5 million for publicity, market development, and consulting contracts.

Clearly, a program intending to recover 3,400 tons per day from New York City's waste stream could take many different shapes. The program set out by EDF was designed with several specific intentions, but was not intended to serve as a model for the *only* way to go about recycling in New York. Key considerations in EDF's design include the following:

- With adequate funding and political commitment on the part of the city, the projected recycling goals could easily be reached in three years. This is comparable to the time it would take to finance and construct the proposed incinerator once permitted, and significantly faster than starting an incinerator from scratch. Many of the programs in the package could be implemented much more quickly.

- The program is broadly based: It targets a wide range of materials and relies on private and nonprofit recycling expertise as well as city collection. This strategy avoids dependence on a small number of secondary-materials markets and, at the same time, takes advantage of the extensive private-sector recycling and processing capacity already in place in New York City. By including many segments of the waste stream, the program holds the capacity for recycling well over 50 percent of the entire waste stream when fully implemented.

- The program builds on existing DOS, nonprofit, and private recycling programs. Whenever possible, data from current New York City recycling programs are used to extrapolate future costs.

- The program attempts to balance the use of incentives and disincentives to promote recycling. For example, rather than counting on higher tipping fees alone to promote commercial office-paper recycling, under this program, the city also provides equipment and training for companies interested in source separation. For landscape gardeners willing to bring yard waste to city compost transfer stations, the program offers a discount in tipping fees.

SUMMARY OF RESULTS FOR NEW YORK CITY

In assembling its analysis, EDF found that the costs of different types of urban recycling programs vary dramatically. In combination, the programs analyzed by EDF are estimated to cost $18 per ton, 60 percent less than $45 per ton estimated for the most realistic incinerator scenario (see tables 4.3 and 4.4). These are present-value, life-cycle costs expressed in 1988 dollars and levelized in real terms. EDF also evaluated recycling costs under adverse conditions, including a 50 percent decline in average market prices that corresponds to a complete collapse of newsprint and green-glass prices, and a substantial softening in other markets, and no savings in conventional garbage collection as a result of recycling waste diversion. In these cases, the package of recycling programs costs 22 percent and 33 percent less than incineration, respectively.

The most expensive program is curbside collection, primarily because of

TABLE 4.3
Summary of Recycling Program Costs
(in levelized, real 1988 dollars)

Program Component	Tons/Day Recovered	Cost Per Ton		
		Baseline	No Savings in Collection Costs	50% Price Collapse
Curbside	418	$44	$92	$44
Apartments	418	31	78	31
Buy-back centers	506	17	26	38
MRF[a]	—	−17	−17	−1
Composting	167	25	25	25
Commercial	520	6	6	6
Const./demo.	539	−7	−7	−7
Institutional	364	6	6	6
DOS bulk	468	28	28	28
Promotion[b]	—	5	5	5
Complete package	3400	$18	$31	$25

SOURCE: EDF, *A Comparative Economic Analysis of a 3,400-ton-per-day Recycling Program for New York City and the Proposed Brooklyn Navy Yard Resource Recovery Facility* (New York: EDF, 1988), p. 7.

[a] The material recovery facility (MRF) is designed to process 835 tons per day from the apartment and curbside collection programs. Revenues from the sales of these materials are enough to pay the costs of the MRF and contribute $17 per ton toward collection costs.
[b] Reflects $5 million in additional annual expenses toward consulting contracts, market development, planning and promotion, applied to the tonnage recovered by all programs in sum.

high labor costs. However, when sales of materials processed by the MRF are factored in, curbside collection is significantly less expensive than the incinerator, even under the most favorable assumptions about incineration electricity revenues. As table 4.3 suggests, apartment collection offers a 30 percent improvement in efficiency over curbside collection. Because materials accumulate in larger quantities, they can be handled by containerized or semi-automated collection vehicle systems that require fewer stops and less manual collection effort.

The different incineration cost scenarios in table 4.4 depend on assumptions about the price of electricity between the present and 1995, and the tax-exempt status of the plant's financing. The most realistic estimate of the 1988 levelized (in real terms) life-cycle cost for the incinerator is the middle scenario, or about $45 per ton.

TABLE 4.4

Disposal Cost Per Ton for Proposed Brooklyn Navy Yard Incinerator (in levelized, real 1988 dollars)

High energy price assumptions	$37.6
Realistic energy prices	44.77
Realistic energy, no tax-exempt finance	55.30

SOURCE: EDF, *A Comparative Economic Analysis of a 3,400-ton-per-day Recycling Program for New York City and the Proposed Brooklyn Navy Yard Resource Recovery Facility* (New York: EDF, 1988), p. 8.

DEALING WITH UNCERTAINTY: ASSUMPTIONS FAVORABLE TO INCINERATION

In planning for even a modest recycling program in a city the size of New York, it is difficult to predict the cost of several important variables with complete certainty. Whenever data were uncertain, EDF's analysis applied figures on the high side, making recycling appear more expensive.

For example, the proposed Brooklyn Navy Yard (BNY) incinerator is to be sited on 13 acres of city-owned land; the lost opportunity for employing this land in some other productive capacity represents a major, real cost to the city that is not reflected in the incinerator tipping fee. On the other hand, industrial real estate required for all major processing, transfer, and buy-back recycling operations described in EDF's study is assumed to be purchased on the private market. The assumed purchase of land for the programs outlined in EDF's analysis adds $6.4 million in additional capital costs to the recycling program.

Likewise, the extensive costs of consulting contracts and planning and administering the city's incinerator program are not reflected in the tipping fee projected for the BNY facility. In contrast, 44 city administrative positions are factored into cost estimates for specific recycling programs, in addition to the $5 million annually programmed for promotion, administration, market development, and other expenses.

Also not reflected in the projected cost of the incinerator are the $47 million direct subsidy granted the plant by the state of New York under the Environmental Quality Bond Act (EQBA), and the legislatively mandated floor price for electricity sales. These subsidies are significant; the EQBA grant alone would pay over half the capital costs of the recycling program.

A NONINCINERATION SOLID WASTE MANAGEMENT PLAN FOR THE TOWN OF NORTH HEMPSTEAD, LONG ISLAND, NEW YORK

Like many communities in the Northeast, North Hempstead, Long Island, is facing the imminent closure of its landfill. In addition, under New York State's Long Island Landfill Law (ECL Section 27-0704), the ten towns of Suffolk County, Long Island, must stop landfilling unprocessed municipal waste by 1990 (i.e., they can only landfill residuals from incineration and recycling operations). The impetus behind this law is that Suffolk County sits above a single aquifer, from which it draws all of its drinking water, that is in danger of contamination from landfills and other industrial sources.

In May 1988, the North Hempstead Solid Waste Management Authority announced that it was awarding a contract to Babcock and Wilcox Company and Ebasco Constructors, to build a 990 tpd incinerator. (The town produces about 923 tons of solid waste per day, of which about 15 percent is construction and demolition debris.) The Authority's announcement fulfills a commitment to incineration first announced in 1985, when a 1,000 tpd plant was recommended.

At the same time the authority was announcing its incinerator proposal, two citizens groups, the Coalition to Save Hempstead Harbor and the Residents for a More Beautiful Port Washington, released a 231-page alternative plan. Like the other studies described in this chapter, the North Hempstead plan incorporates waste composition estimates, life-cycle cost comparisons, detailed estimates of recycling costs and sensitivity analyses of the effects of secondary-materials market price fluctuations and shifts in regular garbage collection costs.[8]

In summary, the combination of two composting facilities, commercial recycling, construction and demolition debris recycling, and aggressive residential source separation is projected to handle 71 percent of the community's waste. The capital costs of the recycling alternative, including interest during construction and bond underwriting fees, were estimated at $93 million, compared to total costs of the Authority's proposed incineration plan and unambitious recycling program of $204 million. On a life-cycle, per-ton basis, the total waste management system cost of the alternative recycling program is estimated at $95 per ton, compared to $122 per ton for system costs when incineration is included.

The key elements of the proposed recycling plan, differences in landfill requirements between the two proposals, and major cost factors are outlined in table 4.5.

TABLE 4.5
Mass-balance Comparison of Solid Waste Management Plans for North Hempstead, NY

Nonincineration Solid Waste Management and Recycling Plan:

	Daily Collection (input) Tons/Day	Mass Reduction Tons/Day[a]	Material Returned to Market Tons/Day	Net Residual to Landfill Tons/Day	Percent Recycled/ Composted	Percent Landfilled
Source-separated Recyclables:						
Computer paper	13	—	12	1	92	8
Newsprint	63	—	60	3	95	5
Office paper	26	—	25	1	96	4
Corrugated	38	—	36	2	95	5
Mixed paper	67	—	64	3	96	4
Glass	38	—	35	1	92	3
Aluminum	2	—	2	—	100	0
Steel	16	—	15	1	94	6
PET/HDPE	3	—	3	—	100	0
Wood	8	1	6	1	88	13
Yard waste	117	42	63[b]	12	90	10
Food waste	60	22	32[b]	6	90	10
Processed Residuals:						
Paper	106	32	48[c]	26	75	25
Glass	30	—	23[d]	7	77	23
Metal	6	—	4	2	67	33
Plastic	51	—	—	51	0	100
Textiles	5	—	—	5	0	100
Rubber	1	—	—	1	0	100

Wood	2	—	1[c]	1	50	50
Food/yard waste	59	18	26[c]	15	75	25
Construction and Demolition Debris:						
Wood	74	6	23[c]	45	39	61
Masonry	63	—	25	38	40	60
Dirt/sand/clay	51	—	20	31	39	61
Metals	24	—	10	14	42	58
TOTALS	923	121	533	267	71	29

North Hempstead Solid Waste Management Authority Plan:

	Daily Collection (input) Tons/Day	Mass Reduction Tons/Day[a]	Material Returned to Market Tons/Day	Net Residual to Landfill Tons/Day	Percent Recycled/ Composted	Percent Landfilled
Mass-burn incineration	459	344	—	115	n/a	25
Source-sep. recyclables	158	—	150	8[e]	95	5
Yard waste/compost	94	33	56	5	95	5
Construction and demolition debris	212	—	—	212	0	100
TOTALS	923	377	206	340	63	37

SOURCE: Coalition to Save Hempstead Harbor et al., *A Non-Incineration Solid Waste Management and Recycling Plan for the Town of North Hempstead, NY* (May 1988), table 3, figures 1, 2.

[a] Mass reduction as a result of composting or mass-burn combustion (solids transformed to gases).
[b] Marketed as Grade 1 compost.
[c] Marketed as Grade 2 compost (separate process from b).
[d] Marketed as aggregate for use in asphalt.
[e] Process residuals split proportionally between recyclables and yard waste.

INTENSIVE RECYCLING ZONES

In small towns, it may be possible to implement recycling programs throughout the entire community at once and make program adjustments (e.g., adding materials) as time passes. It may also be relatively easy to extrapolate costs from a number of existing suburban curbside collection programs to the program under design. In many areas, however, and especially large cities, the maximum, long-term potential of recycling is, to some extent, unknown, even as decisions are being made that would irrevocably commit large fractions of the waste stream to incineration. On paper, variables that are uncertain, such as participation rates, market prices, and the like, can be incorporated into cost comparisons of recycling and incineration. However, cities can do more than this. Instead of waiting years for operational data from large-scale recycling projects to come in, municipalities can undertake experiments over the near term to test empirically the potential for high levels of recycling.[9]

EDF, working with the Citizens Advisory Committee on Manhattan Resource Recovery and the Environment, and with the support of (former Borough President) Mayor David Dinkins, has proposed such an experiment in New York City: an intensive recycling zone. The basic purpose of the intensive recycling zone would be to allow the city to experiment, in a concentrated geographic area, with different source-separation, collection, processing, marketing, and financing strategies designed to achieve the highest feasible levels of solid waste recycling in the most cost-effective and socially acceptable manner. Though the EDF proposal has initially been suggested for part of Manhattan's Upper East Side and part of East Harlem, a number of zones could be implemented in different areas of the city seeking to include a mix of housing and business types, social strata, and so on. DOS has now proposed to site at least one zone in each borough. Some of the details of this conceptual proposal are described below. You may, of course, find ways of improving upon the concept and adapting it to your community.

EDUCATION AND OUTREACH

The intensive recycling zone would be presented to citizens and institutions as an experimental project designed to test the potential of intensive recycling in New York City. A concentrated effort would be made to inform the public of the benefits of recycling and why the city is implementing the zone. Individual buildings, block associations, and community groups would be brought into the education process. The project would also be intended to make citizens aware of the distinct, personal changes in behavior that will be required if New York is successfully to attempt large-scale recycling. This would include opportunities for consumer waste reduction and voluntary alterations in consumption patterns, resulting in positive changes in waste composition.

MATERIALS AND COLLECTION SCHEMES

The materials collected in the intensive recycling zone would include glass, plastics, newsprint, metal cans, magazines, and corrugated cardboard identified for eventual DOS collection in its *White Paper*, the primary strategy document for New York City's recycling program. However, these would not be phased in one by one, as is the current strategy, but would all be collected in the zone from the beginning of the project. In addition, where plausible current or future markets exist, other materials will also be collected, such as residential mixed paper, additional plastics, batteries, food waste, and so on. Food waste could be handled using sealable, wax-coated paper bags distributed to households, for example.

The goals of the collection system would be to minimize net increases in collection costs attributable to recycling, and to maximize reduction of the nonrecycled fraction of trash. In addition, the collection system(s) would be devised to make complicated separation of materials by individual households unnecessary. Materials could be sorted into five categories, for example, containers, newsprint, other paper, food waste, and remaining garbage. Or, the newsprint/other paper categories could be combined and sorted out by later processing. Another variation would be to have all dry recyclables collected commingled, as is the case in the south half of Seattle. Testing these different options against each other might, in fact, be an objective of the intensive recycling zone.

Consistent with the notion of blending high levels of recyclables collection with existing levels of DOS service, a hypothetical one-week collection schedule on a given route might look like this:

	Status Quo Collection System	*Intensive Recycling Collection System*
Day 1	Trash	Food waste*/trash
Day 2	Trash	Food waste/recyclable paper
Day 3	Trash/recyclables	Recyclable containers/trash
Day 4	Trash	Food waste/recyclable paper

* Food waste would include compostible food-contaminated paper.

Such a schedule would, of course, be partially determined by waste composition and participation rates. Since data on these variables may not be completely available at the start of the project or during planning phases, a certain amount of flexibility would have to be built into the initial collection scheme(s). For example, multiple-container recycling trucks could be built with variable-sized bins. In designing the recycling zone, the potential of using DOS packer trucks dedicated to specific materials would be explored, since all of the categories listed above except for containers are compactible.

Since city residents do not pay separately for solid waste pickup, they have no direct economic signals of the costs of collection, processing, and disposal. The recycling zone would, therefore, experiment with financial incentives for residents or entire buildings as a means of facilitating recycling.

Processing

To reduce the costs associated with requiring recycling trucks to drive to multiple locations to unload materials, the project would be served by a nearby processing center/transfer station, located in East Harlem or the South Bronx. Unprocessed materials transferred out of the area would include the remaining garbage fraction and possibly the bagged food waste, which might be composted at the Fresh Kills landfill or at a site outside the city. At the outset, processing services for the zone could also be provided under contract with private transfer stations.

The planning process for the intensive recycling zone would seriously consider the use of privately financed processing facilities and would also consider locating an R2B2-type buy-back center in East Harlem. Such a center would provide an early empirical test of the merits of buy-back versus curbside collection in inner-city neighborhoods.

Planning and Prognosis

As of January 1990, the intensive recycling zone concept has generally been well-received by DOS, and the city council and Board of Estimate have allocated $225,000 for initial planning and a pilot test of the project in one or more neighborhoods. Ongoing planning by DOS is being assisted by EDF, officials from other agencies, and other technical experts and community activists. Waste reduction programs are also being incorporated into planning for the project.

As conceived to date, the project would only apply to DOS-collected material. The planning process might also explore the possibility of creating a contiguous private-sector recycling zone that would require, among other things, a very strong education and training effort on the part of the city to get businesses to source separate in order to test the maximum feasible level of recycling commercial sector wastes.

LEVELING THE PLAYING FIELD

Though recycling may be less expensive than incineration, ample funding is still necessary to make large-scale recycling work. Currently, however, the fiscal policy of most states and cities proposing incinerators is to commit hundreds of millions of guaranteed dollars to incineration projects—often funded by independent bonding authorities—and, at the same time, require that recycling eke out a much smaller budgetary allotment in competition with other government services.

This imbalance must be rectified if recycling is to grow to its full potential. That is, recycling, landfilling, and incineration must be funded on a level playing field. Only under these conditions will spending on solid waste management reflect the waste management hierarchy. Only with equitable access to public funds will the economic advantages of recycling take effect in the marketplace, attracting private-sector financing to major recycling program elements.

The remainder of this section describes the extensive financial advantages that incineration now enjoys over recycling, and means of correcting this imbalance.

CURRENT IMBALANCES IN FISCAL POLICY FOR SOLID WASTE MANAGEMENT

The financial mainstays of incineration are public expenditures and risk-minimization measures designed to make massive private investments attractive and profitable. For example, in New York City, a private bond issue of at least $562 million will be necessary to construct the proposed BNY incinerator. To ensure that these bonds will be paid off, the firm that constructs and operates the plant is counting on a number of public subsidies and risk-reduction measures. To begin with, the plant will receive a guaranteed flow of waste that is delivered free of certain specified materials, such as construction and demolition debris and hazardous waste. The incinerator vendor will also receive a $47 million state grant through the 1972 New York State EQBA, a guaranteed market for energy produced by the facility, free access to ash disposal services provided by DOS, contract clauses that pass certain unexpected costs to the city, and, most important, a substantial monthly service charge, or tipping fee, for disposing of waste.[10] Once the BNY plant comes on-line, the tipping fee will be nondiscretionary and outside the annual budgetary allocation process.

Nothing approaching the extent and value of these risk-reducing measures are available to private or nonprofit recyclers in New York City. Instead, the nuts and bolts of New York City's recycling program— sanitation workers, outreach materials, educational staff, recycling trucks, and the like—are discretionary items, which must be funded on an annual budgetary cycle, along with education, police, fire, housing, welfare, and other city programs.

The fiscal policies of New York State have reinforced this pattern. With the enactment of the 1972 EQBA, New York State authorized grants of some $215 million for incinerators across the state. The New York Department of Environmental Conservation has identified proposals for incinerators that would have a combined capacity in excess of 40,000 tons per day, or 80 percent of the waste stream. For recycling projects, the original 1972 EQBA set aside $1 million, and was amended in 1980 to provide an additional $5 million. The Solid Waste Management Act of 1988 allocated another $6 million to be spent on capital projects, administered through the EQBA structure, $13.5 million essentially for local planning grants, $3 million in grants and loans to industries that use recovered materials, and $3.5 million for state staff, distributed among various agencies.[11] Because of inflation, the disparity between state funds available for recycling and incineration is even greater than it nominally appears. This situation is typical of states in the Northeast and in many other areas of the nation.

In practice, the funding of a solid waste management strategy committed to large-scale recycling and the efficient use of public funds could be very different from the financial imbalance that currently exists in New York and around the nation. New possibilities for providing recycling with the financial base it deserves are described in the following sections.

COMPREHENSIVE REGULATIONS TO PROTECT PUBLIC HEALTH

A cost-effective solid waste strategy that encompasses a strong commitment to recycling has one very important prerequisite: Environmental regulation of landfills, incinerators, and recycling programs must be comprehensive and sufficiently stringent to protect public health and the environment. In a poorly regulated solid waste management system, the economic and environmental costs of, for example, air pollution and groundwater contamination are borne by the public, a situation common across the United States, and particularly in the South and Midwest. More stringent regulations will increase the likelihood that financial expenditures required to avoid damage to public health and the environment (e.g., air pollution control equipment, landfill liners, leachate collection and treatment facilities) are included—or internalized—in the actual cost of each waste management facility. The requirements of such regulations, as they apply to incinerators, are discussed in Part II. EDF and others have extensively commented on regulatory requirements for landfills elsewhere.[12]

UNEARTHING HIDDEN SUBSIDIES

Incinerator and landfill tipping fees are often extensively subsidized, through electricity contracts set above market rates, property tax abatements, donations of public land, and so on.[13] In any comparison of overall expenditures on recycling and incineration, these hidden costs must be taken into account. Uncovering these subsidies and computing their value may make an evaluation of a proposed incinerator more complicated and technical. However, such subsidies play an important role in making incineration appear economically viable, and should be mentioned in even the most basic cost comparisons.

DIRECT COMPETITION FOR FUNDING

The most direct means of allowing market forces a greater role in the selection of solid waste alternatives would be for a municipality to revise the rules that guide the selection of solid waste management facilities to allow for direct competition between landfilling, recycling, and incineration. Under this approach, for example, instead of issuing a request for proposals (RFP) for a 3,000-tpd incinerator and only accepting bids from incinerator vendors, a municipality would ask for proposals to provide 3,000 tpd of waste management capacity. Recyclers would be allowed to bid on single- or multiple-material streams, and the contract would go to the lowest responsible bidder. If delivery of segregated materials by the municipality was necessary, costs of doing so would have to be factored into the bid-selection equation. In this case, an accurate measurement of savings in the conventional waste collection system due to recycling would be very important. If refuse collection is already handled through private contracts, the situation would perhaps be less complicated.

The purpose of allowing consortia of recyclers to compete with incinerator vendors for municipal waste materials and tipping fees is to support private financing arrangements between recyclers and investment banks, following closely along the lines of financing models that have been arranged to support incinerators. Under this model, repayment of revenue bonds for large (e.g., 1,000 tpd) processing complexes would be guaranteed by a municipal tipping fee established through a competitive bidding process. Revenue from the sales of materials would be split between the participants on a formula basis.

Crediting Recycling with Avoided Disposal Costs

Other ways can directly credit recycling for avoiding the costs of other forms of waste disposal. For example, Assembly Bill 2020 (AB 2020), California's modified container deposit law, seeks to internalize the cost of disposal in the scrap value of plastics and glass containers. In essence, AB 2020 requires beverage distributors that sell their products in glass or plastic containers to subsidize the price of glass cullet and scrap plastic at a level that reflects the costs of otherwise disposing of the material. The amount of this subsidy is calculated by the state, and provides for a reasonable profit in each step of the recycling collection, processing, and remanufacture cycle. These payments are passed on to consumers by the beverage industry, and amount to about four cents per container on average.[14]

Under Rhode Island's mandatory recycling law, if a private firm is willing to guarantee that it will accept all available supplies of a given material from in-state recycling programs for a fee equal to or less than one-quarter of the tipping fee at the state's Central Landfill, the state will add that material to its list of mandatory recyclables and ban it from landfill disposal. (The shortcomings of this novel approach should be apparent: Recycling is not given full credit for avoiding landfill disposal costs, and there is no mechanism for accounting for recycling collection costs.)

If unable or unwilling to allow recycling and incineration to compete head-to-head for the same funds (i.e., a city tipping fee), a state could instead require that no funds be spent on incineration until the marginal cost of recycling—the incremental cost of recycling the next ton of materials—was equal to or greater than the average cost per ton of operating an incinerator of a given size. This principal is akin to what is commonly accepted in electric utility regulation as "least cost planning." In many states, before an electric utility is allowed to begin construction of a new power plant, it must show, before the state regulatory agency, that it has exhausted the possibilities of less expensive means of generating electricity, such as conservation, alternative sources, and demand management. Under the New York State Solid Waste Management Act of 1988, by 1992, municipalities in the state must have programs to collect for recycling all materials for which there are economic markets. In the law, economic markets are defined to exist when the net cost of collecting, processing, and selling secondary materials is less than the cost of otherwise disposing of them.[15]

DEDICATED FUNDING TIED TO PROGRAM GOALS

Though the ambitious—50 percent—recycling goals of big cities like Philadelphia and Los Angeles are now an inspiration, in a few years they will become an embarrassment if sufficient funds are not dedicated to make recycling programs work. An alternative to the annual recycling budget competition, which occurs in most cities, is the approach taken in Seattle. That city set high recycling goals based on economic and feasibility studies, and then devised fiscal policies to guarantee a relatively steady, sufficient flow of funds to meet these recycling goals.

This practice can work at the state level as well. Means of providing recycling with a dedicated source of funding include landfill tipping fee surcharges (used in Connecticut, New Jersey, Illinois, and Iowa), general obligation bonds (used in Massachusetts and Michigan, proposed in New York), Exxon overcharge and stripper-well litigation payments (a generally tapped-out source used in New York and elsewhere), earmarked sales tax receipts (Florida), reclaimed bottle deposits (California, proposed in New York), and taxes on difficult-to-recycle packaging (proposed in several states but not passed).[16]

NOTES

1. A variety of studies have been conducted on landfill, recycling, and incineration costs. See: Dresser Camp and McKee, Inc., *North Central Florida Comprehensive Solid Waste Management Master Plan.* (Tampa, FL: CDM, December 1987). This is a detailed study recommending a regional landfill and recycling program and advising against incineration because of high costs and poor local markets for steam or electricity; A Pennsylvania study of curbside

recycling demonstrated that revenue and disposal cost savings exceeded program costs by an average of $27 per ton of recycled material. Carl Hursh, "Curbside Recycling in Pennsylvania," *Resource Recycling*, November/December, 1986, pp. 16–18. Two brief analyses of waste collection, processing, and disposal costs for Minneapolis and Saint Paul found recycling less expensive than alternatives. According to consultant John Madole, costs per ton are approximately $30 for recycling, $65 for yard-waste composting, $85 for current landfilling, $90–$110 for future incineration, and $95–$110 for future landfilling. In Cynthia Pollock, *Mining Urban Wastes; The Potential for Recycling*. (Washington, DC: Worldwatch Institute, 1987 paper no. 76), p. 29. A Minnesota citizens' organization estimated the cost of recycling to be approximately $35 per ton and current landfilling $80 per ton. Citizens League, *The New Weigh to Recycle* (Minneapolis: Citizens League, 1987); The actual benefits of recycling in avoiding landfill costs may be greater than just the per-ton tipping fees comparisons would indicate. Landfills are governed by volume, not weight, and one unpublished study by BFI in San Jose, California, found that many recyclables take up more space in landfills than the same tonnage of mixed solid waste. In Hamburg, New York, a 25 percent recycling rate produced a 34 percent reduction in landfill volume needs. Frank Mulvey, "A Look at Recycling Programs Here and There," *Waste Age*, Waste-to-Energy Recycling Annual 1987, pp. 29–39; California Energy Commission, *Economics of Curbside Recycling in San Jose* (Sacramento, CA: CEC, 1987).

2. Northeast-Midwest Institute, "A Bad Burn; States Are Depending on Incineration Instead of Recycling," *Northeast-Midwest Economic Review*, September 5, 1989, pp. 9–11. Available from NMI, 218 D Street, SE, Washington, DC 20003.

3. Lorie Parker, "Seattle's Road to Recovery," *BioCycle*, June 1989, pp. 28–31.

4. Seattle Solid Waste Utility, *On the Road to Recovery; Seattle's Integrated Solid Waste Management Plan* (1989). Available from the Seattle Solid Waste Utility, 710 Second Avenue, Suite 505, Seattle, Washington 98104; Seattle Solid Waste Utility, *Final Environmental Impact Statement; Waste Reduction and Disposal Alternatives*, vols. I & II, (Seattle: Seattle Solid Waste Utility, 1988).

5. New York City Department of Sanitation, *The Waste Disposal Problem in New York City: A Proposal for Action*, vol. 1 (New York: DOS, April 1984), 6 vols.

6. Environmental Defense Fund, *To Burn or Not to Burn: The Economic Advantages of Recycling Over Garbage Incineration for New York City* (New York: EDF, 1985).

7. John Ruston and Daniel Kirshner, *A Comparative Economic Analysis of a 3,400 Ton Per Day Recycling Program for New York City and the Proposed Brooklyn Navy Yard Resource Recovery Facility* (1988). Available from EDF, 257 Park Avenue South, New York, NY 10010. $10.

8. Coalition to Save Hempstead Harbor et al, *A Non-Incineration Solid Waste Management and Recycling Plan for the Town of North Hempstead, New York* (1988). Available from Steve Latham, Twomey, Latham, Shea and Kelley, 33

W. Second Street, P.O. Box 398, Riverhead, NY 11901. Additional work to upgrade the plan is being conducted by Jeffery Morris at the Sound Resource Management Group and Karen Shapiro at the Tellus Institute. See chapter 2, note 27.

9. An intensive recycling experiment for a less-urban area was conducted by the Center for the Biology of Natural Systems, who is preparing for a similar project in Buffalo, New York. The New York project is proposed to be larger and more permanent; Barry Commoner et al., *Development and Pilot Test of an Intensive Municipal Solid Waste Recycling System for the Town of East Hampton.* Flushing, NY: Center for the Biology of Natural Systems, Queens College, CUNY, 1987).

10. James Tripp and John Ruston, "A State Framework for Solid Waste Management," New York State Bar Association, *Environmental Law Section Journal,* March 1989, pp. 9–15 and note 11; See also: James G. Abert, ed., *Resource Recovery Guide* (New York City: van Nostrand Reinhold, 1983); Stuart H. Russell, *Resource Recovery Economics: Methods for Feasibility Analysis* (New York City: Marcel Dekker, Inc., 1982).

11. Tripp and Ruston, "A State Framework for Solid Waste Management," pp. 9–15.

12. See, for example, "Comments of the Environmental Defense Fund on the Solid Waste Disposal Facility Criteria," submitted on November 30, 1988, to EPA Docket no. F-88-CMLP-FFFFF.

13. See, for example: Robin Kordik, "Environmental Allowance; Refining Traditional Cost-Benefit Analysis Applied to Evaluation of Waste Reduction and Recycling Programs," mimeographed (Olympia: Washington State Department of Ecology, Solid and Hazardous Waste Program, 1987); Oregon Department of Environmental Quality, *An Evaluation of the True Costs of Sanitary Landfills for the Disposal of Municipal Solid Waste in the Portland Metropolitan Area* (Portland: DEQE [prepared by ECO Northwest], 1986); Mark P. Berkman and Frederick C. Dunbar, "The Underpricing of Landfills" (White Plains, NY: National Economic Research Associates, 1987). Berkman and Dunbar point out that, although landfill tipping fees are on the rise, they still typically understate the true (marginal) costs of landfilling. When landfills reach capacity, they must be replaced with new landfills or other means of disposal, which are virtually always more expensive. Every load of garbage hastens the day when new expenditures will have to be made; thus, there is a depletion cost associated with the use of current landfills that is often not taken into account. If land were not used to bury garbage, it could be applied to other uses. The foregone revenue from these (potentially) higher uses is the opportunity cost of landfilling. Finally, the environmental costs of landfills, such as the nuisance to the surrounding community or the expense of cleaning up contaminated groundwater, are usually not reflected in the tipping fee. In some cases, tipping fees do not even cover the annual costs of running the landfill.

14. For information on AB 2020, write AB 2020, Division of Recycling, Department of Conservation, 819 19th Street, Sacramento, CA 95814.
15. Chapter 70, The Solid Waste Management Act of 1988, amending the General Municipal Law Section 120aa.
16. Jim Glenn, "Financing Recycling Programs," *BioCycle*, November 1989, pp. 28–31.

PART II

Health and Environmental Risks of MSW Incineration and Their Control

O NE OF THE CENTRAL MESSAGES of Part I is that rational waste management is, in essence, materials management. It begins with a thorough understanding of waste composition. Source-based measures to reduce the amount and toxicity of materials entering the waste stream represent the most efficient means of waste management. Restricting the use of heavy metal colorants in manufacturing consumer plastics is one such measure. Next, every opportunity to maximize segregation of the waste stream into its various components should be utilized. Developing methods include household-based materials separation programs supported by curbside collection and mixed-waste processing technologies. Waste segregation is a necessary prerequisite in order to direct individual materials to the management methods most appropriate for them.

Recycling and recovery of such materials can yield substantial reductions in energy and raw-materials requirements and wastes associated with manufacturing, and should be the options of first resort. Adoption of measures to stabilize and expand markets for such recovered materials will be critical to their success. With respect to waste management, large-scale separation and recycling can provide the dual benefit of reducing the amount of waste that must be managed and increasing the safety of landfilling or incineration, by removing materials that should not be buried or burned.

171

THE ROLE OF INCINERATION IN MSW MANAGEMENT

Given these principles of a rational waste management system, what is an appropriate role for municipal solid waste (MSW) incineration?

It is critical to recognize the limitations, as well as the advantages, of incineration. Incineration is not a waste disposal method but rather a waste processing technology. It provides the important benefit of reducing the amount, particularly the volume, of waste requiring disposal, but can create air pollution concerns and leaves behind its own substantial burden of toxic ash residues that must be managed and disposed of properly. Decisions to employ incineration—including both the scale of its use and the particular form of incineration technology used—must be preceded by a thorough evaluation of all other options for reducing the volume and toxicity of MSW, including source reduction, separation, and recycling.

The interaction of incineration with these other strategies for waste management is of particular concern. Indiscriminate use of incineration may severely limit other options for waste management. Without careful advanced planning, present or future opportunities to reduce, recycle, or recover components of MSW—management options that are rapidly gaining in both political and economic acceptance—may directly conflict with the contractual arrangements and operating requirements of incinerators that were sized or designed without sufficiently accounting for such opportunities.

Many existing incinerator contracts require that a municipality or region guarantee a minimum tonnage of waste for delivery to the incinerator, often for the several decades over which it will operate. Clearly, incentives to reduce the amount of waste generated through changes in consumption patterns or to implement more aggressive recycling programs may be compromised or entirely eliminated by such long-term contractual obligations.

In addition, alteration of the waste input to an incinerator through recycling or other means can directly affect the efficiency, safety, and even the economy of incineration. Most mass-burn incinerators have restricted operating ranges that delineate minimum waste quantities and calorific values under which the incinerator will operate optimally. Failure to meet these waste feed requirements can result in less efficient combustion and a greater likelihood of generating products of incomplete combustion, such as dioxins. Alternatively, supplemental fuel, such as oil or gas, may be required to maintain proper combustion, which would reduce net energy recovery and significantly affect a facility's operating costs.

For all of these reasons, as well as the risk considerations presented below, whenever incineration is employed, it should be viewed as only one component in an integrated MSW management system. This view is not consistent with current or planned practices in many municipalities. In general, solid waste managers have yet to consider recycling a serious tool of waste management. Rather, the emphasis has been on attempting to implement mass-burn incineration as a wholesale alternative to landfilling. Indeed, hundreds of municipalities are planning or building incinerators with capacities that approach or exceed the size of the entire local waste stream.

Viewing incineration as one part of an integrated waste management system requires planners and managers to step back from the crisis mentality that now dictates many management decisions to consider actions toward waste and risk reduction that can be taken at each step, beginning with materials production and use, and continuing through discard, collection, recycling and recovery, processing, and ultimate disposal.

THE NEED FOR A COMPREHENSIVE ASSESSMENT OF RISKS FROM MSW INCINERATION

The major challenge in MSW management today is how to resolve issues of risk—risk to the environment and public health—and, at the same time, deal effectively and expeditiously with MSW. A major impediment to this resolution has been a failure to comprehensively assess risks associated with various options, particularly with incineration as a method of waste processing.

Although increasingly adopted or proposed as the method of choice for dealing with MSW, incineration is widely perceived as risky and remains highly controversial. Indeed, a number of legitimate risk issues—not the apparent advantages of incineration as a tool for waste management—have emerged as the central focus of the debate concerning this technology. Health and environmental risks, as well as the extraordinary expense, of properly managing the toxic by-products of incineration should give rise to caution in evaluating the utility of indiscriminate (or mass-burn) incineration as a means of waste management.

Despite the clear perception that incineration poses health risks, however, the major focus of the risk debate is only beginning to encompass the full range of such risks. Public and regulatory concern has focused on halogenated dibenzodioxins and dibenzofurans to the exclusion of other toxic constituents of incinerator by-products. There has been a similar fixation on cancer to the exclusion of other adverse health effects, despite the fact that several of the major pollutants released by incinerators (e.g., lead and mercury) are of primary concern because of noncarcinogenic health effects.

In addition, incinerators have primarily been characterized as stationary sources of toxic air pollutants, that is, with reference to their impacts upon ambient air quality. Only recently have risk analyses for proposed incinerators begun to quantitatively assess pathways of exposure to air emissions in addition to direct inhalation. And even preliminary characterizations of the risks from the even larger number of pathways of exposure to incinerator ash are virtually nonexistent. An additional significant limitation is the lack of a sufficient quantity and quality of information needed to support comprehensive risk assessments.

An inaccurate scope of risk assessment encourages inadequate and misdirected strategies for control. The concept of incinerator-associated risks as limited to a few toxic air pollutants fails to comprehend the full range of risks—with respect to the panoply of toxic substances involved and the variety of relevant exposure routes—or our ability to moderate those risks through control over the role that incineration plays in overall waste management.

Moreover, the appropriate consideration of risk issues includes a comprehensive assessment not only of the individual impacts of a specific new source such as an MSW incinerator but, more important, consideration of this source in the context of ongoing exposures to other environmental releases of pollutants. This perspective is particularly critical in evaluating incineration, because at least two of the major toxins released by incinerators—lead and dioxins—are persistent toxins with universal exposure. All persons have been exposed to and carry measurable levels of these pollutants in their bodies. In some populations, existing levels of exposure and body burdens are already in a range associated with detectable adverse impacts. Because of this, the evaluation of incremental inputs—even if they are apparently small when considered in isolation—must be of concern. Consideration of the cumulative nature of both exposure to and the health effects induced by many incinerator-associated pollutants may be critical to the siting of such facilities.

THE NATURE OF HEALTH AND ENVIRONMENTAL RISKS FROM MSW INCINERATION

Incineration yields products that take three forms: energy, gases, and solid residues. Energy (heat) can be recovered partially and used to produce steam for heating or electricity generation; however, this process is not related to the other products of incineration. In modern incinerators, gases exit almost exclusively via the stack, with or without prior conditioning before discharge into the atmosphere. The solid residue emerges from two points within most facilities: at the bottom on the grates, where it is called bottom ash, and at points beyond the combustion chamber, where it is called fly ash. Fly ash may fall out in the boiler or economizer, or it may be deliberately collected by particle trapping devices, such as electrostatic precipitators (ESPs), fabric filters, or scrubbers.

Incineration differs from other methods of waste management, such as compaction and direct landfilling, in that major portions of the waste stream are physically and chemically transformed during the combustion process. Moreover, the products of this process—both solids and gases—differ markedly from the original waste in their environmental and biological behavior.

By way of illustrating these differences, consider the various points of potential environmental release of incinerator by-products. At the facility site itself, opportunities for release of the solid products arise from the moment of their generation, and continue during on-site management, handling, storage, and transport of ash. Further points of release may arise both during disposal (e.g., dust generation during landfilling; runoff or wind dispersal from uncovered ash) and after disposal (e.g., accidental or deliberate discharge of leachate or disposal of leachate treatment residues). Most of these pathways of exposure to waste products are unique to, or far more significant for, incineration than other forms of waste management.

Consideration of potential release points demonstrates another fundamental point: Impacts of incineration on air quality and the nature and amounts of solid residue generated are inextricably linked. In order to condition stack emissions to meet specific health and regulatory goals, modern incinerators are increasingly required to be equipped with such air pollution control technologies as fabric filters, high-efficiency ESPs, and scrubbers. Each of these control devices, however, increases the amount and changes the nature of the solids retained. A growing body of data indicate that as more effective controls are imposed upon stack emissions, the quality of fly ash changes markedly. In particular, both the concentration and leachability of several toxic metals in the fly ash increase.

Failure to understand the essential linkage between air quality control and ash toxicity results in risk transfer, a practice that typically characterizes incinerator operations at present. It is not acceptable to purchase improvements in air emissions at incinerators at the cost of increasing risks associated with uncontrolled or insufficiently regulated disposal of ash.

Part II explores the major risks associated with MSW incineration, and critically examines the available means for assessing and controlling those risks. Chapter 5 provides an overview of the risks posed by the large amounts of ash that remain after incineration, and the types of controls needed to reduce such risks. Chapter 6 summarizes the nature of the air emissions from MSW incineration, and describes the diversity of approaches that can and should be used to control and monitor these releases. Chapter 7 discusses what is perhaps the most controversial risk issue in the debate over incineration: health risk assessment. This discussion is intended to provide the reader with a basic understanding of the risk assessment process. In addition, the chapter presents common deficiencies in health risk assessments conducted for MSW incinerators, in order to provide the reader with the tools necessary to critically evaluate such assessments.

CHAPTER 5

MSW Incinerator Ash

MSW INCINERATORS PRODUCE two distinct types of ash: (1) fly ash, which consists of small particles that travel out of the combustion chamber and fall out of, or are removed by air pollution control devices from, the combustion gases, and (2) bottom ash, which is the material that remains in the bottom of the combustion chamber. Most facilities combine the two types of ash before disposal.

A growing body of data indicate that incinerator ash is a toxic material requiring very careful management. These data demonstrate that:

- ash contains high levels of several toxic metals, and can also contain dangerous levels of organic compounds, such as dioxins;
- by burning up the combustible portions of MSW, incineration concentrates the metals;
- because ash can be dispersed more readily through the environment than unburned MSW and can be inhaled or ingested more readily, incineration provides several new pathways for exposure to these toxins;
- certain of the metals—lead and cadmium, in particular—are readily leachable from ash at levels that frequently exceed the limits defining a hazardous waste under federal law; and
- ash is toxic when tested by several means in addition to the current federal toxicity test.

Each of these characteristics is especially applicable to the fly ash component of MSW incinerator ash.

The enhanced toxicity of heavy metals in incinerator ash illustrates the severe limitations to using incineration to manage heavy metal containing materials in MSW. Incineration essentially destroys the bulky matrix—

177

paper, plastics, or other materials—which contains the metals and which acts to retard their entrance and dispersion into the environment. Once in the form of ash, metals are much more bioavailable than metals in unburned garbage.

Because the metals that make ash toxic are permanent (i.e., cannot be destroyed by any chemical or physical process), reducing the inherent toxicity of ash must be a key objective of environmentally sound ash management. Achieving this objective may require a number of steps: managing fly ash separately from bottom ash; disposing of all ash in secure facilities that do not contain other types of waste; chemically or physically treating the ash prior to disposal; and last, but by no means least, keeping toxic metals out of products that find their way into the municipal waste stream and keeping materials containing such metals out of incinerators.

The remainder of this chapter describes the factors that cause ash to be hazardous and reviews the available toxicity data. Recommended means of ash management are discussed.*

INHERENT TOXICITY OF INCINERATOR ASH

Ash is toxic because it routinely contains high levels of several toxic metals and can also contain high levels of dioxins. Because of a limitation in current federal regulations, most concerns about ash toxicity have focused on the leachability of heavy metals in ash. Although leachability—which reflects ash's potential to contaminate groundwater—is one important consideration, it by no means provides the whole picture.

Rather, the *total* metal (and dioxin) content of ash is the key factor in assessing ash toxicity. Total concentrations must be considered because people or the environment can be exposed to ash through many routes, in addition to contaminated groundwater. For example, humans (and other animals) can inhale ash particles into the lung, after which toxins on the particles can be directly absorbed into the tissue or bloodstream. In addition, they can ingest ash particles, either directly or through contaminated food or water. Because these exposure routes can be highly significant, a full accounting of the hazards posed by ash must begin with knowledge of its total chemical composition.

---

* EDF has developed a model ash permit and model ash regulations that incorporate these and other recommendations. The permit and regulations are available to interested persons through request to EDF.

HEAVY METALS

Table 5.1 compares typical concentrations of lead and cadmium in MSW incinerator fly ash to those found in natural soils, illustrating that fly ash contains several thousand times more lead and cadmium. Bottom ash contains lower concentrations of lead and cadmium than fly ash, but these levels still greatly exceed the amounts found in uncontaminated soils.

Table 5.1 also illustrates how the total metal content of incinerator ash compares to other materials that are classified as hazardous. For example, air pollution control sludge from secondary lead smelters—a waste listed as hazardous under federal regulations—contains lead and cadmium levels akin to those found in incinerator fly ash. The state of Washington has documented levels of several carcinogenic metals in both fly and bottom ash that are sufficiently high to classify the ashes as dangerous or extremely hazardous wastes under state regulations.[1]

Metals are chemical elements, and can neither be created nor destroyed by incineration; their amounts in the waste stream before incineration must therefore equal the sum of their amounts in air emissions and ash left after incineration. Ironically, the growing use of more efficient air pollution control devices on modern incinerators results in ash containing even higher levels of these toxic substances in even more bioavailable forms.

TABLE 5.1
Metals Concentrations in Incinerator Fly Ash, Secondary Lead Smelter Sludge, and Natural Soils

Metal	RANGE OF CONCENTRATIONS (PARTS PER MILLION)		
	Fly Ash[a]	Smelter Sludge[b]	Natural Soils[c]
Lead	2,300–50,000	up to 50,000	10–13
Cadmium	100–2,000	340	0.1–0.2

SOURCES:

[a] NUS Corporation, *Characterization of Municipal Waste Combustor Ashes and Leachates from Municipal Solid Waste Landfills, Monofills, and Codisposal Sites,* 7 vols. Washington, DC: Prepared for EPA, Office of Solid Waste, October 1987, no. 68-01-7310; and EDF database.

[b] EPA *Background Document, Resource Conservation and Recovery Act, Subtitle C—Hazardous Waste Management, Section 3001—Identification and Listing of Hazardous Waste,* book 11 (Washington, DC: Office of Solid Waste, 1980).

[c] H. Vogg et al., "The Specific Role of Cadmium and Mercury in Municipal Solid Waste Incineration," *Waste Management and Research 4* (1986): 65–74.

The process of incineration is uniquely unsuited for managing metals. Incineration essentially destroys the bulky matrix that contains metals in MSW and that acts to retard their entrance and dispersion into the environment.[2] In this respect, incinerators can be compared to secondary metal smelters; by burning combustible materials they release metals, which are subsequently mobilized in air emissions or concentrated in the residues in highly bioavailable form.

Sources of Lead and Cadmium in MSW Incinerator Ash

Many different consumer products contribute the wide variety of toxic metals found in the municipal waste stream. Some of the sources of these metals are obvious, others less so. For lead and cadmium—two of the most troublesome and dangerous toxic metals in incinerators—EPA has recently quantified the major sources, which are briefly discussed in table 5.2.

These EPA data indicate that batteries and plastics are major contributors of both lead and cadmium to MSW. With respect to the levels of metals found in incinerator ash, particularly the leachable fraction, plastics and other pigment uses may well comprise the largest source, given their preponderance in the combustible portion of the waste stream.

Although recycling of batteries through the establishment of collection systems and prohibitions on their disposal are currently the most viable approaches to reducing their contribution of toxic metals to the waste stream, such approaches are far more difficult to institute for plastics and other pigment uses. The ubiquitous and diffuse nature of plastics and pigment uses and the many different types of consumer products containing these materials pose serious economic and logistical, though, it is hoped, not insurmountable, obstacles to efficient recycling. Waste reduction approaches aimed at reducing the amount or toxicity of such materials offer additional alternatives that deserve serious consideration, and may prove essential to reducing the toxicity of incinerator ash.

Health Effects of Metals Mobilized by MSW Incineration

Many of the heavy metals of concern with respect to incineration have well-defined health effects, demonstrable in numerous studies of exposed populations.[3] Their effects are not solely as carcinogens, although many of the heavy metals are carcinogenic; they can also exert a broad spectrum of devastating neurological, hepatic, renal, hematopoietic, and other adverse effects, both in humans and in other biota. Arsenic, cadmium, beryllium, and lead are carcinogenic metals; arsenic, lead, vanadium, cadmium, and

TABLE 5.2
Major Sources of Lead and Cadmium in the Municipal Waste Stream

LEAD

- Lead comes in large part from the disposal of lead-acid automotive batteries, and EPA recently estimated that, nationally in 1986, almost two-thirds of the lead in MSW came from batteries.
- The next largest source of lead is other noncombustible items such as electrical equipment, leaded glass in TV sets, and leaded ceramics. At least some of these sources are unlikely to contribute to the toxic metals found in incinerator air emissions or to the leachable metals found in incinerator ash, since they are bound up in materials that do not burn.
- Of the combustible portion of MSW, which is most likely to contribute to the toxicity of air emissions and ash, EPA estimates that 71% of the lead in this fraction is contributed by plastics, with the largest portion of that coming from packaging materials. Lead is used as a stabilizer in polyvinyl chloride (PVC) plastics, and as a pigment in many different types of plastics. Other uses of lead pigments besides plastics (e.g., in colored printing inks that may be used on paper or plastic packaging) account for another 24% of the lead in combustible MSW.

CADMIUM

- The major source of cadmium in MSW appears to be batteries, in this case, the rechargeable nickel-cadmium batteries used in a growing number of small appliances.
- The next largest source of cadmium in MSW is plastics: 28% of all cadmium in MSW in 1986 came from plastics, with more than one-third of that coming from packaging materials. Like lead, cadmium is used as a stabilizer in PVC and as a pigment in many different types of plastics.
- Of the combustible portion of MSW, almost all (88%) of the cadmium comes from plastics. Other uses of cadmium pigments besides plastics (e.g., in colored printing inks used on packaging) account for virtually all of the rest (11%) of the cadmium in combustible MSW.

SOURCE: Franklin Associates, *Characterization of Products Containing Lead and Cadmium in Municipal Solid Waste in the United States, 1970 to 2000*, (Washington, DC: EPA Office of Solid Waste, January 1989).

mercury are neurotoxic; zinc, copper, and mercury are acutely toxic to aquatic life.

Because of their permanent nature, heavy metals are accumulated both in environmental compartments and within the human body. Thus, long-term releases even at low levels have the potential to increase substantially metal levels in critical environmental compartments (e.g., surface dusts) and humans. The strong correlation in the United States between automobile lead emissions and body lead burdens demonstrates how individually small, but widely dispersed, releases can significantly impact upon general population exposure.

DIOXINS

In addition to metals, dioxins have been detected in all samples of incinerator fly ash tested, in some cases at levels that greatly exceed government guidelines.[4] Unlike metals, dioxins are actually created during incineration. Careful control of the incineration process can minimize the amounts of dioxin formed. Although total dioxin levels appear to be lower in fly ash from newer facilities than ash from older ones, consistently good performance of the newer facilities over the long run remains to be demonstrated.

As with metals, improving the efficiency of air pollution control devices results in transferring any dioxins that are present from the air to the ash. The net effect is that reducing dioxin air emissions through better stack controls may, nevertheless, yield an ash that poses a greater environmental hazard.

LEACHABILITY OF METALS IN INCINERATOR ASH

The leachability of the metals present in incinerator ash is another measure of hazard, one relating specifically to the potential for groundwater or surface-water contamination. Because current federal regulations are geared toward leachable, rather than total, metal content, there is a relative abundance of metal leachability data for ash.

Under federal law, leachability is assessed using the Extraction Procedure (EP) toxicity test.[5] To perform the EP test, a sample of ash is exposed to slightly acidic water for 24 hours, and the amounts of 8 metals that leach into the solution (i.e., dissolve) are then measured. The slightly acidic conditions are designed to mimic the conditions found in a typical landfill, where bacteria create acids as by-products during waste decomposition; those acids increase the solubility of most metals.

Table 5.3 summarizes EP toxicity test data on ash from more than 45 U.S. incinerators tested for leachability. The test data, which include data for ash from new and old facilities using a wide range of technologies, demonstrate that virtually every sample of fly ash ever tested exceeds federal standards defining a hazardous waste, usually for both lead and cadmium. Further, nearly half of the combined fly and bottom ash samples tested also exceed the standards, typically for lead. (A facility-by-facility listing of the EP toxicity test data with references is available from EDF upon request.)

Despite these data, some have questioned whether ash is really hazardous as a scientific matter. (As discussed in chapter 10, EDF is currently involved

TABLE 5.3

Summary of Available Extraction Procedure Toxicity Test Data for Lead and Cadmium from MSW Incinerator Ash

	Lead	*Cadmium*	*Either*
Fly Ash: 23 Facilities			
No. of samples analyzed	185	97	185
No. of samples over EP limit	168	94	173
% of samples over EP limit	91%	97%	94%
Mean of all samples (mg/L)	22.0[a]	37.3	—
No. of facilities over EP limit[b]	20	21	22
Mean of facility means (mg/L)	23.4	31.8	—
Bottom Ash: 22 Facilities			
No. of samples analyzed	773	271	773
No. of samples over EP limit	276	5	278
% of samples over EP limit	36%	2%	36%
Mean of all samples (mg/L)	6.39	0.25	—
No. of facilities over EP limit	9	1	9
Mean of facility means (mg/L)	7.18	0.41	—
Combined Ash: 47 Facilities			
No. of samples analyzed	933	806	933
No. of samples over EP limit	373	115	390
% of samples over EP limit	40%	14%	42%
Mean of all samples (mg/L)	6.45	0.59	—
No. of facilities over EP limit	22	6	22
Mean of facility means (mg/L)	6.26	0.48	—

SOURCE: EDF database; a full list of references is available upon request.

NOTE: Because of the large number of individual samples analyzed from certain facilities, the aggregate data tend to be skewed and overly dependent on the quality of ash from those few dominating facilities. Caution should be exercised in drawing conclusions about overall exceedance rates.

[a] Underlined values exceed EP limits defining a hazardous waste:
   lead: 5.0 milligrams per liter (mg/L); cadmium: 1.0 mg/L.

[b] Number of facilities for which mean of all available samples exceeds limit.

in two lawsuits that raise the separate legal issue of whether such ash is subject to the regulations of the federal hazardous waste system.) In particular, some critics have questioned the suitability of the EP test for evaluating incinerator ash. Those critics assert that because ash is relatively inert (i.e., low in organic matter that can decompose), acidic conditions will not be found at ash disposal sites, so that the use of the EP test yields misleading results.

In addition to arguing for a double standard—other industries' wastes must be tested using the EP test—challenges to the general suitability of the EP test overlook a crucial point: The great majority of incinerator ash is currently disposed of in sanitary landfills along with unburned waste,[6] which is exactly the disposal scenario simulated by the EP test. Moreover, large amounts of incinerator ash are managed by even less-controlled means, such as being used as landfill cover, fill material in marshy areas, or deicing grit on winter roads, or by being mixed with other material and used in construction materials. These uses clearly provide even greater opportunities for dispersal of ash-borne toxic metals or dioxins into the environment than does sanitary landfilling of ash. Finally, certain metals in ash—lead in particular—leach from ash even under non-acidic conditions.

The increased leachability of metals in incinerator ash results from several phenomena that occur during combustion. First, in the high-temperature zone of the incinerator, metals are vaporized; later, as the combustion gases cool, these metals condense onto the surface of fly ash particles. The concentrations of these condensed metals increase with decreasing particle size.[7] The small particle size of ash increases the surface area exposed to leaching,[8] and the presence of metals at or near the surface of such particles also enhances their leachability.[9] In addition, MSW contains large amounts of chlorine from plastics, bleached paper, and other sources. During incineration, chlorine combines with metals to form metal chlorides.[10] These compounds generally are much more soluble in water than most other forms of metals.

Another chemical property of certain metals becomes critical when evaluating the quality of ash generated by facilities equipped with acid-gas scrubbers. Because acid-gas scrubbers are now considered a component of best available control technology (BACT), virtually all new facilities will be so equipped. Scrubbers work by injecting alkaline acid-neutralizing chemicals, usually lime, into the combustion gases. The lime becomes thoroughly mixed into fly ash to form a scrubber residue; that residue is later removed by particulate control devices. At the several U.S. facilities now using such scrubbers, the resulting ash—even the combined ash formed by mixing bottom ash and fly ash containing this scrubber residue—is highly alkaline, with a typical pH value of 11 or higher.[11]

This strongly alkaline ash is chemically very different from ash generated by incinerators lacking scrubbers. Certain toxic metals—most notably, lead—are "amphoteric," meaning that they readily dissolve in water under both alkaline and acidic conditions. In leaching tests of the ash from several of the U.S. incinerators that have scrubbers, lead leached at high levels,[12] often in excess of federal or state standards defining a hazardous waste. Such leaching occurred even when the tests were conducted using ordinary water to simulate conditions where the ash would come into contact with rainfall, rather than the dilute acid used in the EP test. Figure 5.1 illustrates the significant leaching of lead from such ash that occurs under both acidic and alkaline conditions, using leaching data on combined ash from an operating U.S. incinerator.

FIGURE 5.1
Concentration of Lead (Pb) in Leachates of Combined Fly Ash, Bottom Ash, and Scrubber Residue As a Function of Leachate pH.

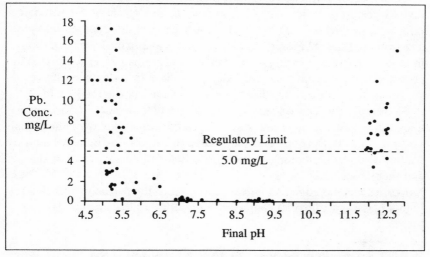

SOURCE: R. Denison, EDF, based on Resource Analysts, "Extraction Procedure Toxicity Test Results for Ash from the New Hampshire-Vermont Solid Waste Project Incinerator," reports on tests conducted for Signal Environmental Systems (Hampton, NH, April 6, 1987; May 30, 1987; and June 29, 1987).

NOTE: The dotted line represents the regulatory limit for lead in the EP Toxicity Test, 5.0 milligrams per liter (mg/L).

Similar results were found in Canadian and Swedish studies.[13] Indeed, the Swedish study found that the amounts of a number of metals—lead, cadmium, mercury, copper, and zinc—leached from the fly ash/scrubber residue mixture were much higher than the amounts leached from fly ash without scrubber residue. Those amounts were much higher than the amounts leached from bottom ash or raw MSW.

The high alkalinity of ash from facilities possessing acid-gas scrubbers also may increase the leachability of organic chemicals. Recent Canadian studies have found that a wide range of organics present in fly ash become much more soluble in water as the ash becomes more alkaline.[14] These findings raise new concerns about the potential for acid-gas scrubbers to increase leaching of dioxins or other toxic substances that are otherwise relatively insoluble in water.

BIOAVAILABILITY AND DIRECT TOXICITY OF INCINERATOR ASH

The hazards of ash must also be evaluated by direct bioavailability and toxicity testing, particularly with respect to the potential for ecological effects. Toxic metals and dioxins present in ash can be absorbed into plant and animal tissues.[15] Moreover, these metals and dioxins have been shown, in some cases, to be directly toxic to plants and animals.[16] In addition to the potential for direct environmental damage, these data document the plausibility of human exposure through contamination of the food chain.

Bioavailability is enhanced by the small particle size of most ash, which allows direct inhalation or ingestion of such particles. Moreover, their small size promotes both short- and long-range dispersion, as demonstrated by studies of metal-containing particles released from a variety of stationary and mobile air pollution sources,[17] including MSW incinerators.[18] These properties take on added significance in light of the permanent (metals) or highly persistent (dioxins) character of the ash's toxic constituents.

ROUTES OF EXPOSURE TO INCINERATOR ASH

Ash can be dispersed not only through releases occurring at the ash disposal site, but also at all earlier stages of ash management: during on-site handling and storage, during transport, and during handling at the landfill. At each step, there is potential for significant airborne and water-borne dispersal of ash. Figure 5.2 illustrates the many exposure routes to air emissions from

FIGURE 5.2
Pathways of Exposure to Emissions from an MSW Incinerator

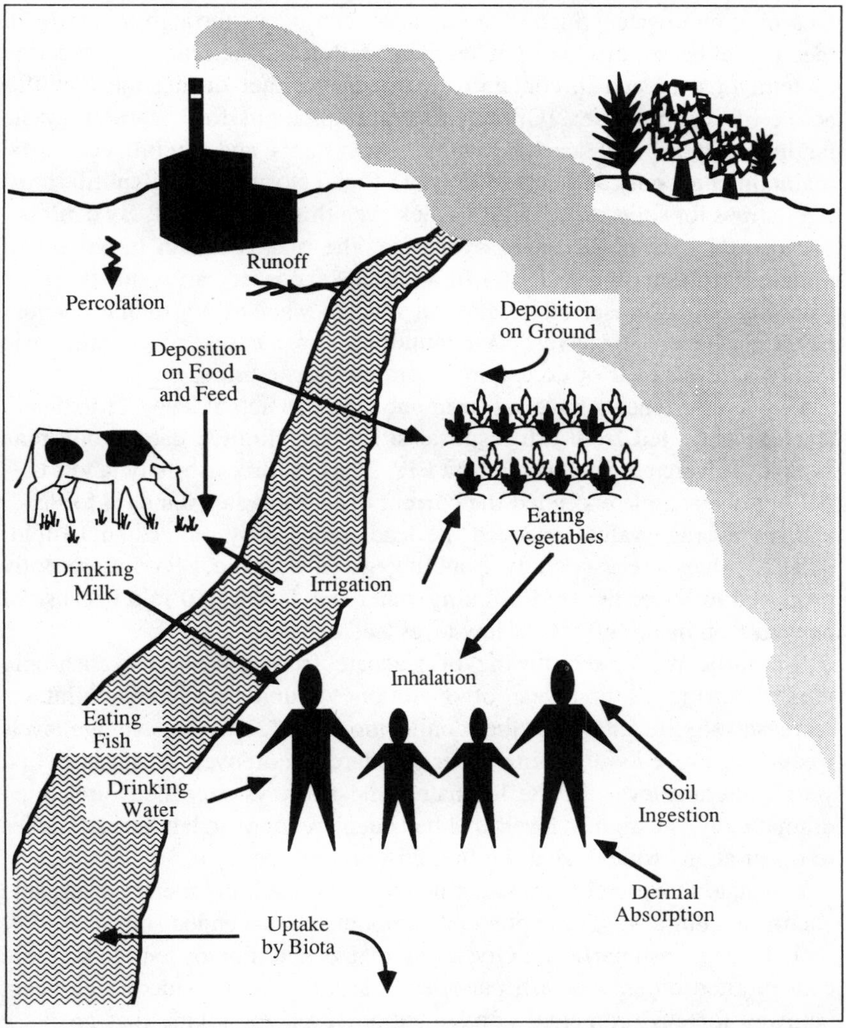

SOURCE: EDF, based on U.S. EPA, *Methodology for the Assessment of Health Risks Associated with Multiple Pathway Exposure to Municipal Waste Combustor Emissions* (Research Triangle Park, NC: Office of Air Quality Planning and Standards, October 1986), cover illustration.

MSW incinerators. These and other routes discussed below are also relevant for incinerator ash.

Even after disposal, leachate from a disposal site can contaminate surface or groundwater. Such contamination can occur through a variety of means: deliberate discharge of leachate, failure of the leachate collection system, or a breach in containment systems, either during the landfill's active life or thereafter. (Current federal regulations for hazardous waste landfills require that leachate collection systems and landfill covers be maintained for only 30 years following official closure of the landfill; most regulations for solid waste landfills lack even this requirement. By contrast, because they do not degrade over time, the metals in ash leachate will remain hazardous indefinitely.) In addition, exposure can result from the handling and disposal of leachate or quench water. Both of these liquid materials have themselves been found, in some cases, to contain toxic metals at levels near or exceeding hazardous waste limits.[19]

Few measurements have yet been published on actual levels of toxins in leachate collected from ash disposal sites. Very limited data—only nine samples—were reported in a recent EPA study of three ash-only landfills.[20] All but one sample exceeded the current drinking-water standard for lead, and the average value exceeded the lead standard by more than 12-fold. (These values are especially troubling given that the EPA has recently proposed to lower the lead drinking-water standard by 10-fold because of new data on health effects of low-level lead exposure.[21])

Similarly, recent monitoring of leachate from a New York ash-only landfill during its first year of operation[22] found that many pollutants increased significantly over the monitoring period, and that average levels frequently exceeded drinking-water standards; moreover, during this first year, pollutant levels in the leachate almost always exceeded, and often dramatically, the highest levels that had been predicted in laboratory studies to occur at any time during the first 25 years of operation.[23]

Leachate may be contaminated not only with soluble metals or organic chemicals, but also with appreciable amounts of suspended solid material, including fine ash particles. Given that metals and dioxins tend to be more concentrated on smaller ash particles, leachate may provide a significant pathway for environmental contamination, even for toxins that are very insoluble.

The ability of ash leachate to result in environmental contamination was amply demonstrated by recent environmental sampling at an ash monofill in Bellingham, Washington. Testing conducted by EPA Region 10 late last year found greatly elevated levels of several metals in groundwater, as well as nearby surface waters and sediments surrounding the ash disposal site. For example, all eight downgradient groundwater monitoring wells showed levels of cadmium that exceeded the drinking-water standard by manyfold: The average level was almost 70 times the drinking-water standard, with levels ranging as high as 133 times the standard.[24]

EPA has recently raised several concerns regarding the effect of ash leachates on clay soils and liners, which are typically the only barrier material present in ash disposal sites. In particular, EPA has stated that the high alkalinity and salt content of such leachates are known to cause rapid deterioration of clay liners.[25] They further state that some data indicate that chloride complexes of lead and cadmium in ashes move rapidly through clay soils.[26] These concerns may well be critical in assessing the proper design for containment systems for ash landfills.

In addition to the permanent or persistent nature of many ash-borne toxic substances, other properties of ash further demonstrate the need for long-term, secure containment. Under certain conditions, ash-borne metals can move through soils to a significant degree; they also can be taken up by plants.[27] These properties are of concern both during a disposal site's lifetime and long after. A long-term perspective is critical because all landfill containment systems will eventually deteriorate. Thus, the potential for erosion of the final landfill cover over time, transport of metals out of the landfill by plant uptake or other means, and future uses of the site following landfill closure (e.g., as a recreational area) must all be seriously considered in assessing exposure routes.

Experience with ash and other ashlike materials, such as metal smelter dusts, amply demonstrates that the various exposure routes described above are by no means hypothetical. Indeed, such studies confirm the reality and significance of virtually all of the exposure routes just discussed, even long after initial disposal.[28]

FUNDAMENTAL OBJECTIVES OF ASH MANAGEMENT

In light of the clear hazards of ash, sound ash management requires taking steps both to reduce the inherent toxicity of ash and to fully contain it during all phases of management more carefully. Meeting these objectives will require the following measures:

- Test and consider managing fly and bottom ash separately.
- Dispose of ash separately from other wastes and only in secure landfills.

- Encourage or require treatment of ash prior to disposal, using methods demonstrated to effectively reduce both its present and future hazards.
- Keep toxic metals out of products that find their way into the municipal waste stream and keep materials containing such metals out of incinerators.

The first three means of reducing the hazards of ash are clearly within the scope of what is normally considered to be waste management. All three involve management at the back end, that is, *after* hazardous ash has been generated. The last objective, often considered to lie beyond the scope of standard approaches to waste management, offers the most effective solution: If steps are taken to remove metals from trash prior to incineration, the resulting ash will be cleaner. Such ash can then be managed in a manner that is inherently more protective than management of a more toxic ash by any currently available method, even disposal in a state-of-the-art landfill.

If less than fully protective—and generally less expensive—ash management provisions are adopted, incentives to reduce the toxicity of ash at the source will be weakened or eliminated. Unfortunately, in EDF's view, the current federal and many state regulations applicable to ash management do not provide sufficient means to accomplish any of these key objectives. (An EDF summary of proposed or adopted state requirements for ash management is available upon request to EDF.) Each of these objectives is discussed briefly below.

Separate Testing or Management of Fly and Bottom Ash

Though it is common for incinerators to mix fly and bottom ash, the two generally exhibit different characteristics and levels of toxicity, and may best be managed separately. Fly ash has a considerably higher concentration of many toxic substances than does bottom ash. In addition, as shown in table 5.3, fly ash has been found to fail the EP toxicity test because of high lead and cadmium levels, even where combined fly and bottom ash does not.

Rather than blindly combining fly and bottom ash, incinerator operators should be required to test them separately, as well as in combined form, and to handle and dispose of the ashes appropriately in light of the test results. Several factors must be considered in using test results to determine proper ash disposal and management requirements. First, present federal regulations require that ash failing the EP toxicity test be managed as a hazardous waste. Although this requirement has been highly controversial and could be changed by passage of legislation now pending before Congress, EPA continues to hold to this requirement.

Separate testing of fly and bottom ash will allow a determination as to whether one or both streams must be managed as hazardous. Unless current regulations that apply to ash are changed, it is highly likely that fly ash will have to be managed as a hazardous waste because it is virtually always EP toxic. As shown in table 5.3, data on ash from more than 20 U.S. incinerators reveal that virtually every sample of fly ash tested using the EP toxicity test has exceeded federal standards defining a hazardous waste, usually for both lead and cadmium.

When such standards are exceeded, all ash generated during the period corresponding to such analyzed samples must be transported and disposed of as hazardous waste, in full compliance with the requirements of Subtitle C of the Resource Conservation and Recovery Act (RCRA), as well as any other state laws and regulations governing hazardous wastes.

The data in table 5.3 also show that combined ash has more frequently displayed leachate levels exceeding federal standards for hazardous wastes than has bottom ash alone. Separate testing and management of fly and bottom ash can thus help to minimize the amount of ash that must be managed as hazardous waste. Incinerators produce 10 to 20 times as much bottom ash as fly ash; put another way, fly ash is only 5 to 10 percent of the total amount of ash. Keeping fly ash separate from bottom ash—a simple task since the two types of ash are generated in separate places in an incinerator—could greatly reduce the total amount of ash that would have to be managed as a hazardous waste.

Separate handling and testing of fly and bottom ash can also determine the effects of mixing the two streams. Such mixing frequently results in little more than dilution of the more toxic fly ash, with a concomitant contamination of a much larger volume of ash. Frequently heard claims of beneficial effects of mixing can only be assessed through testing of both the separate and combined ashes at each facility.

Finally, keeping fly and bottom ash separate would improve our ability to manage toxic ash by means in addition to direct disposal. Containment and treatment technologies are more effective, and cost-efficient, when applied to a smaller volume/more concentrated waste. In addition, any potential for utilization of ash will likely be limited only to bottom ash, yet another reason to at least provide for the capability to manage the two streams separately.

DISPOSE OF ASH SEPARATELY FROM OTHER WASTES
AND ONLY IN SECURE LANDFILLS

Although existing hazardous waste laws and regulations may be sufficient to handle any ash that fails to meet EP toxicity test standards, it is critical that even ash that is found not to be EP toxic be handled carefully during all stages of management and disposed of in secure facilities separate from other solid wastes.

Co-disposal of ash and MSW is recognized by virtually all parties, including the incinerator industry itself, to actually increase the hazards posed by disposal of incinerator ash. As noted above, MSW landfills contain acids that are produced by bacteria in the process of decomposing garbage. The acidic conditions that develop in MSW landfills can increase the leachability of a broad range of toxic chemicals present in ash.

Ash is a much more homogenous material than MSW; when managed separately, it can be compacted to occupy a relatively small volume and to exhibit reduced permeability, which reduces the amount of liquid that comes into contact with the ash and, therefore, the extent of leachate formation and contamination. These factors, together with the exclusion from ash-only monofills of organic material subject to decomposition, produce a smaller, more stable and predictable disposal environment.

The growing use of acid-gas scrubbers on new incinerators has the potential to cause an increase in the amount of lead leaching from the ash produced by such facilities. These data call into question any assumption that monofilling alone suffices to ensure safe disposal. In EDF's view, monofilling is a necessary but not sufficient component of proper ash management. Monofilling should be required, but it does not eliminate the need for full state-of-the-art containment with leachate collection, leak detection, and groundwater monitoring as essential design components of the ash disposal site. In addition, use of impermeable final cover systems and certain operating controls are critical to assuring long-term containment. EDF recommends the state-of-the-art monofill system illustrated in figure 5.3 (and described in more detail in Appendix B).

ENCOURAGE OR REQUIRE TREATMENT OF ASH
PRIOR TO DISPOSAL

The need for treatment, as well as separate management, of fly ash prior to land disposal has been recognized in various studies of ash contaminant leachability, including several excellent studies conducted by the Canadian government.[29] A broad range of approaches is being explored for treating

FIGURE 5.3

Diagram of a Double-lined Monofill with Leachate Collection and Leak-detection Systems

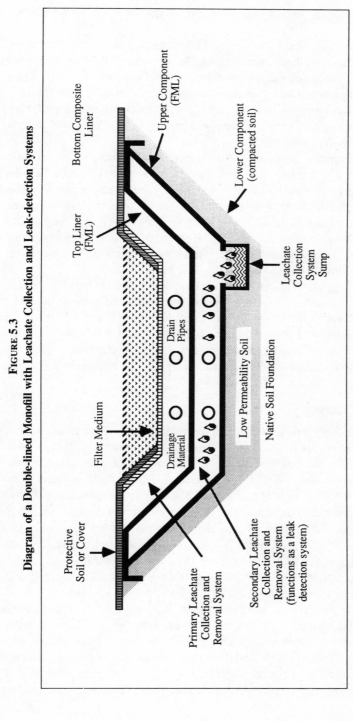

SOURCE: EDF, based on an illustration in *Federal Register* 52 (May 29, 1987) 20226.

incinerator ash to reduce both metal leaching and the potential for dispersal of ash. These methods, most of which are derived from similar methods applied to other hazardous wastes or to coal ash, include techniques for recovering or extracting metals, as well as techniques to solidify and stabilize ash either by adding cement or other chemicals or by "vitrification," heating to a very high temperature so that the ash fuses together to form a glasslike material.

Such methods have considerable potential to reduce ash toxicity and should be aggressively pursued, but they should not blindly be adopted without careful assessment of whether they are effective when applied to incinerator ash, both initially and over the long term. Indeed, given the permanent hazards posed by metals in incinerator ash, any treatment method should be demonstrated to be effective under a range of conditions, such as multiple freeze-thaw cycles, that may occur well beyond the end of the useful life of a disposal facility.

To ensure that treatment is carried out safely and effectively, permits for treatment should be required. Such permits should require the use of a validated type of treatment, and also should require testing of the treated ash and monitoring to assure that the treatment procedure is effective and is conducted in a manner that provides full protection of personnel and containment during all management steps up to and including disposal.

Ash utilization

As increasingly stringent regulations governing ash disposal are developed, interest is rapidly growing in developing beneficial utilization of ash. It is critical to ensure that the risk considerations that have led to more stringent regulation of ash *disposal* are not neglected in assessing the potential for ash *utilization*, an activity that allows the placing of ash or ash-derived products into the general environment rather than a controlled disposal environment. (A separate EDF report—Richard A. Denison, "Ash Utilization: An Idea Before Its Time?"—is available upon request, which discusses this issue in greater detail.) In EDF's view, it is premature to allow full-scale ash utilization before thorough environmental testing has been conducted and the appropriate standards and regulations have been implemented.

Because ash utilization (e.g., in road building or construction activities) allows placing ash or ash-derived products into the general environment, it involves potential exposures that extend well beyond those from ash disposal, both in magnitude and duration. Moreover, our ability for long-term control over ash or for remedial action is lost in most utilization applications, raising the threshhold for demonstrating safety. In the absence of sufficient demonstration of safety, ash utilization may only postpone rather than eliminate exposures.

Based on presently available information, EDF believes that only bottom ash residues should be considered for utilization. This limitation is justified on the basis of the clearly greater toxicity of fly and combined ash; such a limitation is also consistent with the policies and actual practice in other countries.

The need for a complete chemical and physical characterization of ash—both before and after any treatment preceding utilization—is even more critical in this context than for ash destined for disposal. In EDF's view, bottom ash must be thoroughly tested prior to any utilization, using a battery of tests capable of accounting for all routes of both short- and long-term exposure. Leaching tests measure only one of the numerous pathways of exposure to ash that are relevant to evaluating the risks of utilization. The permanent nature of toxic metals increases the relevance of these pathways of direct exposure to ash, as recently noted by EPA's Science Advisory Board:

> Beyond considerations of mobility and identity, the environmental persistence of the compounds [present in incinerator ash] should be explored. Persistence is easily as important to fate prediction as is mobility, since a compound that has the potential to migrate but is not persistent poses little hazard. *Conversely, a compound that does not migrate but does persist can pose a serious problem through mechanisms other than leaching* [author's italics].[30]

Routine testing on a batch or lot basis should be instituted as a precondition for utilization. Performance standards must be established by regulation and met prior to any utilization; these must demonstrate the safety of the proposed utilization under the range of conditions likely to be encountered in the environment (e.g., repeated freeze-thaw cycles; compressive strength tests). In addition, comprehensive environmental monitoring of the utilization environment must be conducted.

Research into the feasibility of ash utilization has only just begun to address the significant environmental and public health concerns involved. In EDF's view, considerable additional research will be needed to provide a sufficient basis for determining whether full-scale ash utilization can be conducted safely and, if so, for what applications and under what conditions. In addition, full-scale ash utilization must be preceded by the development of comprehensive test procedures and a comprehensive regulatory program.

KEEP TOXIC METALS OUT OF PRODUCTS THAT FIND THEIR WAY INTO THE MUNICIPAL WASTE STREAM

The least-expensive and most-effective way to protect public health from the toxic metals in ash is to keep those metals out of the ash in the first place. Doing so can be accomplished through a variety of approaches. At the most fundamental level, manufacturers can reconfigure their products to replace metals, for example, substituting nontoxic organic or water-based pigments for heavy metal-based inks. Where used, metal-containing products can be separated out of the waste stream for recycling, stockpiling, or direct landfilling rather than incineration; for some materials, such as batteries, disposal in hazardous waste landfills would be required.

Such approaches can involve significant expense, but so does improper ash management in the long run. In essence, an insufficiently protective ash disposal system does not account for—indeed, it subsidizes—the continued use and improper disposal of the materials that make ash toxic. It also promotes the continued use of the mass-burn approach to incineration, which disregards the need to dissect the waste stream in order to incinerate only those materials that can be safely burned. Toxic ash results largely from indiscriminate use of incineration. Source-separation programs and preprocessing technologies can provide opportunities to remove materials that contribute toxic metals to the incinerated waste stream; they have been documented to reduce the metal content of both air emissions and ash residues.[31] Source separation and preprocessing can also reduce the frequency of incinerator upsets—reductions in combustion efficiency—caused by feeding noncombustibles into the incinerator.[32] Such upsets can result in large increases in emissions of various pollutants (see further discussion of this issue in chapter 6).

To date, the mass-burn industry has not squarely faced, much less adequately resolved, ash toxicity issues in a way that assures safe, long-term ash management. Perhaps the most graphic illustration of the lack of serious consideration of incinerator ash hazards is that virtually no quantitative risk assessments of the hazards posed by incinerator ash have ever been conducted for a proposed incinerator project.

The growing reliance on mass-burn incineration throughout the United States also threatens to undermine the development of large-scale recycling and other trash-processing technologies. These alternatives could serve both to reduce the amount of incineration and to decrease the volume and toxicity of ash and air emissions. In this respect, recycling and source separation are essential elements in the safe and rational use of incineration. To the extent that the incineration debate continues to give mere lip service to these technologies, we will simply perpetuate the same myth that brought us to the brink of the present landfill crisis—the concept that a single management technique can safely manage our entire municipal waste stream.

NOTES

1. J.C. Knudson, *Study of Municipal Incineration Residue and Its Designation as a Dangerous Waste*, (Olympia, WA: Solid Waste Section, Department of Ecology, State of Washington, 1986).
2. D.C. Wilson et al., "Leaching of Cadmium from Pigmented Plastics in a Landfill Site," *Environmental Science and Technology* 16 (1982): 560–66.
3. L. Friberg, G.F. Nordberg, and V.B. Vouk, *Handbook of the Toxicology of Metals*, 2 vols. (Amsterdam: Elsevier, 1986).
4. NUS Corporation, *Characterization of Municipal Waste Combustor Ashes and Leachates from Municipal Solid Waste Landfills, Monofills, and Codisposal Sites*, 7 vols. (Washington, DC: Prepared for EPA, Office of Solid Waste, October 1987 no. 68-01-7310).
5. Code of Federal Regulations 40:261.24. Hereafter cited as C.F.R.
6. NUS Corporation, *Characterization of Municipal Waste Combustor Ashes and Leachates from Municipal Solid Waste Landfills, Monofills, and Codisposal Sites*; S. Lowrance, Director, Office of Solid Waste, EPA, testimony before the Subcommittee on Transportation and Hazardous Materials, Energy and Commerce Committee, U.S. House of Representatives, July 13, 1989.
7. S.E. Sawell, T.R. Bridle, and T.W. Constable, *Assessment of Ash Contaminant Leachability*, NITEP Phase II-Testing of the FLAKT Air Pollution Control Technology at the Quebec City Municipal Energy from Waste Facility, Industrial Programs Branch, Wastewater Technology Centre (Burlington, Ontario: Environment Canada, 1986); G.A. Norton, E.L. DeKalb, and K.L. Malaby, "Elemental Composition of Suspended Particulate Matter from the Combustion of Coal and Coal/Refuse Mixtures," *Environmental Science and Technology* 20 (1986): 604–09; K. Carlsson, "Heavy Metals from 'Energy from Waste' Plants—Comparison of Gas Cleaning Systems," *Waste Management and Research* 4 (1986): 15–20; R.R. Greenberg, W.H. Zoller, and G.E. Gordon, "Composition and Particle Size in Refuse Incineration," *Environmental Science and Technology* 12 (1978): 566–73.
8. S.E. Sawell, T.R. Bridle, and T.W. Constable, *Assessment of Ash Contaminant Leachability*.
9. G.A. Norton, E.L. DeKalb, and K.L. Malaby, "Elemental Composition of Suspended Particulate Matter from the Combustion of Coal and Coal/Refuse

Mixtures"; A. Wadge and M. Hutton, "The Leachability and Chemical Speciation of Selected Trace Elements in Fly Ash from Coal Combustion and Refuse Incineration," *Environmental Pollution* 48 (1987): 85–99.

10. P.H. Brunner and H. Monch, "The Flux of Metals Through Municipal Solid Waste Incinerators," *Waste Management and Research* 4 (1986): 105–19; T.R. Bridle et al., "Evaluation of Heavy Metal Leachability from Solid Wastes," *Water Science Technology* 19 (1987): 1029–36; P.H. Brunner and Baccini, P. "The Generation of Hazardous Waste by MSW-Incineration Calls for New Concepts in Thermal Waste Treatment," manuscript prepared for the Second International Conference on New Frontiers for Hazardous Waste Management (Pittsburgh, PA, September 27–30, 1987).

11. State of Oregon, Department of Environmental Quality, "Extraction Procedure Toxicity Characterization of Municipal Incinerator Ash from Ogden Martin, Brooks," report prepared by Claude H. Shinn of the Laboratory Division (Portland, OR, 1987); Resource Analysts, "Extraction Procedure Toxicity Test Results for Combined Fly and Bottom Ash from the New Hampshire-Vermont Solid Waste Project Incinerator," reports on tests conducted for Signal Environmental Systems, (Hampton, NH, April 6, 1987, May 30, 1987, June 29, 1987).

12. State of Oregon, Department of Environmental Quality, "Extraction Procedure Toxicity Characterization of Municipal Incinerator Ash from Ogden Martin, Brooks"; Resource Analysts, "Extraction Procedure Toxicity Test Results for Combined Fly and Bottom Ash from the New Hampshire-Vermont Solid Waste Project Incinerator"; Los Angeles County Sanitation District, as reported in the San Gabriel Valley *Daily Tribune*, December 22, 1987; Roy F. Weston, "Framingham Incinerator Ash Sampling and Analysis Report," prepared for ESI, Southborough, MA (Burlington, MA, June 5, 1987).

13. S.E. Sawell, T.R. Bridle, and T.W. Constable, *Assessment of Ash Contaminant Leachability*; J. Hartlen and P. Elander, *Residues from Waste Incineration: Chemical and Physical Properties*, report no. 172, (Linkoping, Sweden: Swedish Geotechnical Institute, June 1986).

14. F.W. Karasek et al., "Determination of Organic Compounds Leached from Municipal Incinerator Fly Ash by Water at Different pH Levels," *Analytical Chemistry* 59, no. 7 (1987): 1027–31.

15. A. Wadge and M. Hutton, "The Uptake of Cadmium, Lead, and Selenium by Barley and Cadmium Grown on Soils Amended with Refuse Incinerator Fly Ash," *Plant and Soil* 96 (1986): 407–12; P.M. Giordano et al., "Mobility in Soil and Plant Availability of Metals Derived from Incinerated Municipal Refuse," *Environmental Science and Technology* 17 (1983): 193–98; M. Van den Berg, K. Olie and O. Hutzinger, "Uptake and Selective Retention in Rats of Orally Administered Chlorinated Dioxins and Dibenzofurans from Fly-Ash and Fly-Ash Extract," *Chemosphere* 12, no. 4–5 (1983): 537–44; M. Van den Berg et al., "Bioavailability of Polychlorinated Dibenzo-p-dioxins and Polychlorinated Dibenzofurans on Fly Ash After Semi-Chronic Oral Ingestion by

the Rat," *Chemosphere* 15, no. 4 (1986): 509–18; M. Van den Berg et al., "Bioavailability of Polychlorinated Dibenzo-p-dioxins and Polychlorinated Dibenzofurans on Fly Ash After Semi-Chronic Oral Ingestion by Guinea Pig and Syrian Golden Hamster," *Chemosphere* 15, no. 4 (1986): 519–33; A. Opperhuisen et al., "Uptake and Elimination of PCDD/PCDF Congeners by Fish After Aqueous Exposure to a Fly-Ash Extract from a Municipal Incinerator," *Chemosphere* 15, nos. 9–12 (1986): 2049–53.

16. J.C. Knudson, *Study of Municipal Incineration Residue and Its Designation as a Dangerous Waste*; D.W. Kuehl et al., "Bioavailability of 2,3,7,8-Tetra-chlorodibenzo-p-dioxin from Municipal Incinerator Ash to Freshwater Fish," *Chemosphere* 14, no. 5 (1985): 427–38; D.W. Kuehl et al., "Isomer Dependent Bioavailability of Polychlorinated Dibenzo-P-Dioxins and Dibenzofurans from Municipal Incineration Fly Ash to Carp," *Chemosphere* 16, no. 4 (1987): 657–66; G. Bronzetti et al., "Mutagenicity Study of TCDD and Ashes from Urban Incinerator 'In Vitro' and 'In Vivo' using Yeast D7 Strain," *Chemosphere* 12, nos. 4–5 (1983): 549–53.

17. Environmental Protection Agency, *Air Quality Criteria for Lead*, 4 vols. (Research Triangle Park, NC: Environmental Criteria and Assessment Office, 1968/600/8-83028aF-dF); M. Harper, K.R. Sullivan, and M.J. Quinn, "Wind Dispersal of Metals from Smelter Waste Tips and Their Contribution to Environmental Contamination," *Environmental Science and Technology* 21 (1987): 481–84; J.O. Nriagu, ed., *Changing Metal Cycles and Human Health* (Berlin: Springer-Verlag, 1984); T.M. Roberts et al., "Lead Contamination Around Secondary Smelters: Estimation of Dispersal and Accumulation by Humans," *Science* 186 (1974): 1120–23.

18. M. Hutton, A. Wadge, and P.J. Milligan, "Environmental Levels of Cadmium and Lead in the Vicinity of a Major Refuse Incinerator," *Atmospheric Environment* 22 (1988): 411; M. Berlincioni and A. di Domenico, "Polychloro-dibenzo-p-dioxins and Polychlorodibenzofurans in the Soil Near the Municipal Incinerator of Florence, Italy," *Environmental Science and Technology* 21 (1987): 1063–69.

19. NUS Corporation, *Characterization of Municipal Waste Combustor Ashes and Leachates from Municipal Solid Waste Landfills, Monofills, and Codisposal Sites*; State of Oregon, Department of Environmental Quality, "Extraction Procedure Toxicity Characterization of Municipal Incinerator Ash from Ogden Martin, Brooks."

20. NUS Corporation, *Characterization of Municipal Waste Combustor Ashes and Leachates from Municipal Solid Waste Landfills, Monofills, and Codisposal Sites*.

21. *Federal Register* 53 (August 18, 1988): 31516.

22. Westchester County, "Leachate Physical and Chemical Parameters," monitoring report for the Westchester County Sprout Brook Residue Disposal Facility, samples taken between October 1, 1986, and May 29, 1987.

23. K.L. Cundari and J.M. Lauria, "The Laboratory Evaluation of Expected

Leachate Quality from a Resource Recovery Ashfill," paper presented at the 1986 Triangle Conference on Environmental Technology (Chapel Hill, NC, 1986).

24. Ecology and Environment, Inc., "Phase 1 sampling summary report for Thermal Reduction Company, Whatcom County, Washington," prepared for Superfund Section, EPA Region 10 (Seattle, WA, February 1989).

25. "Guidance on Municipal Waste Combustion Ash," Draft (Washington, DC: EPA Office of Solid Waste, March 14, 1988).

26. "Status of OSW's Municipal Waste Combustion Ash Efforts," briefing for the EPA Science Advisory Board (Washington, DC, April 26, 1988).

27. A. Wadge and M. Hutton, "The Uptake of Cadmium, Lead, and Selenium by Barley and Cadmium Grown on Soils Amended with Refuse Incinerator Fly Ash"; P.M. Giordano et al., "Mobility in Soil and Plant Availability of Metals Derived from Incinerated Municipal Refuse"; J.S. Mika and W.A. Feder, "Resco Incinerator Residue Research Program: Results, Evaluations and Recommendations," report prepared for Refuse-Energy Systems Company, University of Massachusetts (Waltham, MA, 1985).

28. M. Harper, K.R. Sullivan, and M.J. Quinn, "Wind Dispersal of Metals from Smelter Waste Tips and Their Contribution to Environmental Contamination"; P.J. Landrigan et al., "Epidemic Lead Absorption Near an Ore Smelter," *New England Journal of Medicine* 292, no. 3 (1975): 123–29; H.A. Roels et al., "Exposure to Lead by the Oral and Pulmonary Routes of Children Living in the Vicinity of a Primary Lead Smelter," *Environmental Research* 22 (1980): 81–94; M. Hutton, A. Wadge, and P.J. Milligan, "Environmental Levels of Cadmium and Lead in the Vicinity of a Major Refuse Incinerator," *Atmospheric Environment* 22 (1988): 411.

29. S.E. Sawell, T.R. Bridle, and T.W. Constable, *Assessment of Ash Contaminant Leachability*; S.E. Sawell, T.R. Bridle, and T.W. Constable, "Leachability of Organic and Inorganic Contaminants in Ashes from Lime-Based Air Pollution Control Devices on a Municipal Waste Incinerator," report presented at the annual meeting of the Air Pollution Control Association (New York City: June 21–26, 1987).

30. EPA Science Advisory Board, *Review of the Municipal Waste Combustion Research Plan*, report of the Environmental Effects, Transport, and Fate Committee (Washington, DC: U.S. Government Printing Office, April 1988).

31. E.J. Sommer, Jr. et al., "Mass Burn Incineration with a Presorted MSW Fuel," *Journal of American Pollution Control Assoc.* 39, no. 4 (1989): 511.

32. A. Hershkowitz, "Burning Trash: How It Could Work," *Technology Review*, July 1987, pp. 26–34.

CHAPTER 6

MSW Incinerator Air Emissions

THE MOST OBVIOUS environmental hazard posed by solid waste incinerators is air pollution. Modern incinerators, though vast improvements over their predecessors of a generation ago, still pose significant threats if not carefully controlled.

Incinerators emit a wide range of harmful air pollutants: particulate matter, a variety of heavy metals, acid gases such as hydrogen chloride and sulfur dioxide, nitrogen oxides, and toxic organic compounds such as dioxins and furans. Emissions of these pollutants must be minimized.

Of course, the most effective way to limit air pollution from an incinerator is not to build it in the first place; a less effective though important alternative would be to reduce its size. Assuming that a given incinerator of a given size is to be built, five basic requirements apply. First, the facility should be equipped with state-of-the-art furnace design and combustion and air pollution controls. Second, restrictions should be placed on the kinds of waste materials that may be accepted for incineration. Third, strict specific emission limits must be established for all pollutants of concern. Fourth, comprehensive continuous monitoring and frequent stack testing of emissions must be conducted. Finally, incinerators must be operated and maintained at optimum levels by fully trained personnel.

AIR POLLUTION CONTROL

Emissions from an incinerator will vary according to four factors: (1) the waste that is fed into it, (2) the design of the combustion chamber and furnace, (3) the operating conditions, and (4) the flue gas cleaning devices (end-of-smokestack technology) installed. The worst emissions come from a facility that accepts waste that already contains various toxins, burns it

201

incompletely because of poor design or operation, and lacks effective air pollution control devices. Each of these four factors provides a point of control for air pollution.

It is a mistake to conceive of air pollution control as only consisting of flue gas cleaning devices, such as scrubbers. Certain other elements of incinerator design and operation can also fairly be considered air pollution control measures. These include measures such as employing a furnace design that maximizes the length of time waste and waste gases are exposed to high temperature and using automated combustion controls. In addition, the effectiveness of all such combustion and air pollution controls will depend in large measure on the care with which they are maintained and operated. A much-neglected aspect of incinerator operation in the United States has been operator training. Insistence on careful maintenance, operation by well-trained technicians, and an ethic that the operators' business is not merely waste disposal but pollution control would go a long way to reduce emissions.

An excellent source of information on the variety of approaches that can and should be used to reduce air emissions from MSW incinerators is available.[1]

WASTE STREAM CONTROL

What comes out of the stack is a function of what goes into the furnace in two respects. First, items that are difficult or impossible to burn—for example, because they are wet or because they are not combustible (e.g., metal cans and glass bottles)—reduce temperatures in the furnace, which reduces combustion efficiency, which can, in turn, cause increased emissions of organic substances that would otherwise burn up. Second, notwithstanding the beneficial effects of air pollution control devices, burning wastes that contain toxic substances will cause increased emissions of those substances. Many harmful air pollutants from incinerators are not formed by the incineration process. Rather, they are already present as pollutant precursors in the waste and are simply mobilized by incineration. Such substances include heavy metals, sulfur, nitrogen, and chlorine.

Accordingly, items that do not burn well should be kept out of incinerators. Glass and metal containers are the most obvious examples. Yard and food wastes should also be removed. These wastes actually require more energy to burn than they provide to the incinerator. In addition, such wastes have a high nitrogen content, and a facility that burns large amounts of these wastes will emit much higher amounts of nitrogen oxides (NO_x) than a facility that burns little or none. Because NO_x contributes to a host of environmental ills—acid rain, degradation of water quality, and urban smog—EDF has consistently argued that incinerators should not be allowed to burn yard and food wastes. This strategy not only helps to control NO_x emissions, but also makes such materials available for composting.

Keeping out sources of other pollutants, such as lead and cadmium, can be more difficult. Preventing these metals from entering the waste stream can mean removing them from the consumer products that contain them and that become waste. Most effective will be a combined strategy of reduced use of toxic metals in product manufacture, and source separation and recycling of remaining metal-containing materials from the waste stream to be incinerated.

OPERATING CONDITIONS

To destroy harmful organic compounds that are in the incoming waste or that are created during incineration, a high combustion temperature, sufficient oxygen and mixing, and adequate residence time of combustion gases in the furnace are necessary. (The length of time that combustion gases are actually exposed to the high temperature in the furnace is called "residence time" and can vary with internal furnace design and operating conditions.) Combustion efficiency can be aided through automation affecting parameters, such as temperature adjustment, oxygen flow, and waste feed rate. The optimal conditions vary somewhat from one incinerator to another. Good operating conditions are appropriately considered an important aspect of air pollution control.*

FLUE GAS CLEANING

Generally, air pollution control equipment refers to devices that clean the gases after they exit the furnace and before they exit the stack. There are three basic types of emission controls: particulate controls, acid-gas controls, and NO_x controls.

Particulate Controls

Particulate matter consists of small, unburned solid and condensed particles suspended in the combustion gases. Smoke is a visible form of particulate matter. These particles consist of a variety of different substances. All

---

* Appropriate basic conditions are outlined in model incinerator operating and construction permits that EDF has developed. These are available upon request.

nongaseous emissions from an incinerator exit in the form of particulate matter.

Particulate emissions are related to heavy metal and organic emissions. A large fraction of certain heavy metals and organic substances are emitted in a solid, condensed form, attached to small particulates. Although the furnace chamber temperature is generally hot enough to vaporize many metals and organics, the gases cool when they leave the combustion chamber and these substances then condense to a significant degree onto particulate matter.

Thus, good particulate control goes a long way toward controlling emissions of most organics and heavy metals. However, these chemicals vary with regard to the temperatures at which they vaporize and condense. Mercury, for example, vaporizes and condenses at a relatively low temperature; good particulate control alone will not be effective at controlling mercury emissions. Lead, on the other hand, vaporizes and condenses at a higher temperature, and efficient particulate control will have a substantial impact on lead emissions. For all of these chemicals, optimal control requires a combination of efficient particulate collection, preceded by maximum condensation of the substances onto particulates. Such condensation is most readily accomplished through extensive cooling of the flue gases prior to their entry into the particulate control device.

There are two basic types of particulate controls in use on modern incinerators. The electrostatic precipitator (ESP) has been the most common, although it has recently been giving way to the baghouse, or fabric filter. An ESP operates by giving particles an electric charge and then collecting them on large oppositely charged plates. The plates are periodically rapped to collect the accumulated particles. ESPs typically are built with multiple sets of plates, sometimes called "fields," and usually have from two to five fields. Generally speaking, the greater the number of fields, the higher the degree of particulate removal, as a result of the greater surface area per unit volume of combustion gases. Efficiency will also vary depending on, among other things, the gas velocity through the collector, the nature and size of the particles, and gas temperature and humidity.

A baghouse, or fabric filter, functions much like a vacuum cleaner bag. Flue gases containing entrained particles pass through numerous tubular bags; there can be dozens, hundreds, or even thousands of bags in a single control device. The particles cake up on the surface of the bag; the gases pass through. After brief use, the caked particles themselves help to capture additional particulates. The bags are periodically cleaned by shaking.

A third type of particulate control device is a wet scrubber, sometimes referred to as a "venturi" scrubber, which essentially washes particles out of the gases with a water spray. This device is generally much less efficient than ESPs or baghouses and is not considered an appropriate stand-alone option for MSW incinerator particulate control, although it is favored in Europe for control of acid gases and for condensation of metals and organic compounds. Wet scrubbers generally are not compatible with baghouses, just as introducing mud wreaks havoc on a standard vacuum cleaner.

The relative merits of ESPs and baghouses have been much debated, though a consensus is developing that the baghouse is the device of choice. The superiority of the baghouse lies in two factors: It can generally achieve a higher collection efficiency, and, at any given efficiency, it does a better job than the ESP in collecting very fine particles. This latter factor is especially important because most organics and heavy metals tend to attach more to small particles than to large ones. Smaller particles also pose a greater health risk because they are more easily inhaled. Thus, toxic-control efficiency should be better with a baghouse than an ESP, even if overall particulate control is the same.

ESPs have generally been considered more reliable in long-term operation than baghouses. Recent experience with baghouses has also confirmed their reliability, however, despite the many problems initially encountered. The primary concern as to reliability has been with the potential for fires caused by very hot flue gases. An ESP can handle much hotter gases. If the baghouse is used in conjunction with a scrubber, however, the flue gases are cooled by the scrubber before entering the baghouse.

One general concern with both ESPs and baghouses is related to the ability to monitor their operation in order to detect any malfunction or suboptimal performance. During regulatory testing at a new incinerator in California, a small and undetected defect in the baghouse allowed emissions of several heavy metals to increase by 10- to 100-fold.[2] Instrumentation is commercially available, but not always used, to detect even small baghouse failures and redirect gases to intact bags. Emissions tests at other incinerators have documented wide variations in emissions of dioxins and other pollutants over time at the same incinerator, despite the continual operation of the air pollution control equipment. For example, successive tests conducted four years apart at an incinerator in New York State revealed a ten-fold increase in emissions of particulate matter, apparently reflecting a degradation in the efficiency of the facility's ESP over that period.[3]

Acid-gas Scrubbers

An ESP or baghouse captures only particulate matter. Used alone, they will have little or no effect on acid gases, such as sulfur dioxide, hydrogen chloride, or hydrogen fluoride. Baghouses can be coated with lime, which will result in some removal of acid gases. There is also evidence to indicate that the ash caked on the bags, which is alkaline, can have some neutralizing effect on acid-gas emissions. In state-of-the-art facilities, acid gases are controlled by devices known as "scrubbers."

A scrubber, which is positioned after the furnace but before the particulate control device, neutralizes acid gases by injecting into the combustion gases lime or another alkaline reagent, either as a slurry, which evaporates to produce a dry residue (wet-dry or semi-dry scrubber), or as a powder (dry scrubber). Wet scrubbers, more common in Europe than in the United States, use water or an alkaline solution instead, and produce wet residues and/or wastewaters, which must be further treated.

The actual removal efficiencies for acid gases achieved in practice vary considerably. Under optimal operation, removal efficiencies approaching 99 percent for both hydrogen chloride (HCl) and sulfur dioxide (SO_2) have been achieved. Under less-optimal conditions (e.g., insufficient lime, too high a gas temperature), however, removal efficiencies can be much lower: Values as low as 75 percent for HCl and 30 percent for SO_2 have been reported.[4]

One incidental but, nonetheless, highly significant benefit of using acid-gas scrubbers in conjunction with particulate controls is their ability to increase removal efficiencies for toxic metals and organic chemicals. This enhancement occurs because the scrubber cools the flue gases more than would be the case in the absence of the scrubber, thereby condensing not only more acid gases but also more volatilized metals and organic chemicals onto particles that are subsequently removed by the particulate control device. At the appropriate temperature, heavy metals other than mercury are removed at greater than 99 percent efficiency. Mercury, because of its exceptionally low condensation temperature, requires very careful attention; even modern facilities with baghouses and scrubbers have considerable difficulty in routinely achieving efficient mercury removal. Based on the limitations of current air pollution control technology to adequately control mercury emissions, EPA has recently proposed to require that incinerators be accompanied by programs to remove household batteries from wastes to be incinerated, as part of BACT for mercury emissions.[5]

EPA has also recognized the significance of the incidental benefit of scrubbers in cooling flue gases and promoting condensation of toxic metals and organic compounds. In EPA guidance calling for the use of such scrubbers as BACT (see chapter 10), the agency stated that "performance of the dry scrubber and fabric filter or electrostatic precipitator in controlling acid gases, potentially toxic metals, and potentially toxic organic pollutants is affected significantly by the reduction in flue gas temperature which occurs in the dry scrubber. . . . The control system shall be designed and operated such that the flue gas temperature at the outlet from the dry scrubber does not exceed a specified value."[6] As a result, EPA has recently proposed to require all new and existing incinerators to cool flue gases to at least 450°F prior to entry into the particulate control device.[7] Scrubbers that achieve even lower flue gas temperatures (approaching 250°F) and better metals and organics control are being employed at MSW incinerators in Europe.[8]

Nitrogen Oxide Controls

Neither a particulate control device nor a scrubber has any appreciable effect on emissions of nitrogen oxides (NO_x). Historically, the accepted method of NO_x control has been good combustion conditions. Recently, however, flue gas cleaning devices developed specifically to control NO_x have become available.

Two basic types of such devices are commercially used on MSW incinerators: selective catalytic reduction (SCR) and selective noncatalytic reduction (SNCR). Both work by injecting aqueous ammonia or urea at some point into the furnace or flue gas stream; the ammonia reacts with and breaks down the NO_x gases. Experience with such devices in this country has been limited to date. SNCR using ammonia injection is in place at the Commerce, Stanislaus County, and Long Beach facilities, all located in California. Such technologies are becoming standard equipment in Japan, however, and the same will likely be the case in the United States in the near future, particularly in urban areas subject to NO_x-induced smog.

Waste stream controls over yard and food waste, and controls over incinerator design and certain operating conditions can also help to reduce NO_x emissions. (An excellent paper summarizing a range of approaches to NO_x controls is available.)[9]

EMISSION LIMITS

A facility equipped with a scrubber, baghouse, and NO_x controls will, if properly maintained and operated, be able to hold emissions of air pollutants to a small fraction of uncontrolled levels.

EDF has developed an annotated model air emissions permit, which sets out reasonably stringent but achievable emission limits for a variety of

different pollutants of concern, with references to supporting materials.*
These are limits that EDF deems technologically achievable. This does not
necessarily mean that a facility meeting these limits is automatically acceptable from a public health and environmental point of view. To the contrary, it
should still be subject to close scrutiny and a site- and population-specific
health risk assessment (see chapter 7). Compliance with these limits is, in
EDF's view, a necessary but not sufficient condition for construction and
operation of an incinerator.

Not all of these limits have actually found their way into existing permits or regulations. Many have, however, and those that have not are supported by test data from existing facilities. The burden should clearly
be on the proponent of an incinerator to demonstrate why these limits are
inappropriate.

MONITORING

Frequent or continuous comprehensive monitoring of facility performance
and emissions is essential for three reasons. First, paper obligations to hold
emissions to specified levels will be meaningless unless there is some
guarantee and verification that such levels are actually being achieved on a
continuous basis. There is simply no other means of assuring compliance.
Indeed, wherever possible, direct electronic relay of the outputs of continuous monitoring devices to state regulatory agencies should be required.
This capability, known as "telemetering," is already required in several
state regulations and facility permits.

Second, in contrast to fuels such as oil and coal, municipal solid waste
(MSW) is extremely heterogeneous. The operator has little control over
what the facility burns. Of course, some of the fuel, such as metals, glass,
and dirt, does not burn at all. As a result, conditions vary so often and so
much that a single sampling reveals almost nothing about a plant's overall
operation and emissions.

Third, comprehensive and reliable data on resource recovery facility
emissions during the full range of conditions encountered over the lifetime
of a facility do not exist. Only with more data from individual plants of
differing design and operating protocols will those operating and regulating
these facilities be able to determine optimal design and operating conditions.

*This model permit, as well as a summary of existing emissions limits specified in
state regulations and permits, are available from EDF upon request.

Thus, any incinerator proposal should be accompanied by a full panoply of monitoring requirements. EDF's model operating permit specifies the kinds and frequency of monitoring that should be required. Broadly speaking, monitoring falls into three basic categories: (1) monitoring of emissions, (2) monitoring of combustion and other operating conditions, and (3) monitoring of the ambient environment around a facility.

EMISSIONS MONITORING

Emissions monitoring involves testing of actual emissions from the facility to determine the amounts of various substances of concern for purposes of both assessing compliance with emission limits and determining if air pollution control equipment is functioning properly.

Emissions can be monitored in two basic ways. For many pollutants, especially combustion gases, technology exists that allows for continuous monitoring; these parameters include opacity—an indirect measurement of particulate matter—sulfur dioxide, nitrogen oxides, carbon monoxide, hydrogen chloride (widely used in Europe but often claimed to be unreliable by U.S. incinerator companies), and total hydrocarbons. Wherever technology allows, continuous monitoring is preferable since it provides an uninterrupted flow of information that readily allows an accurate calculation of total emissions. Continuous emissions monitoring devices must be frequently and carefully maintained and calibrated by trained personnel to ensure reliable readings.

For metals, individual organic chemicals, and particulate matter, continuous monitoring is not possible, and stack testing is required. Stack testing involves the collection of an actual sample of the emissions, which is then processed and analyzed using sophisticated chemical methods to determine the concentrations of individual chemicals in the original emissions. It is critical that such testing be conducted on a sufficiently frequent basis to provide a true representation of emissions over the life of the facility.

In addition, testing for individual pollutants should be conducted on the same air sample(s) wherever possible to ensure that all emission limits are being met simultaneously. This is important because emissions of some pollutants are interrelated. For example, increases in combustion temperature to reduce dioxin and carbon monoxide emissions generally increase nitrogen oxide emissions. Separate measurements of these pollutants could indicate compliance with each of the emission limits, but simultaneous measurements might not.

Although virtually all new incinerators are required to conduct initial stack tests, many states do not require subsequent testing, or only require it at intervals that are too infrequent to be of any real use in estimating actual routine emissions from the facility. In addition, infrequent testing on a schedule known to operators well in advance allows both operators and facilities to "be on their best behavior" during the actual testing, again skewing the results away from typical conditions. EDF's model permits set out a schedule for stack testing that EDF considers to be reasonable, recognizing both the variability in emissions and the considerable expense involved.

It is also critical that stack testing be conducted for a broad range of pollutants, including many individual metals and organic chemicals. The list of substances to be tested for should obviously include all of those for which emissions limits exist, and should also include any additional parameters that may be of potential health or environmental concern. Despite the claims of the industry to the contrary, too much variability in emissions and too little comprehensive long-term monitoring data currently exist to justify any narrowing of stack testing to a set of surrogate parameters (i.e., metals or organic chemicals whose concentrations can reliably be used to indicate the concentrations of other chemicals not tested for).

Nor does continuous monitoring of combustion efficiency parameters (e.g., temperature, carbon monoxide emissions) serve as a substitute for direct measurement of individual gases, metals, or organic compounds. Metal and gas emissions are much more related to waste input than they are to combustion conditions. Even for organic compounds such as dioxins, whose emissions do reflect combustion efficiency to a large degree, we do not have sufficient operating experience and emissions data to accurately correlate such emissions with general indicators of operating conditions.

MONITORING OF COMBUSTION AND OTHER OPERATING CONDITIONS

Maintaining a high efficiency of combustion is essential to limiting the emissions of unburned or partially burned waste components, as well as emissions of compounds such as dioxins that can be formed during the incineration process. The three Ts previously discussed—time, turbulence (i.e., adequate oxygen and mixing), and temperature—are primary determinants of combustion efficiency. The basic operating conditions that, in turn, determine the three Ts can and should be monitored on a continuous basis. These include waste feed rate; furnace temperature; auxiliary fuel use; carbon monoxide, carbon dioxide, and oxygen content of the combustion gases; and air flow through the combustion chamber.

In addition, basic operation and efficiency of the air pollution control equipment should be assessed. For a scrubber, measurement of the concentrations of acid gases, such as hydrogen chloride and sulfur dioxide, before and after the scrubber provide a direct assessment of removal efficiencies and, hence, scrubber operation.

MONITORING OF THE AMBIENT ENVIRONMENT

The ideal means of assessing the impact of air emissions from an incinerator on the surrounding environment is to directly measure the concentrations of the pollutants of concern in that environment. Unfortunately, this is easier said than done. First, one needs reliable background data on such concentrations, which requires monitoring to have been conducted prior to incinerator operation. This information is necessary to establish an appropriate baseline against which to measure any increases that may occur after operations begin.

Then, reliable and representative monitoring data need to be collected. Determining the appropriate number of samples to be collected, and the location of the sampling points, is technically highly complex and site specific. Such sampling is also expensive because many samples taken at many locations and at many points in time must be collected and analyzed to provide reliable information.

Ambient monitoring is further complicated by two additional factors: First, many of the pollutants of concern with respect to incinerators are also released into the environment by other sources. For example, lead is released from vehicles burning lead gasoline, from eroding lead-based paint, from other combustion sources such as power plants, and from various industrial facilities. Second, historical accumulations of lead from these and other past sources exist. Sorting out whether any increase over background is attributable to the incinerator or to these other sources is enormously difficult.

Knowing where to look for increases in concentrations of relevant pollutants is also far from straightforward. Although ambient air is the most obvious place to start, many pollutants that are initially released into the air accumulate and pose their most profound risks in surface soils, dusts, water, or food. Assessing the long-term impact of incinerator emissions thus requires measurements of trends in these media, as well as in the air—a very arduous task, given the compounding of all of the factors already discussed.

For these reasons, few incinerator permits contain provisions related to ambient monitoring. EDF's model permits contain some, albeit very limited, proposals for ambient air monitoring. Further discussion of this topic is beyond the scope of this handbook.

NOTES

1. M.J. Clarke, "Improving Environmental Performance of MSW Incinerators," paper presented at the Industrial Gas Cleaning Forum '88 (Washington, DC, November 3–4, 1988).

2. M. Gildart and R. Pasek, "Coordinated Waste, Ash, and Emissions Sampling at the Commerce Waste-to-Energy Facility," in *Proceedings of the International Conference on Municipal Waste Combustion*, vol. 1 (Hollywood, FL: Environment Canada, 1989), p. 5C-31.

3. T.D. Goldfarb, prefiled testimony before the New York Department of Environmental Conservation Office of Administrative Law, in the Matter of the Application of Signal Environmental Systems for permits to construct and operate the proposed Brooklyn Navy Yard Resource Recovery Facility, DEC project no. 20-85-0306 (New York, 1988).

4. M.J. Clarke, "Improving Environmental Performance of MSW Incinerators," p. 20.

5. EPA has recently proposed this requirement as part of its package of emission guidelines for existing MSW incinerators (see *Federal Register* 54, [December 20, 1989]: 52209) and New Source Performance Standards for new MSW incinerators (see *Federal Register* 54 [December 20, 1989]: 52251. See also the discussion of these regulations in chapter 10.

6. "Operational Guidance on Control Technology for New and Modified Municipal Waste Combustors," (Research Triangle Park, NC: EPA, Office of Air Quality Planning and Standards, June 26, 1987).

7. EPA has recently proposed this requirement as part of its package of emission guidelines for existing MSW incinerators (see *Federal Register* 54 [December 20, 1989]: 52209) and New Source Performance Standards for new MSW incinerators (see *Federal Register* 54 [December 20, 1989]: 52251).

8. M.J. Clarke, "Improving Environmental Performance of MSW Incinerators," pp. 15–16.

9. M.J. Clarke, "Technologies for Minimizing the Emission of NO_x from MSW Incinerators," paper presented at the 82nd Annual Meeting of the Air and Waste Management Association (Anaheim, CA, June 25–30, 1989).

CHAPTER 7

Evaluating MSW Incinerator Health Risk Assessments

AN ALMOST UNIVERSAL component of proposals for MSW incinerators is some sort of health risk assessment (HRA). Ideally, but all too rarely, an HRA identifies all health impacts that can be expected to result from all phases of an incinerator's operation, and also considers such risks in light of all other waste management options. However, such assessments virtually always ignore ash-related hazards. HRAs are usually drafted by consultants hired by either the local government or the vendor of a proposed incinerator.

Because quantifying risks is still as much an art as a science, HRAs are frequently highly contested. Unfortunately, they are usually replete with technical jargon. Understanding the terminology and recognizing the limits of our ability to predict health impacts are two crucial steps toward evaluating a risk assessment.

Before describing risk assessment procedures in detail, some critical caveats must be noted. First, all risk assessments entail major scientific uncertainties, both in the methodology itself and in the data on emissions, their toxicity, and the degree of exposure to the emissions. The HRA process involves making a series of assumptions (sometimes guesstimates) about highly complicated phenomena ranging from the potency of various toxic substances, to the potential for various pathways and degrees of exposure, to the efficiency of various pollution control strategies and the resulting levels of pollutants released. If the assumptions used in the HRA are wrong, so are its predictions of risk. Thus, the HRA can at best provide one limited tool for examining potential impacts of a facility.

Assumptions about pollutant emission levels should be scrutinized with special care to ensure that such levels will never be exceeded during actual operation of the facility. Frequently, assumed emissions are far below those that would be set, and enforced, in the facility's permit. Claims of low-risk operations do not substitute for enforceable guarantees to install BACT, use state-of-the-art engineering design, employ trained operators, and require ongoing monitoring of actual operations and releases. (These issues are discussed in chapter 6.) Risk assessments provide one way to estimate the *relative* reduction in emissions, and, therefore, risk, that can be achieved through these controls on design and operation.

Unfortunately, few HRAs candidly acknowledge the tremendous uncertainties inherent in their methods and data. Moreover, many HRAs compound that failing by expressing their results in absolute terms, as estimates of actual risk. Such numbers convey a wholly unwarranted sense of both precision and accuracy. For example, one recent HRA concluded that an incinerator would produce an excess cancer risk of 1.18×10^{-6} (meaning that the incinerator would cause 1.18 additional cancers per million people exposed), even though the underlying data had uncertainty factors of several hundred percent. Because few members of the general public recognize the current limitations in the data on emissions, exposure, and toxicity, presentation of such figures is highly misleading.

Despite their substantial limitations, HRAs can help to answer important questions, such as:

1. Have all significant potential health impacts, exposures, and releases been considered and controlled?
2. Are the projected impacts the minimum that can be achieved within the limits of good operating and engineering practice?
3. How do the risks compare—in a relative sense—to those posed by other waste management alternatives?

If the limitations of risk assessment are fairly appreciated—and fairly translated into equally limited reliance on the results—risk assessments can help translate a morass of information into a more understandable form. This chapter describes a generalized HRA. It discusses the typical content of such a document, the analytical methods that are usually employed, and the limits on its utility as a predictor of health impacts. The chapter also identifies sources of information that can be used to evaluate assertions made in a particular HRA.

FUNDAMENTALS AND LIMITATIONS OF RISK ASSESSMENT

A risk assessment should describe all of the substances that will be released during all stages in the incineration process; review the human health and environmental hazards associated with these substances; quantify the amounts and rates of release anticipated from the incinerator; describe all the pathways of exposure and estimate the degree of exposure of humans and other organisms in the environment to these substances; and evaluate the anticipated risks, or adverse effects, of these exposures on humans and other organisms. It should also evaluate these exposures and impacts in light of already ongoing exposures and impacts to the same population from other sources.

An HRA should be both qualitative and quantitative; that is, it should fully describe the biological properties of each substance and its behavior in the environment (e.g., is it carcinogenic? does it persist in water?), and it should include numerical estimates of the amounts expected to be released from the incinerator, and the impacts on humans and the environment.

The key components of an HRA are:

- a list of all the potentially emitted substances of concern;
- a comprehensive description of the toxicity of these substances;
- information on how much of each substance will be released by the incinerator, and at what rate (for instance, in grams per second or tons per year);
- a comprehensive discussion of how these substances will move through the environment—air, surface and groundwater, dusts and soil—and how people, animals, and plants will encounter them; and
- a description of the real-world environment around the incinerator, including a variety of factors that might affect exposure, such as population density, any special activities, such as farming or fishing, and existing contamination levels from other sources.

Risk assessments can only very roughly estimate risks, and are best used to gauge *relative* risk (e.g., between a facility operating with and without a scrubber). Information on the real-world behavior of these facilities—how many tons of various pollutants they will routinely emit under the full range of actual operating conditions—is extremely limited. On a more fundamental level, we are also still limited in our understanding of the toxicity of many emitted substances, how such substances interact, and how people respond to exposures to complex mixtures of the substances that are released from incinerators. Because there are very few health studies of persons exposed to operating incinerators for long periods of time, either as employees at such facilities or as residents living near them (or near the ash dumps), very few empirical data are available to allow us to evaluate the predictions made by risk assessments. Even now, there is little environmental or human monitoring to determine what sorts of exposures actually result from incinerator operations.

THE HEALTH RISK ASSESSMENT: A THUMBNAIL SKETCH

WHAT IS RELEASED?

An HRA should list and evaluate all substances that are known to be released from incineration of MSW. These include heavy metals, organics, acid gases, particulates, carbon monoxide, carbon dioxide, nitrogen oxides, etc. All of these substances will be released in some amount from an operating incinerator.

The assessment should not only list substances released but should also specify the physical and chemical forms in which they will be released. For example, will a particular metal be released attached to particles or as a fume or vapor (very fine particles or water droplets)? This information is important for evaluating information on environmental dispersion and eventual exposure.

In discussing emissions of particulate matter (sometimes referred to as total suspended particulate, or TSP), the assessment should distinguish between particles smaller and larger than ten microns (a micron is one-millionth of a meter). That distinction is critical in assessing health risks because the smaller particles are respirable, that is, they can be breathed in deeply, reaching the small passages of the lung, where they can be absorbed directly into the body.

WHAT RISKS ARE POSED BY THE RELEASES?

The HRA should provide up-to-date information on the hazards associated with each of the substances released. This part of the HRA, often called the hazard identification stage, should provide information to answer at least these questions:

a. Is the substance known or suspected to cause cancer in humans or experimental animals?[1]
b. Is the substance neurotoxic—does it affect the nervous system?
c. Is the substance toxic to reproduction and development?
d. Is the substance toxic to organs such as the liver, kidney, lung, heart, skin, muscle, or bone?

e. Is the substance mutagenic, for example, does it cause damage to genetic material (DNA)?[2]

f. Is the substance toxic to the immune or endocrine systems?

Substances that fall into these different categories are evaluated by different methodologies. Specifically, one method is generally accepted as appropriate for carcinogens and mutagens (categories a and e); another is applied to substances that fall into categories b, c, d, or f.

Information on toxicity should be supported by up-to-date citations to published information. The best sources are studies or reviews published in scientific journals or by the government after being peer reviewed. Even peer-reviewed publications cannot be unquestioningly accepted, however. For one thing, only a handful of reviewers look at a given document; for another, sometimes the reviewers' comments are simply ignored. Still, on the whole, the peer-reviewed literature is more likely to be accurate and reliable than other sources of information.

In addition to independent scientific journals, two types of government documents can be especially valuable: those published by EPA, particularly the comprehensive Health Assessment Document series, and the Toxicology Profiles now being published by the Agency for Toxic Substances and Disease Registry (ATSDR). ATSDR is part of the U.S. Department of Health and Human Services Centers for Disease Control. EPA and ATSDR documents can be found at U.S. government repository libraries, which include most major universities.[2]

Typically, a hazard identification focuses on human health impacts, measured directly in humans or extrapolated from well-established models for predicting human health effects of toxic substances based on results of studies on animals. However, the hazard identification should not overlook the adverse impacts of these substances on other species. For example, fish and other aquatic organisms are highly sensitive to certain heavy metals and to acid precipitation that results from acid-gas releases. When incinerators and/or ash disposal sites are located near such species' habitats, these considerations become important. Exposures to plants or animals can also translate into human exposure if people eat them.

How Much of Each Substance Will Be Emitted?

In moving from the hazard identification stage to the exposure assessment stage of the risk assessment process, it is essential to have information on the actual amounts of pollutants that will be released from the incinerator. The HRA can, at present, only offer informed speculation because real numbers—measurements of actual emissions over time of all relevant pollutants—have seldom been collected.

In evaluating emissions projections, it is important to check to see to what extent they are based on actual measurements collected through frequent or continuous monitoring conducted during routine operations of incinerators similar to the one proposed, as opposed to models or extrapolations from short-term measurements done during start-up or infrequent testing. Most short-term tests, carefully conducted under the watchful eye of the local or state regulator and often on incinerators when they are new and operated by unusually well-trained personnel, may not be representative of day-to-day operations over the several decades of actual operation.

Finally, the HRA should explicitly acknowledge that emissions from a particular incinerator will vary, and should estimate emissions under the different conditions an incinerator will inevitably encounter. For example, most incinerators must shut each furnace down at least twice a month for routine maintenance and occasionally for emergency repairs; emissions during start-up and shutdown are likely to exceed those during normal operations. In addition, incinerators can suffer upset conditions, during which the incinerator does not function normally. Upsets can occur, for example, when large amounts of uncombustible items or unusually wet garbage (e.g., after a heavy rain) find their way into the furnace or because of mechanical malfunctions in the incinerator itself or its pollution control equipment. As during start-up/shutdown, emissions tend to increase during upsets.

Several cases are available to illustrate the increase in emissions that can occur during suboptimal operating conditions. During recent regulatory testing of a new incinerator in Southern California, dioxin emissions were evaluated during a period when the incinerator was operating at less-than-optimal efficiency. Emissions were 5 to 50 times higher than during other tests conducted under good combustion conditions.[3] Tests at another facility in New York State found a tenfold increase in dioxin emissions during upset conditions.[4]

Despite many operating years, the incinerator industry still has not provided any reliable data or even estimates of the frequency of upsets. HRAs virtually never account for such events when estimating emissions.

HRAs usually describe emissions data in terms of the total amount of a particular substance released per year. Some assessments refer to a rate (i.e., an amount per second), which can be converted into amount per year by multiplying by expected hours of operation per day and days per year. Air emissions may be expressed on a corrected basis, for example, based on a 7 percent O_2 concentration in the stack gases or in units of mass per dry standard cubic foot. These widely used terms allow comparison of emissions from different facilities, correcting for facility-specific factors.

On occasion, HRAs may express emissions in different terms. For example, emissions are sometimes described as amounts per ton of waste burned or, less commonly, per unit of heat produced. In addition, releases of some substances—especially acid gases—may be described as the percentage of the total amount of those substances created in the incinerator that is actually emitted, based on anticipated efficiency of air pollution control devices. Though such data may be useful in some contexts, they are not very relevant in assessing health risks that reflect the total amounts of pollutants released. Thus, every HRA should at least provide data in units that reflect the total mass released per unit time.

HOW WILL THE RELEASED SUBSTANCES BE DISPERSED AND BEHAVE IN THE ENVIRONMENT?

The next part of the HRA usually describes how pollutants move or are dispersed through the environment after being released from the stack. Most of this information is based upon modeling and inference because there are very few real data on what happens to substances released from stacks. The HRA should expressly acknowledge the uncertainties in the data and models.

In What Physical and Chemical Forms Will Pollutants Be Released?

Substances can leave the incinerator either as particles or as vapors/fumes. The specific form of emissions significantly affects how these releases are dispersed. Some substances may be emitted in more than one form; metals, for instance, may be released both as particles and vapors or fumes.

Air pollution control equipment can remove from emissions a significant fraction of particles and certain gases. Once captured, however, the substances do not disappear, but rather are transferred to the ash. Credible risk assessments must examine hazards not just from air emissions but from storage, transportation, and disposal of ash.

In projecting the environmental behavior of releases from incinerators, the chemical characteristics of the pollutants must also be known. Some substances are very persistent in the environment, that is, the normal chemical and biological processes of breakdown act on them only very slowly. Metals such as lead and cadmium are permanent, and cannot be broken down or degraded. Certain metals can be transformed in the environment by bacteria or other processes into different chemical forms. For example, metallic mercury can be transformed into methylmercury, which is far more toxic.

In contrast to metals, the environmental persistence of organic compounds varies substantially. Those of most health concern are generally very persistent, but others change rapidly when exposed to light or moisture, or are readily degraded by bacteria. Unfortunately, studying environmental fate in the real world is quite difficult, and laboratory predictions of environmental persistence may give inaccurate results. For instance, we now know that dioxin in the environment does not break down very quickly, although pure dioxin does break down when exposed to ultraviolet light in the laboratory. This discrepancy is explained by the fact that the dioxin released from incinerators is tightly bound to organic material and is shielded from degradation.

How are the Pollutants Dispersed?

HRAs should describe the environmental behavior of substances released from an incinerator, including local and long-range transport, the highest ground-level concentrations, the range of ground-level concentrations over the area of concern, and the rates at which pollutants are deposited and accumulate over time. Factors that affect transport of emissions close to the incinerator include downdraft and cavity effects, which result from air pockets that affect movement of substances close to the stack. Transport of pollutants can occur over long distances—sometimes hundreds of miles— before they descend to ground or water level.

Ground-level Concentrations: Often, HRAs estimate maximum ground-level concentrations of certain pollutants, using complex mathmatical models that account for variables, such as rates of release, stack height, temperature, and prevailing wind direction. Many such models, however, are not sophisticated enough to address even common features of the local environment, such as hills or buildings. This maximum concentration, usually expressed as the amount of the substance within one cubic meter above the ground, is meant to describe the maximum exposure of a person breathing within that cubic meter of air. It may not, however, represent actual maximum exposures.

Some HRAs also describe a range of ground-level concentrations in particular areas around the incinerator, including residential neighborhoods, hospitals, schools, or farmland. These analyses can highlight special reasons for concern, such as exposures to especially vulnerable members of the community or the potential for food-chain contamination.

Deposition: In addition to presenting information on the concentrations of released substances in air at ground level, the HRA should evaluate the rate of deposition, and accumulation, of releases. Deposition is the process by which airborne particles settle onto surfaces such as water, soils, plants, or human-made structures (roads, houses, etc.). For persistent substances, even slow rates of deposition can result in substantial buildup of the substances in surface dusts and soils. As a result of deposition, the most significant potential for exposure to metals and persistent organics occurs after they settle out of the air rather than during the relatively short period of time they are suspended in air.

Deposition is sometimes divided into wet and dry deposition, that is, the fallout of substances in the presence and absence of rain or snow. Wet deposition rates can be much higher than dry deposition, particularly for gases or very small particles. In HRAs, it is important to consider both types.

After deposition occurs, another critical aspect of environmental behavior comes into play: uptake of the substances by animals or plants within the local environment. Some substances are poorly absorbed; others are readily accumulated. For example, some fish can "bioconcentrate" dioxin about 50,000-fold, meaning that dioxin is present in the fish at levels up to 50,000 times higher than in the surrounding waters. In general, plants do not bioaccumulate most toxic substances as readily as animals; however, deposition of contaminated dusts and soils on leafy surfaces may result in substantial contamination of these parts of plants, so that spinach and lettuce, for instance, may be contaminated.

WHAT IS THE LOCAL ENVIRONMENT?

The HRA for a specific incinerator proposal should include considerable information on the local environment. This is frequently not included. Rather, many HRAs use standard generic models for predicting dispersion of releases, even though local features are very important determinants of the behavior of substances in the environment. At a minimum, the HRA should take into account the actual stack height planned for the facility, its placement in the environment, and the geography surrounding it. In addition, use of accurate and comprehensive information on local meteorological conditions, such as wind directions and rainfall, is important for increasing the reliability of predictions of ground-level concentrations and deposition rates.

Local population patterns are also key factors in evaluating risk. The assessment must consider not only the immediate vicinity of the incinerator, but also areas likely to be impacted by ash transport, disposal or treatment, water discharges, and the like.

Finally, the HRA should disclose and consider the degree to which the local community has already been exposed to pollutants that will be released from incinerators. For instance, in Holyoke, Massachusetts, local public health providers raised objections to the siting of an incinerator in an area with an already high incidence of lead toxicity in young children. The incinerator was rejected on the grounds that any new source of lead exposure was unacceptable.

WHAT IS THE POTENTIAL FOR HUMAN EXPOSURE?

Based upon information about the amounts of various substances released and predictions as to amounts dispersed into air, water, soils, dusts, and the food chain, the exposure assessment estimates what amounts of the substances of concern people will actually encounter. Routes of exposure include the major portals of entry into the body: through the lungs via inhalation, through the stomach via ingestion, and through skin via dermal absorption. Pathways of exposure include the environmental media—air, water, dust, and soil—as well as contaminated food. Pathways and routes may be related in complex ways: For instance, humans can inhale soil particles, ingest soil present on food, and contact soil directly on the skin. *All* pathways and routes of exposure must be considered in this stage of the assessment. (Figure 5.2 illustrates how people encounter pathways of exposure to substances from MSW incinerators.)

Most HRAs use standard assumptions about rates of transfer, that is, the frequency at which people contact their environmental pathways. For example, adults are assumed to breathe ten cubic meters of air per day, although this may vary with the level of physical activity and age of the person. It is also assumed that people drink two liters of water a day. Estimates of soil ingestion are less well established, partly because exposure to soil varies substantially by age. Generally, it is agreed that children under six years are likely to ingest more dirt and dust than adults, as a result of normal play behavior, mouthing, and direct eating of dirt. Inhalation of dust and soil particles is not well studied, though it can be a major route/pathway of exposure.

The final factor in assessing exposure is calculating absorption, that is, how much of the substance encountered in a particular form by a particular route (e.g., lead in inhaled dust) is actually taken up by the body and transferred to places in the body where it exerts toxic effects. To date, researchers have collected little real-world information on absorption; in the absence of such data, HRAs should, and generally do, assume that 100 percent of the substance encountered in each pathway and entering the body by any route will be absorbed. If a figure less than 100 percent is used, that is, absorbed dose is less than exposure dose, good reasons should be provided for this adjustment.

THE BOTTOM LINE: CALCULATING THE RISK

Finally, an HRA calculates an estimated risk to human health resulting from operation of the facility. The risk calculation should take into consideration all of the features described above: the toxicity of the substances and the opportunities for exposure to them that people will have based upon the amounts and rates of release, in light of their environmental behavior. Simply put, the quantitative risk assessment multiplies toxicity times exposure to calculate risks. Risk assessments are, therefore, only as good as the toxicity and exposure information on which they are based.

An HRA may focus on risk of death or disease, or on a particular biological condition (as in the case of lead, where blood levels are a widely used medical indicator of a variety of toxic effects). An HRA should consider the total risk from all exposures to the same substance, whether encountered, for example, in the air after release from a stack or in groundwater after land disposal of ash. Such estimates are generally summed to yield a total risk for each health endpoint (e.g., total cancer risk). Risks are calculated in two different ways, with cancer- and mutation-causing substances assessed through a different approach than other substances.

Cancer Risk Assessments

For carcinogens and mutagens, the EPA and several state health and environmental agencies have adopted a specific method for evaluating the risks from particular exposures, or doses. That methodology also has been extensively reviewed by scientists at the state, national, and international levels.

EPA's methodology is based upon the fundamental assumption that *any* exposure to a carcinogen or mutagen increases the risk that a cancer or a mutation will arise. With very small exposures, the risk is very low; with larger exposures, the risk is greater.

This assumption—termed the no-threshold assumption—reflects current understanding of the biological mechanisms of carcinogenesis and mutagenesis, which are known to begin with changes in genetic material (DNA) or other cellular changes that can be induced by a single molecule.

Based upon this understanding, risk assessments of carcinogens and muta-gens use a linear model, variously referred to as the linearized multistage, Armitage-Doll, or Carcinogen Assessment Group model, to estimate the risk of cancer or mutation resulting from exposures. This model assumes that the risk of cancer or a mutation increases linearly with dose (i.e., the amount of the substance to which one is exposed). At the present time, this is the model that should be employed in assessing cancer risk.

Noncancer Risk Assessments

Substances other than carcinogens are evaluated differently, using the so-called safety-factor approach. The safety-factor approach assumes that each substance has a threshold dose, such that exposure to a lower amount—no matter how often repeated—causes no harm.

Unlike the no-threshold assumption used in cancer risk assessment, the threshold assumption used in the safety-factor model is not based on insights into the underlying biological processes; indeed, frequently less is known about the biological mechanisms of many types of noncancer tox-icity than is known about cancer. Rather, the safety-factor approach simply reflects tradition. That tradition is increasingly open to question, however, as research into noncancer toxic responses suggests that at least certain of these responses may also occur without a threshold. For example, recent research into lead toxicity indicates that there is no threshold below which lead exposure does not cause some neurotoxic response in young children.

To perform a risk assessment using the safety-factor approach, the person conducting the assessment first reviews the scientific literature. In that review, a no-effect level is identified, that is, the highest dose at which laboratory animals show no toxic reaction. This dose is referred to as the no-observable-adverse-effect level, or NOAEL. Alternatively, the lowest-effect level is identified, that is, the lowest dose at which the animals displayed some toxic reaction (referred to as the lowest-observable-adverse-effect level, or LOAEL). Traditionally, a safe dose is then calculated by dividing the NOAEL by 100, or the LOAEL by 1,000.

NOAELs and LOAELs are generally rather imprecise. They are often based on limited data that may not be sensitive enough to detect low-dose effects. In addition, the NOAEL or LOAEL is often based upon experi-ments that focused on one type of adverse response, such as liver toxicity, without investigating whether other types of responses occur at even lower doses. Although some of this uncertainty is compensated for by using the safety factors of 100 or 1,000, the end value can be as much a product of art as science.

SUMMARY: A HEALTH RISK ASSESSMENT CHECKLIST

HRAs are a form of sophisticated crystal-ball gazing. Working from limited data on toxicity, exposure, and local conditions, they try to predict the extent to which some activity—such as operating an incinerator—will affect health or environmental quality. As a result of the serious limitations of risk assessment, EDF strongly believes that efforts to control pollution should be premised on the assumption that facilities must use all technologically feasible means to control their releases rather than simply limiting releases to a safe level. To date, reliable information on safe levels of long-term exposure to pollutants does not exist. Even less information exists on multiple-pollutant interactions and the potentially higher vulnerability of certain segments of the population, such as children, the elderly, and pregnant women.

Unfortunately, HRAs are widely claimed to accurately assess actual risk and, therefore, are used as a basis for justifying the construction and operation of pollution sources. At the very least, HRAs should play fair by their own rules, fully disclosing all releases, all exposure routes, and all uncertainties. The checklist that follows suggests key points to look for in reviewing an HRA.

An **HRA** Checklist

Is the HRA complete? Does it cover:
—All relevant substances
  —Organics (dioxins/furans, PCBs, etc.)
  —Heavy metals (lead, cadmium, mercury, etc.)
  —Others (acid gases, nitrogen oxides, sulfur oxides, etc.)
—All relevant releases
  —Air emissions
  —Ash releases
  —Water discharges
  —Storage, transport, and disposal of ash
—All relevant health effects
  —Cancer
  —Fetotoxicity
  —Neurotoxicity
  —Toxicity to organs (kidney, liver, bone, heart, and lung)
  —Toxicity to systems (immune, blood, etc.)

Are all relevant routes and pathways of exposure discussed? Is post-deposition accumulation of airborne releases considered?

Is the local environment described, or are only general models and predictions incorporated into the risk assessment?

Are carcinogens evaluated by the linear model for risk or is a threshold assumed? What level of risk is calculated for the maximally exposed person? Are overall levels of cancer risk calculated by adding all carcinogens, all pathways and routes of exposure?

Are background levels of exposure and other existing sources of the same substances considered, with special attention given to any locally important sources of high-level exposure, such as nearby factories, disposal sites, etc.?

How much real data are included in the risk assessment, or is it all based on extrapolations and models?

Are the results presented as single values or as ranges reflecting varying assumptions?

Are the claims backed up by good references? Are EPA data used, such as the EPA's cancer-potency calculations? If not, why not?

Are effects on the environment, as well as human health, considered? Are sensitive populations and environments considered?

Are noncancer risks discussed thoroughly, particularly risks of heavy metal poisoning?

Are all assumptions and sources of uncertainty clearly stated?

NOTES

1. For a list of known and suspected human carcinogens, see U.S. Department of Health and Human Services, Public Health Service, National Toxicology Program, *Fourth Annual Report on Carcinogens*, 1985.
2. EPA Health Assessment Documents are also available through: National Technical Information Service (NTIS), 5285 Port Royal Road, Springfield, VA 22161, (800) 336-4700 or Environmental Criteria and Assessment Office, U.S. Environmental Protection Agency, Cincinnati, OH 45268. ATSDR Toxicology profiles are available through NTIS or through: Agency for Toxic Substances and Disease Registry, 1600 Clifton Road NE, Mail Stop E-29, Atlanta, GA 30333.
3. M. Gildart and R. Pasek, "Coordinated Waste, Ash, and Emissions Sampling at the Commerce Waste-to-Energy Facility," in *Proceedings of the International Conference on Municipal Waste Combustion*, vol. 1 (Hollywood, FL: Environment Canada, 1989), p. 5C-31.

4. T.D. Goldfarb, prefiled testimony before the New York Department of Environmental Conservation Office of Administrative Law, in the Matter of the Application of Signal Environmental Systems for permits to construct and operate the proposed Brooklyn Navy Yard Resource Recovery Facility, DEC project no. 20-85-0306 (New York 1988).

PART III

Practical Aspects of Planning, Implementation, and Environmental Review: Strategies for Effective Citizen Participation

T HIS FINAL PART PROVIDES the nuts and bolts of citizen evaluation of, and participation in, a local community's decision whether to build an incinerator, and if so, under what conditions. Chapter 8 discusses some innovative approaches to dealing with a common question that arises with virtually any incinerator proposal: If an incinerator is to be built, how can citizens be sure that all of the promises regarding its performance that are made at the outset will actually be kept?

Chapter 9 places the incinerator proposal into the broader context of solid waste management planning, identifying key elements in any solid waste management plan and approaches to ensuring that the plan addresses all of the available options. Chapter 9 also briefly discusses the highly contentious issue of siting.

Finally, chapter 10 lays out the legislative, regulatory, and judicial framework that underlies solid waste management in general, and the permitting of MSW incinerators in particular. The intent is to provide the reader with a road map through the myriad of federal, state, and local laws and regulations that bear on the decision of whether and how to issue a permit to an MSW incinerator.

CHAPTER 8

Promises, Promises: Screening Out the Bad, Locking In the Good

ALMOST BY DEFINITION, a proposal for a municipal waste incinerator is controversial enough that its proponents are called on to say how it will perform. How much will it cost? What will come out of the smokestack? Will the ash be hazardous? If it is built, will it interfere with the growth of recycling?

Often, the proponents of the incinerator respond to citizen or government concerns by offering promises, either explicit or implicit: "No, the emissions won't be harmful"; "no, the ash won't be toxic"; "no, the incinerator won't preclude expanded recycling." Every time one is made, the question must be asked: Is this a genuine promise? And if so, how can anyone be sure that it will be kept? This chapter discusses a few innovative ways to find out, before final commitments are made.

This chapter also suggests some ways to make sure that such promises are actually kept, not just in the early months or years of operation but throughout the life of the project. Using these techniques during the proposal stage does not imply support for the project; anyone, including the most hardened skeptic, is entitled to know whether the spokespersons for any incinerator are willing to stand behind their promises. If they are not willing to be held to the predictions and assumptions that they are asking the public to accept, then everyone involved in the process is entitled to know that fact from the beginning.

Standards of environmental performance (e.g., how much of which pollutants will come out of the smokestack) are frequently written into permits, and the public is told that the standards are guaranteed because the incinerator will have to obey its permit conditions. Unfortunately, a permit cannot be viewed as a guarantee.

Even if a permit is carefully written, and even if it is legally enforceable, the government has discretion about how vigorously to enforce it. For example, agencies that administer air quality permits often discover violations, but then give after-the-fact permission for the violation to occur, usually in the form of a variance. Even if today's regulators are diligent, the staff of the regulatory agency is sure to change many times during the life of a 30-year incinerator. So may the company and personnel that operates it. And once an incinerator is up and running, with a fleet of loaded garbage trucks arriving every day, government officials are understandably reluctant to interfere, even if the incinerator operator is not complying with permit requirements.

At the outset, then, citizens and officials have a strong and legitimate interest in knowing whether the promises they are hearing are realistic, and whether those promises will actually be kept. Fortunately, citizens do not need to be experts on incineration to find out.

The surest way to find out whether a project's proponents are serious about their assurances is to arrange for the project—not the municipality or the public—to bear the risk if the assurances turn out to be wrong. This put-your-money-where-your-mouth-is approach has two benefits. First, if a project's spokespersons know that the project will be held to their promises, they are far more likely to be realistic about what they say. As a result, the public will get a clearer idea in advance of what standards the project's own experts think they can meet for the full lifetime of the project. In turn, the public and government agencies get a clearer picture of what they are being asked to accept. Second, if something does go wrong later on, the public taxpayer and the public environment will not be the first to suffer.

How can this kind of accountability be created in practice? The key is to do it in advance before all permits are granted and public financing has been authorized. The mechanisms themselves are straightforward. Three examples are given below. A draft resolution that a municipality's governing body could adopt, covering all three examples, is provided in Appendix C.

ASH TOXICITY

In any contract between a municipality and an incinerator, the contract can require that all ash disposal costs be borne by the project proponents, whether the ash is classified as hazardous or not. Incinerator proponents usually claim that their ash will not have to be handled as a hazardous waste, and they submit cost figures on that assumption. If they are wrong, higher costs will almost certainly be passed on to the municipality, for example, through higher tipping fees. Requiring the proponents to agree to cover all ash disposal costs, even if their assumption is wrong, is a way to test the proponents' confidence in their own assumption. If the response to this condition is a steep jump in cost estimates, then all observers have learned that ash disposal poses a serious economic risk.

INJURY TO RECYCLING EFFORTS

The same approach can be used to test the statement that a particular incinerator will not interfere with community recycling efforts.

Waste-to-energy incinerators usually must process a certain amount of garbage per hour to produce the energy that is sold to help cover operating expenses. Thus, most contracts between incinerators and municipalities include a guarantee that the incinerator will receive a certain amount of garbage per day or be paid a penalty. This means that not only the incinerator, but also the municipality signing the guarantee, has a strong interest in being sure there will be enough garbage to meet the contract obligation. If recycling reduces the amount of garbage too much, the municipality may find itself having to pay a penalty, a strong disincentive to maximize recycling. Despite this obvious conflict, incinerator proponents usually insist that incineration is fully compatible with recycling.

Just as the contract can include provisions on ash management, it can also protect recycling. Specifically, the contract can provide that the entity that is guaranteeing to provide the garbage (usually the municipality, at a stated rate of so many tons per day) shall have the right to reduce the amount of garbage provided under contract at any time, without penalty, if the reduction is achieved through either private or municipal recycling efforts. In other words, there will be no penalty for making recycling succeed: If recycling reduces the municipality's flow of garbage, the provision of the contract requiring a municipality to pay a penalty to the incinerator for not providing enough garbage to it simply will not apply. Such an arrangement lets a municipality undertake recycling efforts without any fear that a recycling program would prevent it from being be able to meet its contractual commitment to the incinerator.

Once again, if the response to this contract condition is a sharp rise in estimated costs, observers will know that the risk of competition between incineration and recycling is significant.

AIR EMISSION LIMITS

Air emissions limits are usually incorporated in permits, with the enforcement risks described above. A third condition for the master contract can be a requirement that the incinerator owners enter into a binding private agreement with all local citizens and affected groups who are interested, giving those parties direct enforcement of the air emission limits as a matter of private contract right. Thus, citizens can take enforcement action if government agencies do not.

This approach gives much firmer assurance to affected citizens that the environmental standards set for the project will, in fact, be obeyed, not just at the beginning, but throughout the project's lifetime. If a project refused to accept this condition, it would be particularly telling. The project has presumably already committed to meet the emission limits involved; if project proponents are afraid to provide for private enforcement of these limits, it suggests that they do not believe that government enforcement will be strict.

Project proponents may respond by asking for the emission limits to be relaxed. This is important information since it indicates what level of emissions the proponents think they can actually achieve on a long-term basis during routine operations.

(Drafting the legal agreement between the project and the interested citizens and groups can be technically complex. However, EDF has developed a model contract form, which is available for interested persons to review, and can offer assistance in appropriate cases.)

Conditions like those discussed above were contained in a draft resolution presented to the Board of Supervisors of San Francisco when that body was considering whether to allow the appropriate city officials to enter into negotiations for a proposed 3,000-ton-per-day incinerator for the city. Appendix C is the text of the draft resolution, with names omitted. Had the resolution been approved, the city would have been unable to execute a master contract without the listed conditions. The project proponents were also required to supply cost figures in light of the same conditions.

A similar resolution could be used by any municipality, and proposed by any citizen. In the case of San Francisco, because the Board of Supervisors decided to reject the proposal outright, the draft resolution was never put to a vote.

CHAPTER 9

Important Elements of a Solid Waste Plan

ALTHOUGH THIS BOOK FOCUSES on incineration because many communities are currently considering specific proposals to build incinerators, each community ideally should begin examining the larger topic of solid waste management as a whole before specific proposals are made. One framework for undertaking that process is preparation of a comprehensive solid waste management plan.

Such a plan can be a powerful tool for ensuring that environmentally and economically sound solid waste management practices are adopted. Comprehensive planning allows decision making to proceed rationally, avoiding management-by-crisis. A good solid waste management plan can also save a community money by identifying both existing resources and measures that will be required to accommodate the future needs of the community.

More concretely, the planning process provides an important forum for raising technical issues in a setting somewhat removed from the charged atmosphere of a hearing on a specific proposal. Similarly, the economic aspects of waste management can receive more thoughtful consideration by a government that is developing a solid waste management plan than by one defending a specific incinerator proposal. This section outlines the key elements of the planning process.

IDENTIFYING THE OPTIONS AND ASSIGNING PRIORITIES

Because the results of solid waste planning are frequently controversial, it is important to begin the process on the right foot. One way to make a good beginning is to identify and involve the constituent groups who have a direct interest in the waste management strategy adopted by the community. By giving those groups the opportunity to participate fully in the planning process, and perhaps building early consensus on the proper approach, future problems may be averted.

Key players are likely to include elected officials, public officials, citizens, waste haulers, recycling businesses, vendors, financiers, public interest groups, and local businesses. In addition, if a waste-to-energy facility is under consideration, the energy utility or prospective user of the energy generated should be included. Enlisting these players early not only taps useful sources of information but also decreases the likelihood that they will challenge the conclusions reached during the planning process.

In the past, solid waste disposal options were generally dictated by ready availability of land and limited knowledge of long-term environmental issues. Because landfilling was—for the short run—cheap and easy, local governments favored that option. In recent years, however, environmental contamination from poorly managed landfills has required expensive cleanup. For example, more than 20 percent of the sites on the federal Superfund list of highly contaminated hazardous waste dumps are actually municipal landfills.

Environmental contamination also has prompted increasingly stringent regulation of landfills, with attendant increases in the cost of siting, constructing, and operating a landfill. As a result, the difference between the cost of landfilling and the cost of other options has narrowed significantly in many areas of the country. In evaluating the options discussed below, the key question is whether each waste management option, or combination of them, will manage the waste in an economical manner that protects public health and the environment over the long term.

EPA and several states have chosen to rank the options in a waste hierarchy based on each option's anticipated impacts on public health and safety and the environment. Generally, the waste hierarchy lists the options in the following order of preference: source reduction, reuse, recycling, incineration, and landfilling. EPA designates source reduction, reuse, and recycling as the upper tier, with incineration and landfilling as the lower tier. Establishing a hierarchy among waste management options is also often a first step for a local government to take in developing a waste management plan.

To develop a sound waste management plan, a planning committee should begin by defining its objectives clearly. The objectives may have been set for the committee by a body of elected officials or a planning commission. However chosen, the objectives should be openly and specifically formulated and communicated.

To be an effective tool, a comprehensive solid waste plan should not only set out the elements of the waste management hierarchy but also recommend specific measures that reflect the hierarchy. In doing so, it should answer the following questions:

- What percentage of the waste can/will be handled by each option?
- Is recycling or incineration the priority of the solid waste management plan? How will competition between recycling and incineration for combustible recyclable materials be avoided?
- When will the options be implemented? (An implementation plan should include a detailed timetable.)
- How will implementation of the plan be funded? The plan should identify resources to be allocated to each option, the source of those resources, and when the resources will be obtained and appropriated.

GATHERING ESSENTIAL INFORMATION

After identifying the objectives of the waste management plan, the community should gather and review key information on the composition of the waste stream, current waste management practices, and growth projections for the area. Without that information in hand, thorough evaluation of the available options for waste management is difficult or impossible.

WASTE STREAM ANALYSIS

A waste stream analysis describes the components of a community's waste stream (see chapter 1). In addition to identifying the amounts of recyclable or compostible materials, the analysis may reveal the need for a separate program to handle household hazardous wastes. Such wastes typically include waste oils, used paints, discarded cleaners and pesticides (or their containers), and used batteries. A household hazardous waste program can play a key role in keeping these wastes both out of landfills, thus reducing the threat of groundwater contamination, and out of incinerators, thus reducing the likelihood of toxic emissions and ash contamination.

CURRENT PRACTICES

A Current Practices Report should describe the methods by which wastes are currently collected and disposed. In particular, is waste collected as a public service using government equipment or by private contractors? The type of investment a community has made in collection equipment may profoundly affect future waste management decisions. For example, garbage trucks that compact waste as they collect it are ill suited for some approaches to recycling, because once mixed wastes are crushed, they cannot effectively be separated. Similarly, a community that has invested heavily in equipment designed to haul large amounts of waste to a local landfill may be inclined to favor the construction of an incinerator that could be served by the same equipment. (Of course, the same equipment could be used to haul paper to mills for recycling.)

The report should also describe the capacity, remaining useful life, and budget of each disposal facility now in use, along with any regulations or informal procedures for handling specific wastes, such as bulk items, yard wastes, tree stumps, construction debris, used automobile batteries, used oil, and used tires. Similarly, the report should discuss any existing public or private recycling or reuse programs, such as Salvation Army projects, newspaper collections, etc.

GROWTH PROJECTIONS

Finally, a community should take into account projected growth patterns for the area, looking both at the amount and type of growth (residential, commercial, or industrial). Only a portion of industry wastes are hazardous; the remainder can be legally disposed of in solid waste management facilities. Thus, industrial expansion can affect the local solid waste stream significantly.

EVALUATING THE INSTITUTIONAL FRAMEWORK

At the same time that solid waste planning objectives are identified and background information is being gathered, institutional issues should also be evaluated. Some of the questions that must be addressed are listed below:

Who should be served?

Given the expense of planning and implementing a modern solid waste management plan, local governments may wish to consider banding together to share expenses. Working together, they may be better able to establish a comprehensive solid waste management strategy with each community providing an element of the program. In some cases, a local government may consider planning and implementing a strategy that will serve the needs not only of the community but those of adjacent communities as well.

Who will be involved in the planning phases and how will the public be included?

It is generally wise to assign a role in the planning process to a committee composed of a cross section of the affected communities. Alternatively or additionally, a program for public participation in the planning process may help avoid later controversy over the final strategy.

Is the desired strategy within the economic and physical constraints of the community?

In answering this question, local government decision makers must consider a variety of issues including:

- existence of markets for reusable and recyclable materials and energy;
- cost and reliability of technologies for processing and combustion;
- cost and reliability of environmental controls;
- cost and availability of sites for disposal of residue/ash; and
- cost and availability of sites for disposal of recovered materials not recycled or incinerated.

What constraints exist that could limit successful program implementation in the community?

- The local government should evaluate the legal constraints that may prevent successful implementation of different options. For example, a poorly written flow-control ordinance may need to be revised to support rather than inhibit a source-separation program.
- Existing zoning constraints should be evaluated. For example, if a separation station for recycling falls into the manufacturing category, recycling operations may have difficulty obtaining convenient sites essential to their success.
- Transportation constraints, such as the distance to the nearest disposal facility, and traffic patterns in the study area must be recognized and evaluated. For example, it may be undesirable to transport incinerator ash through residential communities or near vulnerable populations in hospitals, retirement homes, or schools.
- Existing contracts and the potential for future contracts relating to waste supply, recycling, and energy sales should be evaluated.

Is the application politically acceptable?

Among the considerations for evaluating the political acceptability of the strategy are:

- Which constituent groups will be affected by the final strategy?
- What measures can be taken to gather widespread community support for the final strategy?
- Does the strategy conform with the existing political structure and fall within the authority of the local government(s)? And, if not, can the existing structure be modified? These questions are particularly important when a regional waste management strategy is being considered. Local governments may lack the authority to enter into the legally binding agreements that are necessary to implement a regional plan.
- Is the financing strategy acceptable and is the commitment within the budgetary constraints of the affected community?
- Should the facility(ies) required be publicly or privately owned? Are service contracts with private owners/operators appropriate?
- What criteria will be used to site the facility(ies) and how will those criteria be developed? (See Appendix D for a list of questions relevant to siting a solid waste management facility.)

Obviously, development of a solid waste strategy is a complicated process that requires evaluating a community's existing waste stream and a variety of options for managing it safely and effectively. Frequently, a community will retain an outside consultant to provide expertise not available on staff. Consultants also may be retained by local officials in an effort to provide an impartial study, particularly if the issue has become politically sensitive. In many cases, however, consultants are viewed—often legitimately—as less than objective, or even predisposed toward a particular viewpoint, based on factors such as their previous work for incinerator vendors or other clients with a vested interest in seeing certain options prevail over others. (A discussion of the consultant selection process is included in Appendix E.)

PARTICIPATING IN THE DECISION-MAKING PROCESS

One way for citizens to participate in the planning process is through their local elected officials. Often, a first step is persuading local officials to form a solid waste task force to evaluate solid waste management options in the community. Citizens should advocate citizen representation on advisory committees, ask to be included on mailing lists for all committee meetings, and ask to attend the meetings.

If this strategy fails, citizens can evaluate opportunities under state and federal law to force their community to develop a plan. Under the federal Resource Conservation and Recovery Act (RCRA), states with federally delegated solid waste management programs are required to develop state plans. Table 9.1 lists states that have received federal RCRA authorization. Some states also require or encourage local plans.

Although a review of each state's planning and permitting requirements and procedures is beyond the scope of this handbook, such materials may be available from officials in the state's environmental agency. Those materials may also be available from public interest groups at the state or local level. Using those materials, citizens should learn about waste management in their state and how to effectively participate in the permit process. If laws are inadequate, citizens can contact their state legislators and urge that the laws be strengthened to require local planning, including citizen participation.

TABLE 9.1
States with RCRA/HSWA Authorization
(status as of November 1989)

States with Baseline (RCRA) Authorization:

All states except:

Alaska	Idaho
California	Iowa
Connecticut	Wyoming

States with Final Authorization for HSWA:

Georgia
Minnesota
Utah

States with Partial Authorization for HSWA:

Colorado	Missouri
Florida	Nebraska
Kentucky	New Jersey
Illinois	Washington
Michigan	Wisconsin
Mississippi	

SOURCE: EPA RCRA Hotline (800-424-9346).

NOTE: Baseline authorization is for the basic hazardous and solid waste program. HSWA authorization is for the additional regulatory provisions arising from the 1984 Hazardous and Solid Waste Amendments to RCRA.

SITING

One of the most complex and controversial steps in devising a solid waste management plan is selecting sites for particular facilities. To some extent, this process can be simplified—and perhaps made less controversial—by using a two-step process: first, identifying the criteria that will be used in selecting the sites, and second, choosing the sites themselves. Though such a strategy can help produce a more orderly process with a more rational result, it does not guarantee that all interested parties will be pleased.

A full-fledged discussion of the siting process is beyond the scope of this handbook. Instead, this section offers some technical information on the types of criteria that should be taken into account in choosing sites that will best protect public health and environmental quality over the long term. Other types of factors are also summarized (see Appendix D).

As with other aspects of the planning process, public participation in selecting siting criteria and particular sites is essential. Siting criteria should be subject to public comment to ensure that the community's concerns are reflected in the criteria. Doing so also helps educate members of the community about the technical reasons for including or excluding potential sites.

SITING CRITERIA

Environmental factors are of key importance as siting criteria. These factors, which reflect the physical characteristics of the air, groundwater, and surface-water patterns at and around a site, include the following:

Air	*Groundwater*	*Surface Water*
—prevailing wind direction	—depth to groundwater	—proximity to site (especially for waters
—downwind land uses	—soil permeability	used for fishing,
—proximity to already polluted areas	—direction of water flow (toward or away from drinking water sources)	swimming, or that are ecologically significant)
		—proximity to a floodplain

Environmental factors also require consideration of vulnerable groups within the population, including the elderly, the very young, and the ill.

Thus, proximity of a site to retirement communities, day care centers and schools, and hospitals should be taken into account, particularly in light of prevailing wind and groundwater patterns. In addition, related factors such as traffic patterns, including routine and emergency access to the site, should be identified.

Economic criteria will also play a role. All other factors being equal, a less-expensive site will be preferred. However, in analyzing economic costs, all costs of using the site should be taken into account. Thus, in addition to the direct expense of purchasing a site, any necessary site modifications should be explicitly acknowledged. Further, effects on adjacent property values should be noted, along with associated tax-base effects. Traditional cost-benefit analyses generally fail to assess the full range of effects on health, environmental quality, and secondary economic effects. Thus, such analyses should be used cautiously, if at all, in the siting process.

Finally, equity issues need to be factored into siting criteria. If controversial facilities are already located in a particular area, residents of that area may believe that it is inappropriate for additional facilities to be sited nearby.

APPLYING SITING CRITERIA

There are several ways that siting criteria can be applied. Some of these methods are described below:

Suitability Mapping

Using transparencies, constraints derived from the criteria can be mapped and laid over a map of the jurisdiction. The areas identified by overlaying the sheets have potential for accommodating a facility. Constraint mapping is most effective with a limited number of criteria.

Some potential problems with the use of this technique include (1) key data, such as groundwater patterns, may not be available; (2) connections between criteria may not be recognized; and (3) political constraints can find their way into the mapping, which can create substantial public outcry. In addition, any method that identifies potential facility sites can have the effect of generating opposition by nearby residents. In spite of these drawbacks, constraint mapping can be a valuable tool in identifying potential sites if the mappers use the best-available data and adhere to strictly technical criteria.

Location Standards

Although good engineering design is a fundamental part of minimizing risks from a solid waste management facility, location standards can provide an additional measure of protection. For example, although engineers can attempt to flood proof a facility sited in a floodplain, a state or community may decide that the overall risk from such a facility would remain unacceptable. In that event, the state or community could adopt a location standard that prohibits siting facilities within the 100-year floodplain.

Alternatively, instead of imposing flat prohibitions, location standards can require additional protective measures for facilities sited in sensitive or marginally suitable areas. Thus, a standard could require that facilities built in the 100-year floodplain be constructed to prevent washout by a 200-year flood.

Location standards can also require use of buffer zones. Such zones can be especially effective as a means of reducing risks from accidental releases. For example, in the event of groundwater contamination, groundwater monitoring in the buffer zone can provide the opportunity to detect and react to releases before they affect adjacent water supplies.

Numerical Ranking

Site suitability may also be evaluated by assigning numerical values to different criteria. For example, a site where the distance to the nearest public drinking-water supply is one mile could be assigned a ranking of one; one within 200 feet would get a ranking of ten. Each site is ranked according to the criteria, the numerical scores tallied, and the site with the best score is selected.

Numerical rankings have the potential drawback of giving an undue air of objectivity to the fundamentally subjective process of assigning relative importance to various criteria. Moreover, there is no way to account for interrelationships between factors; consequently, a multifaceted issue may be counted several times, giving it an unreasonable weight. Because of these criticisms, numerical ranking can fuel public opposition to a facility. Although useful as an initial screening methodology, numerical ranking probably should be only one input in choosing among final candidate sites.

Matrix Models

To accommodate for the failure of various methodologies to account for interrelationships and cumulative impacts, mathematical matrices can be used. These models can provide a more sophisticated approach to numerical ranking. Still, they suffer from some of the problems discussed above in relation to other evaluation tools. In particular, some criteria may be subject to double or triple counting, giving them greater weight than they deserve.

Combination

Each of these approaches suffers from various weaknesses. At the risk of stating the obvious, there is no easy way to make difficult decisions about where to place necessary but unpopular facilities. The best approach uses a combination of tools to evaluate different sites. Ultimately, however, the final decision must be made by well-informed, courageous decision makers who are responsive to and can balance the needs and demands of the public.

C H A P T E R 10

Permitting and Review
for MSW Incinerators

IF A COMMUNITY HAS DECIDED, at least tentatively, to go forward with an incinerator, the focus is likely to shift to the permitting and review process prescribed by federal, state, and local law. This chapter focuses on the requirements that must be satisfied before a proposed project can proceed. Because a different, less stringent set of requirements applies to facilities that already exist, this chapter concludes with a brief survey of requirements that may apply to such facilities.

A variety of federal, state, and local laws require an incinerator proponent to obtain one or more permits before building or operating the facility. The permit typically includes certain general conditions, including a requirement that the facility comply with all regulations in effect at the time the permit is issued, as well as various specific requirements. Mere existence of those requirements, however does not guarantee they will be enforced.

Because an incinerator project cannot proceed until the permit is issued, the permit-issuance process offers a key opportunity for citizens to help in determining whether a permit should be granted and, if so, to shape the specific requirements to be imposed. On the other hand, by the time a project reaches the permitting stage, it will have developed a good deal of momentum. Legal challenges at that stage have limited ability to reshape a project's fundamental outlines or defeat it outright. Active involvement before a project actually pursues its permits is vital if nonincineration alternatives, such as recycling, are to be fully considered.

246

ENVIRONMENTAL IMPACT STATEMENTS
AND RELATED REQUIREMENTS

NATIONAL ENVIRONMENTAL POLICY ACT

NEPA requires that before commencing "major federal actions" that will have a "significant" effect on the environment, federal agencies must prepare an environmental impact statement (EIS).[1] The EIS must evaluate the project's unavoidable adverse environmental effects, and a range of alternatives to the project, including the "no action" alternative (i.e., not going ahead with the project at all).

To determine whether the proposed action crosses the threshold of having a "significant" effect, an agency must prepare—for virtually any action—a preliminary "environmental assessment." If that assessment concludes that the threshold is not met, the agency makes a Finding of No Significant Impact (FONSI); otherwise, the agency must undertake a full-blown EIS. The relevant agency must give public notice of the FONSI and seek public comment on it. (Alternatively, the agency can skip the preliminary assessment and go directly to the EIS stage.) The first step in EIS preparation is often a public scoping meeting, at which agency determines which issues and alternatives will be analyzed in depth in the EIS.

NEPA's EIS requirement generally does not apply to resource recovery facilities. Though EPA must issue permits for many incinerators, and though permit issuance counts as a "major federal action," EPA-issued permits are exempt from the EIS requirement on the theory that EPA's permitting process is the "substantial equivalent" of the EIS process. The NEPA EIS requirement may be triggered, however, if federal real estate is leased for the site, if federal funding is used for the construction, or if the incinerator will be federally owned or operated.

Most NEPA lawsuits either have challenged the adequacy of an EIS or have asserted that one should have been prepared but was not. By and large, efforts to infuse NEPA with further substantive content have failed. NEPA allows approval of projects that will have significant environmental impact, as long as their full impacts and all alternatives have been considered; it requires agencies to "look before they leap," but doesn't prohibit them from leaping once they have looked.

This essentially procedural requirement, nonetheless, can have practical significance. At the very least, preparing an EIS and fighting over its adequacy can take an extremely long time. Thus, simply going through the

EIS process creates some incentive to deal carefully with environmental issues. At times, too, the process can produce significant improvements in a proposal.

MINI-NEPAS

Many states have passed statutes modeled on NEPA that impose similar requirements. Table 10.1 lists these mini-NEPAs. In some states, the mini-NEPA reaches significantly further than its federal counterpart, both procedurally and substantively. First, the state EIS requirement is much more likely to be triggered by a municipal incinerator proposal. Some states require an EIS for any incinerator above a certain size or, more generally, an air pollution source that will emit more than a certain amount of pollution. Moreover, the issuance of state permits may trigger the state EIS requirement.

Second, some state environmental laws go beyond the procedural EIS requirement. For example, New York (State Environmental Quality Review Act) and Michigan (Michigan Environmental Protection Act, which does not include an EIS requirement) both impose a substantive requirement on all persons and entities to minimize or avoid the adverse environmental impacts of their activities. Such an open-ended, unspecific obligation is an important tool in efforts to block or alter an inadequate incinerator proposal.

AIR POLLUTION LAWS

FEDERAL CLEAN AIR ACT

National Ambient Air Quality Standards

At the heart of the federal Clean Air Act's scheme for controlling pollutants from stationary sources are the National Ambient Air Quality Standards (NAAQS). Primary (health-based) and secondary (welfare-based) standards exist for six substances: sulfur oxides, nitrogen oxides, particulate matter less than ten microns in diameter (PM10), carbon monoxide, ozone, and lead. NAAQS are ambient standards, that is, they establish allowable pollutant levels for an area, rather than setting the amount that can be emitted by any particular source. In implementing NAAQS, each state is required to devise a State Implementation Plan (SIP). Based on a survey of all emission sources in the specified area, the SIP sets specific limits for particular facilities as necessary to meet each of the NAAQS.

TABLE 10.1
States with Mini-NEPAs

California	Cal. Pub. Res. Code Sec. 21000 et seq. (West Supp. 1974). Amended by Stats. 1978, C. 760, C. 1093 (West Supp. 1979).
Connecticut	Conn. Gen. Stat. Ann. Sec. 22a-1, et seq. (West Supp. 1979).
Delaware	Del. Code Ann. Tit. 7 Sec. 7001 et seq. (Supp. 1972 as amended 61 Del. Laws c. 116, effective July 6, 1977 (Supp. 1978).
Georgia	Ga. Code Ann. Sec. 32-10-64(5) (Michie 1982).
Hawaii	Hawaii Rev. Stat. ch. 343, as amended 1983.
Indiana	Ind. Code Ann. 13-1-10-1 et seq. (Burns).
Maryland	Md. Code Ann. N.R. Sec. 1-301 to 1-305 (1975). As amended, L. 1975 Ch. 129 (Supp. 1978).
Massachusetts	Mass. Ann. Laws ch. 30 Sec. 61, 62 to 621, as amended L. 1977, 947 (Supp. 1978).
Minnesota	Minn. Stat. Ann. Sec. 116 et seq. as amended 1982.
Mississippi	Miss. Code Ann. Sec. 49-27-11(i) (Supp. 1974).
Montana	Mont. Code Ann. Sec. 75-1-101 et seq.
Nevada	Nev. Rev. Stat. Sec. 704.820 et seq. (1973).
New Mexico	N.M. Stat. Ann. Sec. 74-77-1 et seq. (1983).
New York	N.Y.E.C.L. Sec. 8-0101 et seq. added by L. 1975 ch. 612. As amended L. 1977 Ch. 252 effective June 10, 1977.
North Carolina	N.C. Gen. Stat. Sec. 113A-1 et seq. (1973).
Puerto Rico	P.R. Laws Ann. Tit. 12 Sec. 1121 et seq. (Supp. 1973).
South Dakota	S.D. Comp. Laws Ann. Sec. 34A-7-1 et seq.
Virginia	Va. Code Ann. Sec. 10-177 et seq. (1973) Sec. 10-17-107 et seq.
Washington	Wash. Rev. Code Ann. Sec. 43.21c.010 et seq. (Supp. 1973).
Wisconsin	Wis. Stat. Ann. Sec. 1.11 (West Supp. 1974-5).

SOURCE: F. P. Grad, *Treatise on Environmental Law,* vol. 2 (New York: Matthew Bender & Co., 1987), chp. 9.

An area that meets an NAAQS is said to be "in attainment" for that pollutant. Attainment status for one NAAQS is independent of the status of another NAAQS; for example, a given area can be in attainment for carbon monoxide, oxides, lead, and particulate matter, but not for ozone or nitrogen oxides.

The NAAQS approach leaves a good deal to be desired. Many of the NAAQS are inadequately protective; they may, for example, fail to account for exposure pathways other than direct inhalation. In addition, back calculating from ambient levels to individual sources requires use of models; such models are flawed by our limited understanding of air pollutants' physical and chemical behavior, and by sparse data. Finally, some states have devoted inadequate resources to designing—much less enforcing—their SIPs. For example, ten years after the federal NAAQS for ozone was issued, most metropolitan areas of the nation have yet to attain that standard.

Prevention of Significant Deterioration

Arguably, the most important provisions of the Clean Air Act affecting new incinerators are the Prevention of Significant Deterioration (PSD) requirements. The PSD program is designed to slow or avoid deterioration of air in attainment areas. Each SIP must "contain emission limitations and such other measures as may be necessary . . . to prevent significant deterioration of air quality."[2] Specifically, any new major emitting facility to be located in an attainment area must obtain a PSD permit. That permit is issued by EPA; however, EPA can delegate its permitting authority to the state, and has done so in virtually all states.

The PSD permit requirements apply only to "major emitting facilities."[3] These include all incinerators that will emit over 250 tons per year of any pollutant; also covered are incinerators that have the "potential to emit" (taking pollution control devices into account) over 100 tons per year of any pollutant if the incinerator's charging capacity (the amount it can burn) exceeds 250 tons per day.

In practice, these thresholds are low enough that all but the smallest MSW incinerators are covered by the PSD program. A PSD review must be conducted for every pollutant emitted in "significant" amounts. EPA regulations define such amounts for each pollutant regulated under the act.[4] In general, MSW incinerators exceed these amounts for all regulated pollutants. Specific PSD requirements include the following:

- No permit can be issued to a facility if it will cause violation of any NAAQS.
- Emissions from the new facility can only cause local air quality to deteriorate to a degree, that is, until they use up part of the gap between existing air quality and the NAAQS. The act itself establishes increment limits for sulfur oxides and particulates. Although EPA is supposed to establish similar limits for other criteria pollutants, it has yet to do so, and is now under a court order to promulgate such limits for nitrogen oxides.
- Each PSD permit must require use of best available control technology (BACT) for all pollutants regulated by any of the act's programs. Those pollutants are:

Pollutant	Type of Regulation
Lead	NAAQS
Ozone	
Sulfur oxides	
Nitrogen oxides	
Particulate matter (PM10)	
Carbon monoxide	
Arsenic (inorganic)	NESHAP*
Asbestos	
Benzene	
Beryllium	
Mercury	
Radionuclides	
Vinyl chloride	
Particulate matter	NSPS*

* NESHAP = National Emission Standard for a Hazardous Air Pollutant
NSPS = New Source Performance Standard
The NSPSs for MSW incinerators are about to be revised. These programs are discussed below.

A given BACT requirement not only specifies use of a particular control technology, but also sets an emission limitation "based on the maximum degree of reduction [feasible] . . . taking into account energy, environmental, and economic impacts and other costs." Thus, BACT is determined on a case-by-case basis. In practice, however, BACT specifications and limits for resource recovery facilities do not vary greatly from one situation to the next. BACT can also include fuel cleaning or preprocessing, an authority that EPA is using to support its proposed incinerator NSPS that requires a limited degree of source separation and recycling as part of BACT.

- In its proposed NSPS for new MSW incinerators, issued in December 1989, EPA defined BACT to consist of acid-gas scrubbers, together with fabric filters or electrostatic precipitators. The proposal also specifies certain combustion controls and "good operating practices."[5] Accordingly, new or modified incinerators located in attainment areas should be so equipped with few, if any, exceptions.
- The PSD permit authority must hold a public hearing, at which interested members of the public may "submit written or oral presentations on the air quality impact of such source, alternatives thereto, control technology requirements, and other appropriate considerations."[6]

- Although the PSD provisions of the statute do not explicitly refer to monitoring or sampling, the EPA administrator has plenary authority to require monitoring and stack testing.[7] PSD permits, therefore, generally include monitoring requirements and are an important avenue for establishing such requirements.
- The PSD permit emission limitations only apply to those pollutants actually regulated under the stationary source provisions of the act. Thus, the permits issued under current regulations need not address such critical pollutants as dioxins, furans, other organics, or most heavy metals. However, EPA has adopted a policy that requires that, in selecting appropriate control technologies for BACT, permit writers should take into account unregulated pollutants.[8]
- A PSD permit is a construction permit. Construction cannot begin until a permit is issued, and must begin within 18 months after permit issuance. Once the facility has been constructed, no separate operating permit is needed. Some PSD permits, however, expressly reserve the right to lower the emission limits in light of data from actual stack tests performed once the plant is up and running.[9]

To date, the BACT requirement has been ineffective in ensuring effective nitrogen oxides (NO_x) control. Generally, BACT for NO_x has been deemed to be good combustion practices. Good combustion practices are undeniably better than bad combustion practices, but they should not alone suffice as BACT. At the very least, some control over the waste stream should be undertaken (e.g., no burning of yard waste, which releases large amounts of nitrogen). In addition, flue gas cleaning for NO_x has become available, and a compelling argument for de-NO_x controls as BACT can now be made.

EPA's proposed NSPS for incinerators, issued in December 1989, for the first time specifies an emissions limit for NO_x, based on the use of selective noncatalytic reduction or an equivalent de-NO_x technology as BACT. The emissions limit applies only to large (greater than 250 tons per day) new incinerators, however, and would not be applied to existing facilities through retrofitting.[10]

On the whole, PSD permits can be a powerful tool for requiring that incinerators proposed to be built in attainment areas use sophisticated pollution control devices and perform frequent monitoring. Citizens can use the PSD permit process to ensure that state and federal regulators impose such restrictions.

Nonattainment Provisions

The PSD program applies only to areas that are already in attainment or to areas that are nonclassifiable (i.e., areas where the state or EPA has insufficient information to determine the attainment status). Separate, more stringent requirements apply with regard to construction in nonattainment areas. This program is generally referred to as New Source Review; confusingly, that term is sometimes used to refer to the PSD permitting scheme as well.

Contrary to popular belief, nonattainment provisions of the Clean Air Act do not altogether forbid new polluting facilities in nonattainment areas. Rather, those provisions are designed to avoid any further degradation of air quality. Each state SIP must include a permitting program for facilities to be located in nonattainment areas. Because many areas are in attainment for some pollutants but not others, the PSD review and the nonattainment review usually are performed together, with the permitting authority applying the PSD requirements with regard to some pollutants and the nonattainment requirements to others. The two key provisions of the nonattainment program are:

1. Each facility must employ pollution control technology that will achieve the lowest achievable emission rate (LAER). This is stricter than BACT. LAER is defined as the lowest emission limit that has been required in any state SIP, which would include any permit, or that is achieved in practice. LAER and BACT are often treated as interchangeable in practice, but they are not the same. The statute plainly requires that a facility located in a nonattainment area must limit emissions of the relevant pollutant(s) to absolutely the lowest level possible.
2. Under the so-called offset requirements, a new facility must balance its emissions by arranging for an equivalent reduction in emissions at another facility. Many states have attempted to exempt resource recovery facilities from the offset requirements; indeed, EPA's original offset rules allowed resource recovery facilities to be constructed without offsets if none could be found before construction began, though they still had to be obtained in the end.[11] This exemption is clearly illegal under the Clean Air Act and has since been rejected by the EPA when proposed in specific SIPs. Thus, the offset requirement should be enforced against waste-to-energy facilities. Under the statute, the offset must result in a positive net air quality benefit in the nonattainment area.

New Source Performance Standards

Under Section 111 of Clean Air Act, EPA has established New Source Performance Standards (NSPS) that apply to particular categories of facilities, including incinerators and resource recovery facilities. These standards are technology based. In other words, each NSPS reflects EPA's evaluation of what emissions levels the best-demonstrated, cost-effective control technology can achieve for a particular category of facility.

NSPS is not enforced through a permit scheme. Rather, the NSPS automatically applies to any facility constructed after the standard's effective date. (As noted above, in selecting the BACT in the context of a PSD review, the permit-writer must adopt a BACT at least as stringent as any relevant NSPS).

The current NSPS for incinerators is virtually an antique.[12] Adopted in 1971, the NSPS applies to incinerators with a capacity of over 50 tons per day and limits particulate emissions to 0.08 grains per dry standard cubic foot (gr/dscf). This requirement is technologically obsolete and has, in effect, become irrelevant. Application of BACT (in attainment areas) or LAER (in nonattainment areas) or a specific state standard will always result in a particulate emission limit far stricter than 0.08 gr/dscf.

EPA has recently proposed a new, more stringent, and broader NSPS for MSW incinerators. The standard was proposed in December 1989 and is expected to be promulgated in final form in December 1990.[13]

A separate NSPS already applies to resource recovery facilities. In November 1986, EPA adopted an NSPS for steam-generating units.[14] That NSPS, expressed in terms of pounds (lb) of pollution emitted per million BTUs (mbtu) of heat input, limits particulate emissions to 0.1 lb/mbtu. This translates to a little less than 0.05 gr/dscf; again, this is too high to be of any real importance. Similarly, the NSPS limits opacity to 20 percent, except for one six-minute period per hour when opacity can reach 27 percent. This is also too lax to be of any real use. The NSPS does require continuous monitoring of opacity.

The steam-generating-unit NSPS also limits emissions of nitrogen oxides (NO_x) to 0.3 lb/mbtu, a relatively strict requirement. The limit applies, however, only if at least 10 percent of the total heat input comes from natural gas. Newer resource recovery facilities equipped with auxiliary burners have the capacity to accept 10 percent of the heat input from auxiliary burners. Unfortunately, the regulation does not clearly indicate whether it is triggered by potential, as opposed to actual, heat input from fossil fuels. EDF has taken the position that the NO_x limit does apply to a facility where auxiliary natural gas burners could contribute more than 10 percent of total heat input; EPA has yet to clarify the applicability of the standard.

EPA's proposed regulations for MSW incinerators issued in December 1989 are comprised of two separate rules. The first rule takes the form of nonbinding emissions guidelines for existing incinerators,[15] which would assume the force of law only after individual states incorporate them into their own regulations. The proposed standards include emission limits for opacity, particulates, hydrogen chloride, sulfur dioxide, and dioxins and furans. The actual emission limits for these pollutants vary according to size and type of technology employed (e.g., mass-burn versus RDF), and are generally less stringent than those proposed for new or modified facilities.

The second proposed rule comprises NSPS for new and modified MSW incinerators.[16] The proposed NSPS includes emission limits for opacity, particulates, hydrogen chloride, sulfur dioxide, and dioxins and furans for all new, modified, and existing incinerators. As with the emissions guidelines, the actual emission limits for these pollutants vary according to size and type of technology employed (e.g., mass-burn versus RDF). An emission limit for NO_x is also proposed, but it would only apply to new facilities larger than 250 tons per day.

The proposed rules would also require use of certain "good operating practices," including limits on the level of carbon monoxide emissions, an indicator of combustion efficiency, and a maximum flue gas temperature at the point of entry into pollution control devices. Finally, the proposal would require that areas served by incinerators remove lead-acid vehicle batteries from wastes to be incinerated, develop household battery collection programs, and develop and implement source-separation or preprocessing programs or technologies capable of diverting 25 percent of the local waste stream for recycling.

EDF has prepared a table that lists the standards proposed by EPA for existing, modified, and new MSW incinerators in a format that allows comparison to standards contained in existing state regulations and individual facility permits. This table is available from EDF upon request.

National Emission Standards for Hazardous
Air Pollutants (NESHAP)

If the EPA administrator determines that an air pollutant causes an increase in mortality or serious illness, he or she may list it as a "hazardous air pollutant" under Section 112 of the Clean Air Act.[17] Once having listed a pollutant under this section, the administrator must either find that it is clearly not a hazardous air pollutant or establish an emission standard that will protect public health. These health-based standards apply to new and existing facilities alike. By and large, the Section 112 process has been slow and not very fruitful. EPA has never been enthusiastic about developing health-based standards with such broad application.

EPA has established a handful of NESHAPs for certain specific pollutants in certain specific contexts.[18] None applies directly to emissions from incinerators. The beryllium NESHAP might apply if certain beryllium-containing wastes were incinerated; the mercury NESHAP applies to the incineration of sewage sludge. It is highly unlikely that either would apply to an MSW incinerator unless it was exceptionally careless about what it burned.

EPA has begun the NESHAP standard-setting process for cadmium.[19] If and when it does establish a cadmium NESHAP, it would certainly apply to incinerators, which are the second most important existing sources of ambient cadmium and can be expected to grow in relative importance. Final issuance of such a standard is, unfortunately, a very long way off.

Finally, EPA recently entered into a settlement agreement with the Natural Resources Defense Council and the states of New York and Florida, under which EPA agreed to propose regulations for new and existing incinerators by November 30, 1989, and to issue those regulations in final form by December 31, 1990.[20] These regulations are being developed under the authority of Section 111 of the Clean Air Act. Under the settlement, the plaintiffs reserved their right to bring additional litigation to seek establishment of standards under Section 112—the provisions of the Clean Air Act authorizing the agency to develop NESHAPs—if they believe a significant risk still remains after the Section 111 regulations are issued.

Dioxins

Conspicuously absent from the discussion of current Clean Air Act regulations has been any mention of dioxins—the incinerator pollutants that have generated perhaps the greatest amount of public concern. Although the U.S. Congress and EPA profess to share that concern, so far the situation has been like the old adage about the weather: Everybody complains about it, but nobody does anything. In other words, there are not yet any federal statutory provisions or regulatory standards relating to dioxin emissions from incinerators. EPA has finally proposed dioxin emission limits for new and existing incinerators and has ruled that, in determining BACT, the effect of various different pollution controls on dioxin emissions must be taken into account.

STATE AIR POLLUTION LAWS

All states have some sort of air pollution laws. All states must also have a SIP and some type of permitting program for sources of air pollution.

Because the details vary from one state to the next, this handbook cannot describe state laws and programs in detail. However, the key points follow.

State Permits

A new incinerator will have to obtain a state permit. It is likely that the state law requirements will be similar to the federal requirements. However, in many states, the opportunity for public participation is greater than with regard to a PSD permit issued by EPA. Often, a public adjudicatory hearing is available if interested parties are able to make a responsible showing that they have something of value to contribute to the review.

In addition, the substantive requirements of state law may be more stringent or, more likely, more broadly worded than the federal requirements and, thereby, offer an avenue for imposing stricter operating and emission requirements. For example, some states impose a general prohibition on air pollution. This opens the door for citizens to make a showing that a given facility will have unacceptable effects.

Ambient Standards

Few states have established ambient standards stricter than their federal counterparts, but some states do have ambient standards for a greater number of pollutants. By and large, however, state ambient standards will not prove useful in working to improve an incinerator proposal.

Emission Standards

Many states have recently developed or are in the process of developing emission standards for incinerators, either in the form of specific regulations or as BACT guidelines. Rarely are these limits as strict as technology allows, though some of the limits on individual pollutants are appropriate.

A state incinerator standard is a two-edged sword. On the one hand, it establishes a minimum level of control. In New York, for example, the regulatory limit for hydrogen chloride can only be met if the incinerator has a scrubber; that limit thus translates into a valuable provision. On the other hand, standards that are too lax or inadequately comprehensive present an obstacle to developing more stringent requirements either in general or in the context of a specific facility.

County Permits

Many counties also have jurisdiction to issue air contaminant permits. In practice, county permits generally just track state permits. However, the county procedure offers another forum for public participation, and may be worth participating in as such.

In theory, federal BACT requirements are superior to state emission standards for controlling emissions of toxic substances since they are site-specific and are supposed to take into account advances in technology. In practice, however, BACT requirements do not vary much from one situation to the next, and often emission standards in certain states exceed federal standards based on BACT.

SOLID WASTE LAWS

FEDERAL RESOURCE CONSERVATION AND RECOVERY ACT (RCRA)

Federal Incinerator Standards

The Federal Resource Conservation and Recovery Act (RCRA) is the major federal statute that addresses hazardous and solid wastes. Under RCRA's authorities, EPA has established regulations for hazardous waste incinerators but not for municipal waste incinerators. There is no such thing as a federal solid waste facility permit, nor are there any federal standards other than those established under the Clean Air Act that apply to municipal incinerators as such.

EPA has, however, developed guidelines for the operation of MSW incinerators.[21] These are nonbinding recommendations that largely reflect standard operating procedures; they do not, by any stretch of the imagination, guarantee that an incinerator is environmentally acceptable. Most existing facilities already comply with these recommendations.

State Solid Waste Plans

Subtitle D of RCRA, dealing with nonhazardous wastes, calls on states to produce solid waste management plans. It does not require such plans outright, but does hold the promise of federal financial assistance for those states that adopt an approved plan. In the late 1970s, when federal funds were indeed available, the inducement was significant and many states developed plans. More recently, the federal funding has entirely dried up. By and large, those states without plans have not developed them and those states with plans have allowed them to grow dusty and out of date. New mandates for state solid waste management plans are likely to be included when RCRA is reauthorized in the near future.

It is, nonetheless, worth determining whether your state has such a plan. If it does, the document may include a general endorsement of recycling and waste reduction, or something more specific, that could be useful but not legally binding. Under RCRA and its implementing regulations, a state plan must give serious consideration to the obstacles and potential for recycling and waste reduction. Some plans, however, tend to treat waste-to-energy incineration and materials recovery as of equal value.

When Congress amended RCRA in 1984, it included a set of provisions that indicates a distinct preference for recycling over waste-to-energy incineration. The statute expresses Congress' intent that, in sizing a waste-to-energy facility, the needs of local recyclers should be taken into account.[22] The practical usefulness of this expression of concern is uncertain. The American Paper Institute has petitioned EPA to promulgate regulations implementing these provisions and ensuring that recyclable paper is not routed to incineration. Thus far, EPA has shown little interest in issuing such regulations.

Because the 1984 provisions do not directly require or forbid anything, it would be hard to say that a particular facility violates these provisions. Yet, clearly any state solid waste plan must place the needs of recyclers before the desires of an incinerator proponent. A reasonable argument can be made that a facility that can be shown to take materials from recycling for incineration is inconsistent with the statute.

Ash Disposal Requirements

The best-known RCRA provisions are those that pertain to the identification, storage, transport, treatment, and disposal of hazardous wastes. MSW incinerator ash frequently qualifies as a hazardous waste; however, there is a dispute as to whether a loophole in RCRA exempts such ash from the regulations.

RCRA does not require a generator of hazardous waste to obtain a permit to create such wastes. Generators must, however, determine whether their wastes are hazardous, and if so, send the waste to an appropriate disposal or treatment site. If a generator fails to identify a waste as hazardous, that waste slips (illegally) out of the hazardous waste management system altogether. Generators must also meet a number of record keeping and reporting requirements. RCRA forbids disposal of any waste—hazardous or not—in an open dump. (As defined in convoluted EPA regulations, that provision essentially just prohibits contamination of surface water or off-site groundwater.)[23]

RCRA also imposes an array of restrictions on wastes that qualify as hazardous. MSW incinerator ash frequently qualifies as hazardous because it exceeds the standards for leachable lead and cadmium as determined by the Extraction Procedure (EP) toxicity test. A solid waste qualifies as hazardous either if it is listed as hazardous by EPA—incinerator ash is not—or if it has any of four characteristics, one of which is EP toxicity. (The other three are ignitability, corrosivity, and reactivity.)[24]

The status of incinerator ash under RCRA has given rise to considerable legal controversy. The incinerator industry argues that ash from resource recovery facilities (though not from incinerators that do not recover energy, unless they burn exclusively household waste) is automatically excluded from regulation as a hazardous waste by a specific provision of RCRA known as Section 3001(i).

In the view of the environmental community and EPA, however, Section 3001(i) creates no such loophole. As a result, ash that fails the EP toxicity test should be considered and handled as a hazardous waste. In January 1988, EDF took this question before the courts in two similar but separate federal suits: one against a private facility in Westchester County, New York, owned and operated by the largest U.S. incinerator company, Wheelabrator Technologies; and the other against a public facility owned and operated by the city of Chicago. Each of the suits challenges the incinerator operator's failure to comply with hazardous waste requirements, despite clear evidence that its ash routinely fails the EP toxicity test.[25]

Shortly before this book went to press, both courts rejected EDF's legal argument, ruling that ash is exempt from hazardous waste regulation if incinerator operators take certain steps to exclude hazardous wastes from the wastes they burn. EDF intends to appeal the decisions, but must first complete additional factual proceedings in both courts.

As of this writing, a number of proposed amendments to RCRA are pending in Congress that would establish specific requirements for the handling and disposal of ash. Most of these proposals would exclude ash from regulation as a hazardous waste but would impose numerous protective requirements, including disposal in lined landfills or monofills with leachate collection systems and groundwater monitoring. In addition, about a dozen states have proposed or adopted their own ash management legislation, regulations, or policies. (A summary of these state requirements is available from EDF upon request.)

Finally, EPA recently proposed to revise its regulations on MSW landfills.[26] As proposed, these regulations were extremely weak. A final rule is due to be promulgated in 1990. In the event that the courts rule against EDF in the pending ash lawsuits and hold that ash is exempt from the hazardous waste regulations, the final form of EPA's MSW landfill proposal would take on an even greater importance. Unless states impose more stringent requirements or until Congress mandates federal ash management regulations, it would constitute the standard for all ash disposal sites.

STATE SOLID WASTE LAWS

Most states require MSW incinerators to obtain solid waste management facility permits. Such a permit controls all aspects of the plant's operation other than air pollution: noise and odor control, acceptance of waste, maintenance, inspections, and any general waste management requirements. In addition, most states have a general set of regulations for solid waste management facilities, including incinerators as well as landfills, transfer stations, etc. These vary significantly in stringency from state to state.

MISCELLANEOUS REQUIREMENTS

ARMY CORPS OF ENGINEERS PERMITS

Only a few incinerators—those to be located directly in or adjacent to wetlands or major waterways—are likely to require Army Corps of Engineers permits. Specifically, if the facility will involve any construction in the navigable waters of the United States, it will require a permit under Section 10 of the Rivers and Harbors Act or Section 404 of the Clean Water Act. Such permits are also required if construction will involve discharge of dredged material or filling of wetlands.

The requirements associated with these two permit programs are neither detailed nor substantial. The Army Corps has largely unfettered discretion with regard to whether to issue a Section 10 permit. As for the Section 404 program, the Army Corps undertakes a broad "public interest review" and applies EPA regulations ("the 404[b] guidelines").[27] The public interest review amounts to little more than a vague examination of whether the project seems like a good idea.[28] The heart of the 404(b) guidelines is a requirement to consider all alternatives; if there is a prudent and feasible alternative that will not involve discharges into waters or the filling of wetlands, it must be undertaken. In the case of activities, such as the construction of an incinerator, that are not water dependent, such alternatives are presumed to exist; this requirement can actually have some teeth as a result. In addition, if a proposed incinerator is to be sited next to a navigable water, these permit programs may come into play in incinerator proceedings.

WATER DISCHARGES

The operation of an incinerator may involve various uses, and subsequent contamination, of water. For example, in order to extinguish and cool the smoldering ash, most incinerators dump their ash into a water-filled pit— the quench pit—under or near the furnace chamber. Some incinerators simply reuse the water; others discharge it from time to time. Incinerators that discharge water must comply with certain requirements; the specifics depends on where the water goes. Under the Clean Water Act, any industrial facility that discharges effluent directly into waters of the United States must obtain a National Pollutant Discharge Elimination System permit from EPA or from the state if EPA has delegated permitting authority to the state.

Rather than directly discharging its wastewater, a facility may send it to a sewage treatment plant, also known as a publicly owned treatment works (POTW). Before doing so, however, the facility must obtain permission from the POTW to hook into the municipal sewer system and possibly meet pretreatment standards if required by municipal law.

FEDERAL AVIATION ADMINISTRATION APPROVAL

If a proposed incinerator's smokestack would be near an aircraft flight corridor, the Federal Aviation Administration can refuse to issue a no-hazard determination. Although such a determination does not actually prohibit the construction of the smokestack, no insurance company will insure a facility under those circumstances.

GENERAL CONSIDERATIONS

WHETHER TO BUILD AN INCINERATOR

State and federal laws have a fair amount to say about just what sort of incinerator you can build if you decide to build one. But they do little to influence that initial choice. The BACT provisions, for example, only require that each facility do what it can to control emissions.

There are three ways in which the legal requirements discussed above, however, can affect overall solid waste management decisions. The first is through programs—such as NEPA and its state counterparts—that mandate examination of alternatives. That examination offers a critically important forum for looking at the bigger picture, including whether an incinerator is really needed and, if so, of what size. The question of alternatives is also central to consideration of a Section 404 permit, should one be required due to the incinerator's effect on wetlands or waterways.

A final avenue for the examination of alternatives is the PSD permitting process. The public review that precedes a permit must include a discussion of alternatives. In addition, EPA has proposed to expand the scope of the required BACT analysis to include specific consideration of recycling and source separation. This requirement, if adopted, could provide an important tool for citizens and regulators to use to significantly alter the size and type of incinerator proposed in a given locale.

The expanded BACT requirement, and other existing legal requirements, could thus be used to influence overall planning decisions through reliance on integrated waste management as a pollution control measure for incinerators. Most obviously, the less waste burned, the less pollution that will result. To date, that argument has met with little success in limiting the size of an incinerator.

More promisingly, existing requirements can provide the basis for arguing that certain items (e.g., yard wastes, batteries, noncombustibles) should be kept out of the incinerator to improve combustion efficiency and reduce the amount and toxicity of ash and air emissions. Such pressure for integrated waste management fits comfortably into the federal air pollution control program, as well as under many state air pollution laws, and is the motivation behind EPA's proposal to expand the scope of BACT for MSW incinerators.

In particular, fuel preprocessing is an accepted approach under the Clean Air Act. Preprocessing requirements can already be imposed as part of the case-by-case BACT requirements in PSD programs within attainment areas. In addition, EPA has ample authority to support its proposal to impose such requirements in its NSPS to be finalized by December 1990.

The preprocessing approach has seldom been invoked with regard to mass-burn incinerators. Such incinerators have misleadingly been sold on the basis of their supposed ability to burn the entire unprocessed waste stream. However, an integrated waste management scheme—one that includes source separation and recycling of toxic or noncombustible items— is a type of fuel processing that should be utilized both for its own sake and to reduce incinerator emissions and ash toxicity.

Finally, the decision whether to build an incinerator, and if so, the determination of its size, should be made in the context of overall solid waste planning. Although RCRA does not force states to develop solid waste management plans, it does encourage such planning and establishes guidelines for doing so. In response, some state legislatures have explicitly required the development of state plans. Often, state law provides that state grant money is available for a project only if it conforms with a state or local plan. Even if no state plan exists, common sense dictates that no incinerator project should be developed in a vacuum, without reference to or consideration of other solid waste management practices and alternatives.

THE ROLE OF SPECIFIC STANDARDS

Existing legal requirements are both a help and a hindrance to efforts to ensure that MSW incinerators are built only where necessary and then in proper fashion. On the one hand, specific regulatory requirements help to ensure that a facility is operated correctly. The general disappearance of the uncontrolled incinerators of the past is directly attributable to increasingly stringent regulatory requirements.

On the other hand, the existence of specific standards is often interpreted as meaning that society implicitly approves any facility that meets those standards. Opponents of a specific incinerator project will almost certainly be told, "we will comply with all applicable standards," and that may well be true. But those standards are themselves often inadequate; for example, there are no federal standards for air emissions of dioxins or heavy metals. Furthermore, the state of the art continues to evolve, and specific standards can become obsolete quickly. For example, witness the current federal NSPS for incinerators relative to EPA's recent proposed NSPS.

For these reasons, a flexible requirement, such as BACT, can often be more useful than a specific regulatory emission limit. At the same time, that flexibility means that active public involvement in permitting proceedings is vitally important. By insisting on stringent permit conditions, using legal handles such as BACT, LAER, and state prohibitions on air pollution or environmental harm, protections can be developed that go beyond the weak standards that may now exist.

In addition, public participation in developing stronger incinerator standards is also vital. Increasingly, states are stepping into the void left by federal inaction and are developing their own incinerator requirements. For example, New York State recently adopted comprehensive new incinerator regulations. Citizen vigilance played a significant role in strengthening the standards in those regulations.

STRATEGIC CONSIDERATIONS

If you find yourself embroiled in an incinerator battle with local decision makers or state or federal permitting authorities, there are three key strategic considerations to make your voice effective.

1. *The power of information.* Be armed with as much information as you can gather. The other side will have fancy consultants, slick presentations, and reassuring tales of successes elsewhere. Unless you have hard facts, and maybe even some outside experts, you will get nowhere. In the context of local decision making (e.g., before a city council or county waste management board), you will be heard out but ignored. In the context of an actual permitting proceeding, you may not even be heard out.

2. *The ratchet effect.* With regard to the specifics of a proposal, insist on the best that anyone has gotten anywhere else. This approach is particularly important in the context of a permitting proceeding, but also applies elsewhere. Identify protective requirements imposed on incinerators in other communities and demand clear explanations of any proposal not to adopt such requirements in your community.

3. *Alternatives.* Incinerator proposals tend to arise in an atmosphere of crisis, dominated by an apparent urgent need to find immediate means of disposing of growing amounts of garbage when the local landfill approaches capacity. Many officials may have their doubts about incineration; few are likely to have doubts about the need to do *something*. In such situations, flat opposition is unlikely to persuade officials to forego incineration. The investigation of alternatives via an EIS or general political avenues will be unsuccessful—and verge on the socially irresponsible—unless those opposed to the incinerator are also in favor of something else. Recycling and source reduction programs can provide important alternatives to incineration in many communities. Similarly, arguments that proposed pollution control equipment is inadequate will get nowhere unless they are backed by feasible suggestions of alternative controls.

EXISTING FACILITIES

The above describes the various legal requirements triggered by an incinerator proposal. What about a facility that already exists? What requirements apply to it?

PERMITS

Unless the incinerator is extraordinarily old or very small, it will have a permit. The first question to ask is whether the facility is complying with the requirements of that permit. Frankly, it probably is, since many older permits contain conditions that are easily met. But the first concern is to determine, through the state environmental agency, if the facility is complying with its own permit.

Second, some of the legal requirements discussed above are not imposed via a permit scheme and do not apply only to facilities that began operations after the effective date of the requirement. Most notably, the RCRA ash disposal requirements apply to any incinerator. In addition, the entire controversy over the claimed exemption of ash from hazardous waste regulations pertains only to waste-to-energy facilities. An incinerator that does not recover energy is not exempt unless, under an EPA regulation, it is burning exclusively household waste—a very rare circumstance.

CLEAN AIR ACT STANDARDS

Of the Clean Air Act requirements, both NESHAP and NSPS have some application to facilities that existed when the standards were adopted. Any NESHAP would apply in full force. Unfortunately, none of the NESHAP now in effect addresses pollutants that are likely to be emitted by municipal incinerators. If EPA ever completes a NESHAP for cadmium or lead, this situation could change dramatically, but such developments are not imminent.

As the name New Source Performance Standard implies, NSPS does not apply directly to existing sources. However, the states are supposed to make some effort to bring existing facilities up to the standard.[29] At present, neither the current incinerator NSPS nor the resource recovery NSPS is of much significance. When the revised incinerator NSPS is finalized, it could have important consequences for existing facilities.

Specifically, EPA currently plans to issue final guidance for existing facilities at the same time it issues the revised NSPS in final form.[30] EPA has also indicated that it intends to require states to submit plans for upgrading existing incinerators that incorporate the new emissions guidelines, with submittal of such plans expected within nine months after the guidance is released.

The ambient standards set forth in the NAAQS may present a more immediate avenue for action. Where an existing incinerator is located in an area that has not attained all the NAAQS, an individual citizen cannot seek relief against the facility for contributing to NAAQS violations. The state, however, can act against individual facilities pursuant to its obligation to achieve overall compliance with the NAAQS. Thus, the state environmental agency should be encouraged, or formally petitioned, to require better controls on, or even closure of, a dirty incinerator in a dirty air area.

NOTES

1. The quoted material in this section comes directly from the National Environmental Policy Act of 1969 (42 U.S.C.A. 4321 to 4370a).
2. U.S. Code 42:7471. Hereafter cited as U.S.C.
3. The quoted material in this section comes directly from the Clean Air Act (42 U.S.C.A. 7479).
4. Code of Federal Regulations 40:52.21.23. Hereafter cited as C.F.R.
5. *Federal Register* 54 (December 20, 1989): 52251.
6. U.S.C. 42:7475(a)(2).
7. U.S.C. 42:7475(a)(7).
8. See *North Country Resource Recovery Associates*, PSD Appeal No. 85-2 (Washington, DC, 1986) (decision of the EPA administrator noting the value of scrubbers in controlling dioxins in the context of considering whether scrubbers are BACT for sulfur dioxide.
9. See, for example, Florida Department of Environmental Regulation, final determination and permit for Hillsborough County Energy Recovery Facility (lead limit); EPA, Region 9, PSD Permit for TriCities Resource Recovery Facility (general reservation of authority to lower emission limits).
10. *Federal Register* 54 (December 20, 1989): 52251.
11. C.F.R. 40: Part 51, Appendix S, II(A)(19).
12. C.F.R. 40:60.50-54 (Subpart E).
13. *Federal Register* 54 (December 20, 1989):52251.
14. C.F.R. 40:60.40b-49b (Subpart Db).
15. *Federal Register* 54 (December 20, 1989):52209.
16. Ibid., 52251.
17. Clean Air Act (42 U.S.C.A. 7412).
18. C.F.R. 40:Part 61.
19. *Federal Register* 50 (*October 16, 1985*):42000.
20. State of New York et al. v. U.S. EPA, D.C. Cir. no. 87-1463, 1987.
21. C.F.R. 40:Part 257.
22. U.S.C. 42:6943(d).
23. C.F.R. 40:257.3.
24. See generally C.F.R. 40:Part 261.
25. EDF v. Wheelabrator Technologies. no. 88-0560 (Southern District of New York, filed January 27, 1988); EDF & Citizens for a Better Environment v. City of Chicago, no. 88-0769 (Northern District of Illinois, filed January 27, 1988).
26. *Federal Register* 53 (August 30, 1988):33314.
27. C.F.R. 40:230.
28. C.F.R. 33:320.4.
29. See Section 111(f) of the Clean Air Act (42 U.S.C. 7411).
30. *Federal Register* 54 (December 20, 1989):52209 and 52251.

APPENDICES

Location and Status of MSW Incinerators in the United States

State	Operating	Under Construction	Planned	Blocked/Cancelled/Delayed	Shut Down
AL	Tuscaloosa		Huntsville		Huntsville
AK	Juneau Prudhoe Bay Shemya Sitka		Ketchikan		
AZ			Mesa		
AR	Batesville Blytheville Hope Hot Springs N Little Rock Osceola Stuttgart		Craighead Co	El Dorado (C) Fayetteville (B)	
CA	Commerce Long Beach Modesto		Glendale San Marcos San Mateo	Alameda Co (D) Compton (B) Contra Costa (C) Freemont (B) Gardena (B) Irwindale (B) Los Angeles (B) Miliken (B) Puente Hills (B) Redwood City (B)	Susanville

CO			Denver	Riverside (C)	
				San Diego (B)	
				Sanger (D)	
				Ukiah (D)	
				Visalia (D)	
CT	Bridgeport	Wallingford	Danbury	Middletown (B)	
	Bristol		Lisbon	Naugatauk (C)	
	Hartford		Preston		
	New Canaan		Stratford		
	Stamford (2)		Wallingford		
	Windham				
DE	Wilmington (2)		Sussex Co		
DC	Washington				
FL	Dade Co	Broward Co (2)	Escambia Co	Lake Co (D)	Pompano Beach
	Hillsborough Co	W Palm Beach	Jacksonville	Leesburg (C)	
	Key West		Pasco Co	Naples (C)	
	Lakeland		Pinellas Co	Orange Co (C)	
	Mayport Naval Sta				
	Panama City				
	Pinellas Co				
	Tampa				
GA	Savannah	Atlanta			
HI	Honolulu	Honolulu			

State	Operating	Under Construction	Planned	Blocked/Cancelled/Delayed	Shut Down
ID	Burley			Bannock Co (C)	
IL	Chicago–NW		Chicago–South Crestwood E St Louis Ford Heights Rockford Springfield		Chicago–SW
IN	E Chicago Indianapolis			Bloomington (D)	
IA	Ames		Des Moines		
KS			Kansas City		
KY	Franklin Louisville			Campbellsville (C)	
LA	Shreveport				
ME	Auburn Biddeford Frenchville Harpswell Orrington Portland		Lewiston	Bath (C)	
MD	Baltimore		Cockeysville	Anne Arundel Co (C)	

	Baltimore Co Harford Co		Montgomery Co St. Mary's Co	Kent Co (B) Prince Georges Co (B) Pulaski (C)	
MA	Agawam Fall River Framingham Lawrence Millbury N Andover Pittsfield Rochester Saugus	W Haverhill	Hull Taunton Webster Weymouth	Boston (B) Holyoke (B) Lowell (C) Somerville (C)	
MI	Clinton Jackson Mount Clemens Detroit	Grand Rapids Kent Co	Albion Macomb Co Marquette Co Muskegon Co Oakland Co	Kalamazoo Co (D)	Oakland Co
MN	Alexandria Duluth Eden Prairie Elk River Fergus Falls Newport Olmstead Co Perham Red Wing	Hennepin Co Polk Co	Dakota Co	Winona Co (D)	Collegeville

State	Operating	Under Construction	Planned	Blocked/Cancelled/ Delayed	Shut Down
(MN cont)	Rochester				
	Savage				
	Thief River Falls				
MS	Pascagoula				
MO	Ft Leonard Wood		Independence		
	St Louis		Joplin		
			Springfield		
			St Louis		
MT	Livingston				
NV	Reno				
NH	Auburn	Concord	Manchester		Portsmouth
	Candia		Portsmouth		
	Canterbury		Seabrook		
	Claremont				
	Durham				
	Groveton				
	Litchfield				
	Meredith				
	Nottingham				
	Pittsfield				
	Wilton				
	Wolfeboro				

NJ	Warren Co Fort Dix	Camden Co Essex Co Gloucester Co	Atlantic Co Bergen Co Cape May Co Hudson Co Mercer Co Middlesex Co Monmouth Co Passaic Co Pennsauken Somerset Co Union Co Salem Co Sussex Co	Morris Co (D) Ocean Co (D) Woodbine (B)	
NM			Los Alamos		
NY	Albany Babylon Brooklyn (2) Cuba Dutchess Co Glen Cove Huntington Long Beach Niagara Falls Oneida Co Oswego Co Oyster Bay	Dutchess Co Hempstead Hudson Falls Huntington New Cordell	Bronx Brooklyn Broome Co Lackawanna Co Manhattan N Hempstead Onondaga Co Oyster Bay Rockland Co Queens St Lawrence Co Staten Island	Islip (D) Saratoga Co (C) Washington Co (C)	Monroe Co Poughkeepsie Queens

277

State	Operating	Under Construction	Planned	Blocked/Cancelled/Delayed	Shut Down
(NY cont)	Queens Skaneateles Westchester Co				
NC	New Hanover Co Wrightsville	Mecklenburg Co	Charlotte Gaston Co	Cumberland Co (D)	
ND				Willingston (C)	
OH	Akron Columbus Euclid Montgomery Co (2)		Greene Co	Franklin (C)	
OK	Miami Tulsa			Oklahoma City (C)	
OR	Brookings Coos Bay Marion Co		Portland		
PA	East Penn Twnshp Easton Harrisburg Westmoreland Co	Potter Co York Co	Berks Co Bradford Co Bethlehem Chester Erie Falls Twnshp Glendon	Bucks Co (C) Delaware Co (C) Lancaster Co (D) Monroe Co (C) Morgantown (C) Philadelphia–S (C)	Philadelphia–NW Philadelphia–East Central

			Hanover, Lackawanna Co, Mercer Co, Mifflin Co, Montgomery Co	
RI			Blackstone Valley, Johnston, Quonset Point	N Kingston (D)
SC	Berkeley Co, Hampton, Johnsonville	Charlestown Co	Cherokee Co, Lee Co	
TN	Dyersburg, Gallatin, Hohenwald, Lewisburg, Madison, Nashville		Cocke Co, Knoxville, Nashville	Tullahoma (D)
TX	Bay City, Borger, Carthage, Center, Cleburne, Gatesville, Palestine, Waxahachie		Texas City	Galveston (D), Grand Prairie (D), Houston (C), Lubbock (D)
UT	Davis Co			

State	Operating	Under Construction	Planned	Blocked/Cancelled/Delayed	Shut Down
VT	Rutland				
VA	Alexandria Galax Hampton Harrisonburg Newport News Portsmouth Salem	Fairfax Co Petersburg	Prince William Co Suffolk		
WA	Bellingham Friday Harbor Skagit Co	Spokane Co	Clark Co Pierce Co Snohomish Co	Maryville (D) Seattle (B) Tacoma (D)	
WI	Barron Co La Crosse Co Madison Sheboygan St. Croix Co Waukesha Co		Dakota Co Muscoda Outagamie Co	Eau Claire Co (D)	

Total incinerators:
  Operating: 163
  Under construction: 26
  Planned: 107
  Blocked/cancelled/delayed: 63
  Shut down: 12

SOURCES:

"1988 Refuse Incineration and Refuse-to-Energy Listings," *Waste Age*, 19, no. 1 (November 1988) pp: 195–212.

Citizen's Clearinghouse for Hazardous Wastes, Inc., *Incineration Fact Pack* (Arlington, VA, January 5, 1989).

Radian Corporation Progress Center, *Final Report: Municipal Waste Combustion Industry Profile* (Research Triangle Park, NC, September 16, 1988).

Radian Corporation Progress Center, *Planned and Projected Municipal Waste Combustors Profile Update* (Research Triangle Park, NC, May 18, 1988).

The United States Conference of Mayors Natural Resource Recovery Association, *City Currents* 7, no. 4 (October 1988).

EDF Proposal for Design of MSW Incinerator Ash Monofills

EDF proposes that ash monofills be designed with two liners and two leachate collection systems and, after filling, be covered with a composite cap, overlain by a vegetative cover. Specifically, the liner system should consist of an upper (primary) flexible membrane liner (FML) constructed of, or equivalent to, a 60-mil thickness of high-density polyethylene (HDPE). The lower (secondary) liner should be a composite liner consisting of two components: an upper FML identical to the primary liner, immediately underlain by a minimum three-foot thickness of clay or other natural soil compacted to a maximum hydraulic conductivity of 1×10^{-7} centimeters per second (cm/sec).

A primary leachate collection system should be required to be installed above the primary liner, capable of maintaining a hydraulic head not to exceed 12 inches. A secondary leachate collection system, which serves the additional function of a leak detection system for the primary liner, should be required to be installed between the primary and secondary liners.[1]

Upon closure, monofills should be required to install a final composite cover consisting of an upper FML immediately underlain by a minimum two-foot thickness of clay or other natural soil compacted to a maximum hydraulic conductivity of 1×10^{-7} centimeters per second (cm/sec). The cover system should be overlain by a vegetative cover graded to control run-on and runoff.

The remainder of this paper will describe the rationale for this design and then present available cost information on our recommended design, demonstrating its cost-effectiveness.

RATIONALE: EACH ELEMENT OF THE RECOMMENDED BASELINE DESIGN IS NECESSARY FOR PROPER LANDFILL FUNCTION

EDF considers the standard for ash monofill design described above to be necessary not only from the perspective of environmental protection but also to enable any landfill containment system to function properly. Each of the components is an essential element of the containment system.

Our recommended standard is consistent with—indeed, is necessary to achieve—the goals of EPA's liquids management strategy, which was developed in the context of hazardous waste disposal but applies similarly to monofills.[2] This strategy has two objectives: (1) to minimize leachate generation in waste management units and (2) to maximize leachate removal at the earliest practicable time. Achievement of these two goals provides the framework for the following discussion of the rationale for inclusion of each of the design components recommended by EDF.

1. *Need for a Double Liner with Double Leachate Collection.*

One of the advantages of a double-lined system over a single-lined one is obvious: Liners are neither impermeable nor permanent, so some degree of what may appear to be redundancy is needed to provide effective containment. As EPA has clearly stated on several occasions:

> Although a liner is a barrier to prevent migration of liquids out of the unit, no liner can be expected to remain impervious forever. As a result of waste interaction, environmental effects, and the effects of construction processes and operating practices, liners eventually may degrade, tear, or crack and may allow liquids to migrate out of the unit. . . . It is evident to the agency that single-lined units allow substantially greater migration of hazardous constituents than would double-lined units.[3]

Efficient leachate collection and removal is a second advantage of a double-lined system. As EPA stated in 1987, "The double-liner system is the mechanism by which leachate collection and removal can be maximized."[4] In addition to providing two systems for collecting and removing leachate, buildup of any appreciable hydraulic head on the ultimate barrier—the secondary liner—is avoided by collecting the great majority of leachate off of the primary liner. Thus, even where leaks exist in the primary liner, in most cases, the majority of leachate can still be removed and prevented from ever reaching the secondary liner.

Early leak detection is a third critical advantage of double-lined systems. The leachate collection system between the liners serves several functions: It collects and removes any leachate that migrates through the primary liner, thus minimizing the hydraulic head on the secondary liner; it provides a means of detecting leaks in the primary liner at a time before such leaks have allowed contaminants to migrate out of the unit; and it provides a means of assessing the magnitude of such leaks, thereby increasing both the ability to respond to leakage and to assess the effectiveness of such responses. Obviously, a leak detection system offering these significant advantages is not possible without a double-liner system.

2. Need for a Secondary Composite Liner.

The bottom liner in a double-lined system needs to provide several functions: (1) maximization of the detection capability of the leak detection system; (2) maximization of leachate collection and removal from the secondary liner; and (3) minimization of migration of leachate and contaminants through the liner and into the environment. On all three counts, EPA and others have clearly documented the need for a composite bottom liner, rather than either a synthetic or natural liner alone.[5]

The use of an upper FML component in the composite liner provides a highly impermeable layer off of which to collect leachate; the minimal migration of leachate through such a liner also increases the sensitivity of leak detection. In contrast, use of a more permeable natural soil or clay liner alone allows significant amounts of liquid to penetrate into the liner and eventually migrate out of the unit; such penetration also greatly reduces the ability to both detect and assess the extent of leakage.

The lower compacted clay or natural soil component of the composite liner optimizes liner function in several ways: It serves as a backup in the event of a breach in the FML component; its greater thickness reduces the likelihood of puncture or other damage during installation or landfill operations; it provides some attenuation of certain leachate contaminants that are capable of chemically binding to such soil materials; and, because it is in immediate contact with the overlying FML, it helps to plug any leaks in the FML that may exist or develop over time. EPA has indicated that a minimum thickness of three feet is necessary to assure the stability of the clay or other natural soil component of a composite liner.[6]

Finally, EPA has raised several concerns regarding sole reliance on clay liners for containing ash leachates. In particular, it has stated that the high alkalinity and salt content of such leachates are known to cause rapid deterioration of clay liners.[7] EPA further states that some data indicate that chloride complexes of lead and cadmium in ashes move rapidly through clay soil.[8] These concerns offer additional rationale for the need for bottom composite—rather than compacted clay—liners in ash mono-fills.

3. Need for a Composite Final Cover.

Although these design elements are intended to contain and effectively remove liquids that enter or are generated in landfills, an equally important objective of EPA's liquids management strategy is to minimize leachate generation in waste management units. In addition to controls over liquids disposal, which the agency has proposed largely to prohibit, the major controllable element in reducing leachate generation is to reduce infiltration of liquid into the unit, which primarily enters in the form of precipitation. The final cover is critical in this regard in that it, along with appropriate run-on/runoff controls, provides the most effective means for reducing infiltration, particularly after closure of an active unit. As EPA stated in 1982 when it required composite final covers for hazardous waste landfills: "While liners may remain effective at preventing migration from the unit until well after closure, their principal role occurs during the active life. After closure, EPA believes that a protective cap becomes the prime element of the liquids management strategy."[9]

A principal factor in determining the nature of the final cover is the permeability of the unit's liner system, since a cover that is more permeable than the liner(s) can result in the buildup of liquid in the unit—the so-called bathtub effect. For this reason, EPA has generally required final cover materials to be no more permeable than the unit's liner system. This, in turn, dictates the use of FML covers for landfills that employ FML liners. The greater durability and thickness of clay materials, along with the advantages of using a combination of FML and clay liner materials rather than either alone, provide technical justification for the proposed requirement of a composite final cover.[10]

4. Need for Additional Operating Practices to Minimize Leachate.

Given the predominant role of infiltration of precipitation in the formation of leachate, especially during the active life of a landfill, steps must be taken to minimize the period of time during which wastes are exposed to precipitation. It is increasingly recognized that a phased-filling operation can greatly decrease leachate generation. Phased filling involves the sequential filling of landfill cells, which are relatively small areas that can be filled quickly and then sealed with final cover.

We strongly support the use of a phased-filling operation. In our view, a maximum period of time during which an active cell may remain open must be specified. Based on state regulatory or permit requirements, we recommend a maximum active cell life of no more than 12 to 18 months.

COST DATA

Several sources of information on the cost of designing a landfill to meet the double-liner standard we recommend are available. EPA itself commissioned an extensive study of the costs of compliance with its revised hazardous waste landfill rule that would require such a design. The EPA study[11] derived estimates that allow a direct comparison between the costs of the double-liner system we propose and a single composite-liner system. That is, the study estimates the incremental cost of adding an additional FML and leak detection system (LDS) to a design consisting of a leachate collection system underlain by a composite (upper FML and lower clay) liner. Moreover, it estimates these costs as a function of landfill size. Average annual incremental costs per ton of waste (assuming a 20-year time frame) for the additional design components vary according to landfill size (expressed in tons per year, or tpy) as follows:

TABLE B.1
Cost of an Additional Liner and Leak Detection System as a Function of Landfill Size

TPY	1 Composite Liner, 1 LCS ($/ton)	1 FML/1 Composite Liner + 2 LDS ($/ton)	Added Cost ($/ton)	% Increase
550	$647.82	$676.18	$28.36	4.4
1,100	402.55	418.91	16.36	4.1
2,200	277.73	287.45	9.73	3.5
6,600	181.82	186.36	4.55	2.5
16,500	81.91	84.73	2.82	3.4
38,500	60.09	61.91	1.82	3.0
66,000	51.64	53.09	1.45	2.8
110,000	45.91	47.09	1.18	2.6
165,000	41.45	42.36	0.91	2.2

These cost estimates, which include labor and materials, indicate a modest increase (2.2 to 4.4 percent) in total landfill costs for the added liner and leak detection system. For landfills serving 100,000 or more people (about 66,000 or more tpy of waste), added costs would be on the order of $1.50 per ton or less. Even for smaller landfills, although per-ton costs are higher, the percent increase in total landfill cost for the added protection is still small and relatively constant with size.

The above cost data are expressed in terms of costs per ton of MSW. Costs for disposal of incinerator ash could be substantially less because of the greater density of ash (see below).

Several other sources of cost data provide support for this relatively minor increase in cost to add an additional synthetic liner and LCS. New York State recently prepared cost estimates for its new regulations that require double-composite liners for all new MSW landfills. It did not examine economies of scale for landfills of various sizes, but it did provide unit costs (i.e., cost per unit area for liners and leachate collection systems). These cost estimates are summarized in table B.2. The New York cost data have been converted into cost-per-ton-of-ash estimates by assuming a 60-foot depth of ash at capacity, which represents 18 tons of ash per square yard of filled area (at 1,800 pounds per cubic yard).

Using these unit costs, as well as the costs for the requisite drainage layers, filter fabric, etc., New York estimates that its double-composite liner/double leachate collection system would cost $49.05 per square yard, or $4.09 per ton of MSW. A final composite cover with a gas venting layer is estimated to cost $24.70 per square yard, or $2.06 per ton of MSW. After accounting for the greater density of ash (typically, 1,800 pounds per cubic yard, versus 1,200 for MSW), these costs would be $2.73 per ton of ash for the liner system and $1.37 per ton of ash for the final cover.

EDF's proposed liner and cover design standards differ somewhat from New York's more stringent requirement; using New York's unit cost, EDF's double-liner proposal would be slightly less expensive: $2.61 per ton of ash.

TABLE B.2
New York State Unit Cost

Component	Cost/Yd²	Cost/Ton of Ash
40-mil FML (for cover)	$ 4.63	$0.26
60-mil FML (for liner)	6.42	0.36
Clay liner, 3 feet thick (10⁻⁷ cm/sec)	15.33	0.85
Leachate collection system	1.22	0.07

NOTE: Cost figures include materials, installation, and quality assurance/quality control.

Adding to this the cost of EDF's composite cover design ($1.17 per ton) results in a total additional design cost of $3.78 per ton of ash.

This value can be further translated into two other useful cost estimates. Because incinerators significantly reduce the weight of MSW, a ton of MSW generates considerably less ash. Assuming a typical weight reduction of 75 percent, the increase in the incinerator tipping fee—the amount charged per ton of MSW received—that would result from EDF's proposed design would be only $0.95 per ton (i.e., 25 percent of $3.78). *The added cost to an individual citizen, who typically generates about two-thirds of a ton of MSW each year, would therefore be about $0.63 per year, a truly trivial expense for the added protection of EDF's design.*

Several other studies provide comparable estimates of unit costs for the same or similar materials. It is not clear, however, whether these estimates include only materials or also installation costs. These studies and their estimates (expressed in terms of dollars per ton of ash) are as follows:

TABLE B.3
Other Estimates of Unit Costs for Landfill Containment System Components

MBS*	60-mil FML ($/ton)	
	0.25	
GLEBS†	??-mil FML ($/ton)	3 feet Clay ($/ton)
	0.25–0.50	0.05–0.19

* Multinational Business Services (MBS), "Potential Subtitle D Compliance Costs for Municipal Landfills—An Analysis," June 1987.

† R. T. Glebs, "Landfill Costs Continue to Rise," *Waste Age,* March 1988, pp. 84–93.

Actual construction costs for an ash monofill provides further support for these estimates. A six-acre monofill with capacity for 202,500 cubic yards of ash equipped with a composite liner and a composite cover was recently constructed in Marion County, Oregon; county officials report that the total cost (for land acquisition, design, and construction, and operating and maintenance) was $16.50 per ton.[12]

The EPA, New York, MBS, Glebs, and Marion County data are all relatively consistent, and indicate modest incremental costs for meeting the design standard we recommend for ash monofills, subject to only slight economies of scale; total landfill costs should be increased by considerably less than 10 percent. When judged in the context of the tremendous increase in containment system performance and the concomitant environmental benefits, we simply see no justification for requiring anything less.

NOTES

1. This system is essentially identical in design to the primary leachate collection system; its location between the liners allows it to function as a leak detection system for the primary liner.
2. *Federal Register* 52 (May 29, 1987): 20221.
3. Ibid., 20220–21.
4. NUS Corporation and GeoServices Consulting Engineers, "Background Document on Bottom Liner Performance in Double-Lined Landfills and Surface Impoundments," report prepared for EPA (Washington, DC: Office of Solid Waste, 1987, no. 530-SW-87-013).
5. *Federal Register* 52 (April 17, 1987): 12566; *Federal Register* 52 (May 29, 1987): 20218; and "Background Document on Bottom Liner Performance."
6. *Federal Register* 52 (March 28, 1986): 10710.
7. "Guidance on Municipal Waste Combustion," draft (Washington, DC: EPA Office of Solid Waste, March 14, 1988).
8. "Status of OSW's Municipal Waste Combustion Ash Efforts," briefing (Washington, DC: EPA Science Advisory Board, April 26, 1988).
9. *Federal Register* 47 (July 26, 1982): 32285.
10. Ibid., 32314 for further discussion.
11. Pope-Reid Associates, "Engineering Costs Documentation for Baseline and Proposed Double Liner Rule, Leak Detection System Rule, and CQA Program Costs for Landfills, Surface Impoundments, Waste Piles, and Land Treatment," report prepared for EPA (Washington, DC: Office of Solid Waste, March 1987, no. 68-01-7310).
12. Randall Franke, Marion County Commissioner, presentation at a seminar on MSW Incinerator Ash sponsored by the Northwest Center for Professional Education (Orlando, FL, December 1, 1988).

Model Resolution

[Creating Conditions in Advance for Master Contract between City and Facility]

RESOLUTION permitting the [authorized City official] to conduct negotiations with [owner of proposed incinerator] for a resource recovery facility to be located in [location], under specified conditions.

The [authorized City official] is authorized to conduct negotiations with [owner] over a proposed agreement for a resource recovery facility to be located in [location], for the purpose of determining the acceptability and approximate cost terms of such an agreement, PROVIDED THAT the proposed agreement include all of the following conditions:

1. That the City shall be free at any time to reduce the amount of garbage provided to the facility when the reduction is the result of recycling, in any amount and with no penalty or other economic risk;
2. That the facility owners and their successors shall bear all direct and indirect costs attributable to ash resulting from the project, including but not limited to handling, storage, and disposal, whether such ash is required to be classified at any time as a hazardous waste, a special waste, or otherwise, so that in no event shall the City bear any such costs; and
3. That, before any commitment by the City takes effect, the facility owners and their successors shall have bound themselves by enforceable private contract with any affected groups and private individuals desiring to enter into such contract to comply with specified emission limits for specified air contaminants throughout the lifetime of the facility, in a form that insures direct enforceability by such private individuals and groups;

AND FURTHER PROVIDED THAT the [authorized city official] CAO promptly obtain from [owner] its current estimate of the full costs of building and operating the facility under the foregoing conditions.

No further negotiations shall take place until after the cost figures referred to in this resolution have been obtained and provided to the Board.

No negotiations shall take place at any time concerning any agreement for participation in a resource recovery facility unless such agreement contains and implements all three of the foregoing conditions.

Pertinent Issues and Questions

This list of questions is primarily intended for use in communities where discussion of new waste management facilities or approaches is in an early stage. For readers who have been in the midst of such discussions, many of these questions may appear obvious or even naive, but can still serve as a checklist of issues needing consideration.

I. Needs assessment and planning
  A. Is this facility needed? How was need established?
    1. Local or regional survey?
    2. Is the proposed facility compatible with the survey?
  B. Is the proposed facility an improvement over those now in use? Will the facility replace an outmoded/worse polluting one?
  C. What geographical area will it serve? Is a more regional approach to waste management the preferred option?
  D. Has a waste management hierarchy been established? (e.g., prioritization of waste management options in the order of source reduction, reuse, recycling, incineration, landfilling)
    1. Have the elements of the local plan been fit into the waste management hierarchy?
    2. Are reduction and recycling receiving top priority?
    3. How will the competition between recycling and incineration for combustible recyclables be handled?
    4. Does the waste management plan establish a percentage of waste to be handled by each option, consistent with the hierarchy?

NOTE: This list was adapted for use on solid waste management facilities from a list for hazardous waste management facilities prepared by the Keystone Siting Process Group for the Texas Department of Water Resources, January 1984.

    5. How does the proposed facility fit into the hierarchy?

E. Is this facility part of a master plan to provide waste management? Who developed the plan?

F. Are there plans for future expansion?

    1. Are additional facilities planned?

    2. What types of additional facilities are planned?

    3. What time frame is anticipated?

II. Sources and nature of wastes being managed

A. What kinds and amounts of wastes will be handled? What are their physical and chemical characteristics?

B. How will special wastes be handled?

    1. Used automotive batteries

    2. Tires

    3. Used oil

    4. Asbestos

    5. Paints

    6. Laboratory waste

    7. Household hazardous waste

    8. Infectious waste

    9. Yard wastes

C. Where will the wastes come from? How will wastes from various sources differ in composition and quantity? How will these characteristics vary during the course of the year?

    1. Households

    2. Commercial establishments

    3. Industries

    4. Waste from other locations

        a. Regional

        b. State

        c. Out of state

D. What facilities will be needed to store source-separated recyclable materials, and how will they be provided?

E. What wastes will not be handled by the facility? How will they be identified and excluded? Where will such wastes be sent?

III. Technologies to be used—general questions

A. Why was this technology chosen?

    1. Are others available? Why were they rejected?

    2. Can wastes to be handled be recycled or reduced to avoid the need for the facility or to reduce its size?

    3. What engineering design and operating techniques are neces-

sary to compensate for any special waste characteristics or site deficiencies?

B. Reliability of technology
   1. What are past experiences with the selected technology?
   2. What are the potential environmental impacts associated with it?
   3. How will long-term optimal performance be assured?

C. Sequence of waste handling at the facility from arrival of waste to the end of processing at the facility (flow chart)
   1. Unloading
   2. Storage
   3. Processing
   4. Disposal or treatment
   5. Will there be any residuals requiring further handling? How will they be managed?
   6. Monitoring
   7. Closure
   8. Postclosure

IV. Technologies to be used—specific questions
   A. Recycling
      1. How will it be accomplished (e.g., source separation, curbside collection, pre-processing, materials recovery facility)?
      2. What materials will be recovered?
      3. Are the recovered materials marketable?
      4. What is the long-term demand for the recovered materials?
      5. What steps can be taken to strengthen markets?
   B. Storage
      1. How and where will the wastes or source-separated materials be stored?
      2. How long can/will they be stored?
      3. How much material can be stored on-site?
   C. Incineration
      1. What percentage reduction of the waste stream, by volume and by weight, is anticipated?
      2. How will unprocessible or bypass wastes be managed?
      3. What air quality protection measures will be utilized?
      4. What is the anticipated air quality impact?
      5. What monitoring will be done, and how frequently?
         a. Emissions from stack
         b. Operating conditions of incinerator and air pollution control devices

      c. Ambient air

      d. Adjacent surface waters

      e. Adjacent soils

      f. Groundwater

   6. What are the procedures to be followed in case of an upset?

   7. How will the ash be handled at the facility?

   8. Where will the ash be stored pending the results of testing?

   9. How will the ash be transported?

 10. Where and how will the ash be disposed of?

      a. Specially designed ash monofill

      b. Codisposal with unburned MSW

 11. Will the incinerator make additional demands on the existing water supply?

D. Land disposal

   1. Processing or treatment preceding land disposal

   2. Measures to prevent or detect groundwater contamination

      a. Liners

      b. Distance from bottom of liner system to groundwater

      c. Groundwater monitoring system

      d. Leachate collection and leak detection systems

      e. Leachate treatment and management capacity

   3. Daily and intermediate cover

   4. Run-on/runoff control systems

   5. Closure plans

      a. Interim partial closure of each cell

      b. Final closure of full facility

      c. Financial responsibility

   6. Postclosure plans

      a. Periodic monitoring and maintenance

      b. Length of the postclosure period and nature and frequency of required monitoring and maintenance

      c. Financial responsibility

      d. Responsibilities of facility operator, land owner, local and state units of government

      e. Future uses of site and use/deed restrictions

V. Site characteristics

A. Characteristics to be considered

   1. Site geology

   2. Hydrology

   3. Topography

   4. Soil properties

    5. Aquifer characteristics
       a. Relationship to water table, including seasonal variations
       b. Wells presently in or planned for the area
       c. Flow rate and direction of groundwater flow
       d. Groundwater quality and quantity
       e. Connection/proximity to other aquifers
       f. Aquifer recharge area
       g. Does the site overlie a sole-source aquifer?
       h. Current and projected usage
    6. Climatic conditions
       a. Extent of precipitation
       b. Potential for natural disaster (e.g., floods, hurricanes, tornadoes)
    7. Proximity to environmentally sensitive areas
       a. Wetlands
       b. Shoreline
       c. Flood-prone area
       d. Aquifer recharge zone
       e. Endangered or threatened species critical habitat
       f. Hurricane storm surge area
       g. Prime agricultural area
       h. Seismic zone or otherwise unstable area
       i. Other
    8. Evidence of stability or subsidence
    9. Proximity to residential areas
   10. Proximity to vulnerable populations
       a. Schools
       b. Retirement homes
       c. Hospitals
       d. Medical institutions
       e. Prisons
   11. Current character of surrounding area
   12. Zoning of site and areas nearby
   13. Current or future plans for site and area
   14. Transportation routes
  B. Reasons for site selection
    1. Were other sites considered?
    2. Are alternate sites still under consideration?
    3. Why were other sites rejected?
VI. Environmental quality
  A. Surface drainage

1. Is the site in a floodplain?
    a. What type of floodplain (e.g., 25-year, 100-year)?
    b. How current are maps or other data used to make determination?
    c. What is the elevation of the land?
    d. What flood-proofing provisions have been made? How large a storm has been planned for?
2. Storm-water management
    a. How will it be controlled?
    b. How will the discharges be treated?
    c. What effect will effluents have on receiving waters?
3. Hurricane vulnerability
    a. Is site in an area subject to storm surges?
    b. What storm design specifications were used?
    c. What damage from wave action is possible?
    d. For what levels of wind speed is facility designed?
B. Groundwater protection
    1. Groundwater resources
        a. Current or future use of aquifer; location of wells
        b. Proximity to surface water
    2. Soil
        a. Hydraulic conductivity and homogeneity
        b. Barrier capacity of the soil
            (1) Depth to the nearest aquifer
            (2) Depth to bedrock
            (3) Cation exchange capacity
        c. Soil pH
        d. Erodibility
        e. Other
    3. Geology
        a. Nature and extent of underlying layers
        b. Earthquake potential
        c. Slope
        d. Fissures or other irregularities
    4. Leachate collection
        a. How will leachate be collected and managed?
        b. How will leachate be treated?
        c. How will the resultant treatment residues be managed?
        d. For how long will leachate be collected? Treated?
        e. How will sufficient leachate management capacity be assured?

5. Liners
   a. Design and construction requirements
      (1) Type: clay or synthetic
      (2) Thickness
      (3) Construction method: quality assurance/control
      (4) Compatibility with wastes or leachates
      (5) Number of liners
      (6) Leak detection capability
   b. Areas of the facility to be lined
   c. Remedial action in the event of a breach in the liner(s)
6. Final cover
   a. Design and construction requirements: same questions as for liners
   b. Erosion control
   c. Prevention of water standing on site, correction of settlement
   d. Postclosure maintenance
C. Air emissions
   1. Anticipated emissions
   2. Air emission controls
   3. Potential for release of unregulated pollutants
   4. Monitoring
   5. Odor control plans
   6. Affected communities
   7. Direction of prevailing winds
   8. Frequency of bad-air conditions in vicinity of facility
   9. Frequency of upset conditions at facility
   10. Distance to surface drinking-water supply
   11. Significance of this source's emissions to other sources in the vicinity and to existing background levels of pollutants
VII. Transportation
   A. Mode of transportation now and in future
      1. Truck
      2. Rail
      3. Barge
   B. Containment of waste during transport
      1. Vehicle covers or closed containers
      2. Measures to prevent waste releases
   C. Parties responsible for transport
      1. Record of company responsible for transport
      2. Training of drivers

D. Timing of arrivals
   1. Days of the week
   2. Hours of the day
E. Routing
   1. Routes to be used
   2. Existing restrictions
      a. Enforcing agencies
      b. Penalties for noncompliance
   3. Effects on area traffic
   4. Effects on area road conditions
   5. Proximity of routes to vulnerable population
F. Spill response
   1. Whose responsibility is spill response?
   2. What cleanup techniques will be employed?
   3. How will the cost of cleanup be handled?
VIII. Operations
A. What actions will be taken when there are operating problems?
   1. History of downtime
   2. Backup systems planned
   3. Start-ups and shutdowns and unanticipated upsets
      a. Effects on permitted emissions
      b. Frequency/longevity anticipated
   4. Notification of regulatory officials
B. Emergency response
   1. What is included in the contingency plan?
   2. How will fire protection be provided?
      a. On-site equipment
      b. Mutual aid agreements
      c. Alarm systems
      d. In the event of a fire, is there adequate containment to prevent firefighting water from contaminating nearby surface waters?
C. Site security
   1. Controlled entry
   2. Fencing
   3. Warning signs
   4. Surveillance systems
D. Personnel
   1. Experience and certification of training required
   2. Technical levels and working experience of staff
   3. Training plans

   4. Participation in quality assurance/safety programs
IX. Enforcement
 A. Regulations
   1. Which regulations apply to this facility and site?
    a. Local
    b. State
    c. Federal
   2. What permits are needed?
    a. Which agencies are involved?
    b. Are there opportunities for public participation?
   3. What are the penalties for noncompliance?
 B. Monitoring to ensure environmental protection
   1. Techniques used
   2. Equipment available
   3. Frequency of monitoring
    a. By owner/operator
    b. By governmental agencies
    c. Other
   4. Citizen review committees planned (e.g., an operations review committee)
   5. Provisions for public notification in the event of a release (e.g., emissions from a malfunctioning incinerator)
 C. Who is responsible for enforcement?
   1. Owner/operator—self-reporting system
   2. Local level
    a. City
    b. County
    c. Regional or special district
   3. State level
   4. Federal level
 D. Sequence and timing of possible enforcement actions
   1. Corrective measures prescribed
   2. Penalties assessed
   3. Administrative orders, consent orders, and litigation
 E. What is the government's capability to ensure compliance?
X. Economic considerations
 A. Profit expectations
   1. High or low risk
   2. Longevity of the proposed facility
    a. Expansion anticipated

      b. In what time frame?
- 3. Who owns the facility?
- 4. Are the owners financially backed by others?
- 5. Who are the competitors?
- 6. Flow controls on waste

B. Facility operators
- 1. Prior experience/operating record
- 2. Will the company that owns also operate the facility?
- 3. Who will seek permits?
- 4. How can operators' expertise be evaluated if new to this field?

C. Economic effects on community
- 1. Possible effects on property values
- 2. Who will receive any increase in tax base?
- 3. How much tax revenue may be generated?
- 4. Will public costs rise?
  - a. Police protection
  - b. Fire protection
  - c. Road maintenance
  - d. Emergency response equipment and facilities

D. Potential for compensation to community
- 1. Donated equipment community may need as a result of facility locating nearby
- 2. Fees to general revenue fund
- 3. Property value guarantees
- 4. Parks, etc.
- 5. Closure of existing waste management facilities that are not up to today's higher standards
- 6. Community waste accepted free of charge at proposed facility
- 7. Household hazardous waste collection days
- 8. Construction of wastewater treatment facility for the community and for treatment of leachate

E. Closure and postclosure
- 1. When is closure anticipated?
- 2. Who is responsible for the site after closure?
- 3. What assurances will there be that the site will be closed in accordance with the plan?
- 4. What financial assurances have been made to establish the capability of facility owners/operators to handle problems after closure?

5. Who certifies that the facility is properly closed?
6. What controls or protections are in place regarding future uses of the property (e.g., zoning or dead restrictions)?

F. Corrective action

1. What measures are to be taken in the event of releases from the facility to the environment?
2. What financial assurances have been made to establish the capability of facility owners/operators to undertake any necessary corrective action?

Consultants, Requests for Qualifications, and Requests for Proposals

There are three basic ways consultants are selected. First, single-source procurements can be used, usually in cases where a particular highly specialized consultant is known to have the necessary expertise and knowledge of the situation at hand; this is most common for very technical, involved projects or for a project that demands immediate action. Second, selection can be done on the basis of qualifications from a pool of pre-qualified candidates. Although these selection processes can save a community time, they are also vulnerable to criticism that the consultants are biased or too close to the contracting agency.

A third selection process is based on the results of a formal request for qualifications (RFQ), a notice to qualified consultants requesting them to submit descriptions of their qualifications to perform a given task. RFQs should contain a brief description of the problem, project objectives, and minimum desired qualifications for consultants wishing to be considered. RFQs are generally developed by a technical review committee also responsible for reviewing the responses. A properly prepared RFQ for consultants to perform a solid waste management survey should be designed to attract consultants with a broad experience, ranging from waste stream composition studies to collection and recycling systems to waste treatment and disposal.

The completed RFQ should be published in newspapers and professional journals. Responses from applicants usually contain a description of the

SOURCE: Adapted from Efraim Gil et al., *Working with Consultants*, American Planning Association, Planning Advisory Service, report no. 378 (*Chicago*, 1983).

types of services performed by the firm, the principals, key personnel and their experience, completed projects and references. Based on the submissions, the technical review committee staff evaluates a firm's reputation, its past relationships with clients, its record for meeting deadlines, problem-solving ability, and quality of its reports. The technical review committee pares the list down to three to five consultants, which subsequently are interviewed or asked to submit an informal proposal. In addition to evaluating the technical expertise offered by the consultants, reviewers should also consider the following points:

- Identify the role of the principals. Will they be involved in a distant oversight capacity or will they be actively involved as the project managers?
- Have any of the consultant's projects been constructed? Are they operational? How accurately was the consultant able to project costs? What sort of cost overruns were involved? How much downtime was experienced?
- What was the consultant's actual involvement in the projects he or she lists? Large multifaceted projects may involve many consultants, each studying a specific aspect of the project. Any single consultant's affiliation with the project may be misinterpreted as being indicative of a broader range of experience than is actually the case.
- Is the consultant affiliated with any other firm, which would prejudice the study to one viewpoint? For example, there are consultants who have developed a relationship with specific incinerator vendors. Because of their close working relationships, the recommendations of these consultants may be vulnerable to criticism as being biased.
- Does the consultant understand the legal framework within which the community must operate?
- How does the consultant perceive the relationship of recycling to incineration and sizing an incinerator? In many cases, recycling has been considered only after the incinerator is sized to accommodate the majority of the waste stream, and then recycling is restricted to those materials whose removal will not interfere with operation of the incinerator.
- What is the consultant's record with dealing with the public? What is the attitude of the principals toward public participation in the decision-making process? Waste management decisions are controversial. If confronted by the press or the public, it is critical that the consultant be able to explain the project and its ramifications clearly and concisely in an objective, nonconfrontational manner.

- Is the consultant familiar with the physical area under study? Has the consultant joined in a partnership with a local firm? Does the consultant have a local field office? These practical concerns relate to the wise expenditure of the moneys budgeted for the project. A partnership with a local firm can provide the consultant team with in-house experience on the history of the area, sources of information, contacts, etc.

Particularly if project costs are large, communities may elect to publish a request for proposals, or RFP. An RFP is a solicitation to consultants for formal proposals to complete a project outlined by the client, in this case the local government. It may be handled in a manner similar to an RFQ, in that it may be published in a professional journal to encourage a large pool of consultants to submit proposals. More frequently, the final selection process employed is a two-step one, which requests the most-qualified consultants that responded to the RFQ to submit an RFP. RFPs should contain the following information: a background statement; project description; anticipated end results; project scope including time frame, staffing, and budget; a discussion of services that will be provided to the consultant by the contracting agency; a description of the evaluation process; and instructions, such as format, organization, and deadline for submittal.

Because the project will only be as good as the consultant's qualifications and understanding of the project objectives, the contracting agency must be very specific in describing the project. In some cases, a presubmission conference may be appropriate.

RFPs need not specify that a particular technology or even a particular waste management option be used. For example, instead of issuing an RFP for a 3,000 tpd incinerator and only accepting bids from incinerator vendors, a municipality could ask for proposals to provide 3,000 tpd of waste management capacity. Recyclers would be allowed to bid on single or multiple material streams, and the contract would go to the lowest responsible bidder. If delivery of segregated materials by the municipality was necessary, costs of doing so would have to be factored into the bid-selection equation. In this case, an accurate measurement of savings in the conventional waste collection system as a result of recycling would be very important.

To evaluate an RFP, many of the same considerations applying to the evaluation of RFQs apply. In addition, reviewers should consider:

- The consultant's understanding of the problem and agency objectives; clarity of the analysis; and creativity of the approach to problem solving.

- Is the proposed schedule reasonable? Are intermediate milestones proposed? Are there opportunities for interaction with and reporting to agency staff contained in the schedule?
- Is the consultant able to manage the project? Are the project staff qualified to perform the work?
- Is the proposal well organized and well written?
- Does the proposal address all of the tasks described in the RFP?
- Is the final product described? Can the consultant perform the task under the constraints of the budget? Given the constraints of the budget, will the final project be conducted in enough depth to be valuable?
- Are the contracting agency and the consultant team compatible?

The last step of selecting a consultant is the negotiation phase, where the final details of the project are settled. In this phase, the actual agency personnel commitment may be made, and terms of payment, a final implementation plan, and provisions for resolving disputes agreed upon. It is critical that the consultant and contracting agency agree upon the project objectives and their respective roles in achieving those objectives. Finally, provisions should be made in the event that the project is extended.

Knowing the limitations of using consultants is another important aspect of the consultant selection process. Consultants can be very useful for certain types of projects, but are not a substitute for development of in-house staff and expertise. If use of a consultant is being considered in an information-gathering project, for example, it will be important to ensure that an agency staffer shares the task, so that as much of what is learned is retained by the agency that pays for it.

APPENDIX F

Abbreviations

ATSDR	Agency for Toxic Substances and Disease Registry
BACT	Best available control technology
BNY	Brooklyn Navy Yard
DOS	Department of Sanitation
EAC	Environmental Action Coalition
EDF	Environmental Defense Fund
EIS	Environmental impact statement
EPA	Environmental Protection Agency
EQBA	Environmental Quality Bond Act
ESP	Electrostatic precipitator
FML	Flexible membrane liner
HDPE	High-density polyethylene
HRA	Health risk assessment
IPC	Intermediate processing center
LAER	Lowest Achievable Emission Rate
LOAEL	Lowest-observable-adverse-effect level
MPC	Material-processing center
MRF	Material recovery facility
MSW	Municipal solid waste
NAAQS	National Ambient Air Quality Standards
NESHAP	National Emission Standard for Hazardous Air Pollutant
NEPA	National Environmental Policy Act
NOAEL	No-observable-adverse-effect level
NPL	Superfund National Priority List
NSPS	New Source Performance Standard
POTW	Publicly owned treatment works
PSD	Prevention of Significant Deterioration
RCRA	Resource Conservation and Recovery Act

RDF	Refuse-derived fuel
RFP	Request for proposals
RFQ	Request for qualifications
SCR	Selective catalytic reduction
SNCR	Nonselective catalytic reduction
SIP	State Implementation Plan
tpd	Tons per day
USDA	U.S. Department of Agriculture

INDEX

309

Also Available from Island Press

Ancient Forests of the Pacific Northwest
By Elliott A. Norse

The Challenge of Global Warming
Edited by Dean Edwin Abrahamson

The Complete Guide to Environmental Careers
The CEIP Fund

Creating Successful Communities: A Guidebook for Growth Management Strategies
By Michael A. Mantell, Stephen F. Harper, and Luther Propst

Crossroads: Environmental Priorities for the Future
Edited by Peter Borrelli

Economics of Protected Areas
By John A. Dixon and Paul B. Sherman

Environmental Agenda for the Future
Edited by Robert Cahn

Environmental Restoration: Science and Strategies for Restoring the Earth
Edited by John J. Berger

The Forest and the Trees: A Guide to Excellent Forestry
By Gordon Robinson

Forests and Forestry in China: Changing Patterns of Resource Development
By S.D. Richardson

From *The Land*
Edited and compiled by Nancy P. Pittman

Fighting Toxics: A Manual for Protecting Your Family, Community, and Workplace
By Gary Cohen and John O'Connor

Hazardous Waste from Small Quantity Generators
By Seymour I. Schwartz and Wendy B. Pratt

In Praise of Nature
Edited and with essays by Stephanie Mills

Last Stand of the Red Spruce
By Robert A. Mello

Natural Resources for the 21st Century
Edited by R. Neil Sampson and Dwight Hair

The New York Environment Book
By Eric A. Goldstein and Mark A. Izeman

Overtapped Oasis: Reform or Revolution for Western Water
By Marc Reisner and Sarah Bates

The Poisoned Well: New Strategies for Groundwater Protection
Edited by Eric Jorgensen

Race to Save the Tropics: Ecology and Economics for a Sustainable Future
Edited by Robert Goodland

Reforming the Forest Service
By Randal O'Toole

Reopening the Western Frontier
From *High Country News*

Research Priorities for Conservation Biology
Edited by Michael E. Soule and Kathryn Kohm

Resource Guide for Creating Successful Communities
By Michael A. Mantell, Stephen F. Harper, and Luther Propst

Rivers at Risk: The Concerned Citizen's Guide to Hydropower
By John D. Echeverria, Pope Barrow, and Richard Roos-Collins

Rush to Burn: Solving America's Garbage Crisis?
From *Newsday*

Saving the Tropical Forests
By Judith Gradwohl and Russell Greenberg

Shading Our Cities: A Resource Guide for Urban and Community Forests
Edited by Gary Moll and Sara Ebenreck

War on Waste: Can America Win Its Battle with Garbage?
By Louis Blumberg and Robert Gottlieb

Western Water Made Simple
From *High Country News*

Wetland Creation and Restoration: The Status of the Science
Edited by Mary E. Kentula and Jon A. Kusler

Wildlife of the Florida Keys: A Natural History
By James D. Lazell, Jr.

For a complete catalog of Island Press publications, please write:
Island Press
Box 7
Covelo, CA 95428

or call: 1-800-828-1302

Island Press Board of Directors